Mothers and Daughters

Mothers and Daughters

Living, Loving, and Learning over a Lifetime

Suzanne Degges-White and
Christine Borzumato-Gainey

ROWMAN & LITTLEFIELD
Lanham • Boulder • New York • Toronto • Plymouth, UK

Published by Rowman & Littlefield
4501 Forbes Boulevard, Suite 200, Lanham, Maryland 20706
www.rowman.com

10 Thornbury Road, Plymouth PL6 7PP, United Kingdom

British Library Cataloguing in Publication Information Available

Library of Congress Cataloging-in-Publication Data

Degges-White, Suzanne.
Mothers and daughters : living, loving, and learning over a lifetime / Suzanne Degges-White and Christine Borzumato-Gainey.
pages cm.
Includes bibliographical references and index.
ISBN 978-1-4422-1931-1 (cloth : alk. paper) -- ISBN 978-1-4422-1932-8 (electronic)
1. Mothers and daughters. 2. Motherhood. I. Borzumato-Gainey, Christine. II. Title.
HQ755.85.D43 2014
306.874'3--dc23
2013034335

™ The paper used in this publication meets the minimum requirements of American National Standard for Information Sciences Permanence of Paper for Printed Library Materials, ANSI/NISO Z39.48-1992.

Printed in the United States of America

Contents

Contents

Preface

It is with great pleasure that we share this book and the wisdom of many mothers and daughters with you, our reader. As both of the authors are indeed daughters and mothers of daughters, we realize that no single mother-daughter relationship is like any other. We know that every relationship has its own nuances and qualities, but we believe similarities abound in the types of struggles and joys that are experienced within this very intense dyad.

While there are many different paths that can lead to motherhood, the focus of this book is on the relationship, not the etiology, of mothers and daughters. Many books focus on the variety of special circumstances that can land us in the role of mother or daughter—adoption, foster care, surrogate mothering, artificial insemination, and so on. Within this book, we may include stories of women who share details about their experiences of becoming mothers, or even finding their own mothers. However, these narratives will be presented within the overall framework of the book, which presents a chronological exploration of the mother-daughter relationship followed by an exploration of the messages passed along from mothers to daughters. Although there are so many diverse ways of finding oneself in a mother-daughter dyad, we must work with a limited number of pages. Therefore, our focus is necessarily delineated by the topics listed in the contents for this book. Whether a mother, a daughter, or someone who would like to understand better this complex relationship, we believe you will recognize bits and pieces of yourself or those you love within the pages of this work.

RESEARCHING THE RELATIONSHIP

To prepare for this project, we gathered a substantial amount of information via several methods. First, we developed a structured questionnaire that was a part of a large, qualitative study in which women of all ages, from eighteen years on up, were invited to share their experiences as mothers or daughters. The Institutional Review Board at the University of Mississippi approved this study. Next, due to the wealth of experience we have as counselors for women from their late teens well into older adulthood, we also recounted and described composite stories of clients we have had who have dealt with the struggles or shared narratives of the joys found in the mother-daughter relationship.

We have included the stories of a very diverse group of women within these pages, and although we have occasionally included a woman's ethnic identity as part of the descriptor, this is done so only when it is felt to be a relevant piece of data. In all other cases, we ask readers to refrain from making assumptions about the ethnicity of any of the individuals whose stories we shared. Women who represented many backgrounds and lifestyles shared many perspectives and experiences. In fact, approximately half of our sample was comprised of women of color.

Asking women to share their mother-daughter stories and experiences can bring about any number of divergent responses. Younger women are eager to share their stories about their relationship with their mothers, as they are often at the beginning of the shift that occurs in the relationship as mothers begin to recognize their daughters have become women. Budding friendships and shared interests were highlighted by many of this age group. Women in their middle years were often more hesitant to share the challenges in their relationships with their mothers, as there is often another shift going on during this period. Women are often at the point in life in which they are able to see their relationships more clearly, and the hurt and trauma they may have experienced, or perpetrated, often are too raw to reveal. However, if these same women had daughters of their own, they were often much more willing to share about this generation of the mother-daughter relationship. Women who have lost their mothers often shared the positive and uplifting stories that typified their relationships, although, conversely, there were a number of women who had been unable to reconcile with their mothers before their mothers passed away.

ORGANIZATION OF THE BOOK

This book is organized in four sections. The first section, "The Maternal Instinct—American Style," addresses the biological aspects of becoming a mother—from evolutionary patterns to current influences on pregnancy and birthing daughters. The second chapter addresses social and cultural forces that shape the motherhood role and how contemporary influences have redefined priorities and expectations. Our second section, "Mothers and Daughters over the Life Course," opens with a chapter that provides an overview of the expected challenges in the mother-daughter relationship as a function of the psychosocial development of daughters. We then provide chapters that cover the experience of mothering daughters from birth to adulthood and ending with a chapter addressing the turning of the tables when adult daughters must care for their aging or ill mothers.

Our third section, "A Mother's Influence," provides insight on the lessons that daughters learn from their mothers—either overtly or covertly. These chapters address topics such as sex and romance, parental divorce, social support, career, and finances. Our final section is titled "The Maternal Legacy." It opens with a chapter that addresses the transformation of the word *daughter* from noun to verb. We describe the ways in which mothers must allow their female offspring "to daughter" their mothers and fathers. We address four aspects of a daughter's development and describe how these transitions can play out in life. The next chapter is an ethnocultural exploration of the ways in which diversity of many types (ethnicity, social economic status, religion, and so on) influences the development of daughters into women. This section ends with a chapter that celebrates the positive outcomes and healthy relationships that women can find with their mothers.

In conclusion, we recognize that the mother-daughter relationship is perhaps the most intense and challenging relationship that women may experience. In the following chapters, we address some of the external, interpersonal, and intrapersonal forces that drive and shape this relationship. We share firsthand stories of the difficulties faced in successfully raising daughters as well as the pure joy that this relationship can yield for both individuals involved. We hope you enjoy reading this book and that you are able to recognize something of yourself within the pages as well as take hope that this intimately defining relationship can shift and improve over time.

Acknowledgments

Thank you to all of the wonderful individuals who opened their hearts with us to allow this book to be created! We had the pleasure of speaking to daughters from their early years through older adulthood and to mothers across the life span. We are grateful for the honesty and vulnerability exhibited as you shared your experiences and memories.

We also would like to thank our editor at Rowman & Littlefield, Suzanne Staszik-Silva, who saw the value of the project and supported its development from its conception to its publication.

S. E. D. & C. B. G.

I am deeply indebted to my amazing family—my partner, Ellen, and our kids, Georgia, Andy, and David. Our family constellation provides just one example of the ways in which more than just one person may mother us in our lifetimes. I am grateful for their unfailing support throughout the years. While the kids are now young adults and setting up nests of their own, the role of mother seems to grow only more deeply layered as our children mature. And for this, I am grateful!

S. E. D.

I am honored to have had the opportunity to be a small part of such a meaningful book. Thank you, Suzanne.

C. B. G.

I

The Maternal Instinct—American Style

ONE
Becoming a Mother
Biology Influences Culture

Many of us assume that the "maternal instinct" is encoded into the genes of every female baby conceived; however, the desire and ability to mother a child successfully are not necessarily inherent to the biological ability to conceive and deliver a child. Feminists have spent decades exploring the myth that motherhood is or should be the ultimate role for personal fulfillment for women.[1] As Adrienne Rich noted in her seminal work on motherhood, *Of Woman Born* (42), "The institution of motherhood is not identical with bearing and caring for children."[2] The art of becoming a mother is more complex than just the biological construct of reproduction; it requires an investment of altruistic care and the giving of oneself to another without surety that the love will be returned. The patriarchal culture shaped the cultural expectations of how "motherhood" should look, although good mothering does not necessarily mirror the "myth of the good mother" created by men. Aside from some highly unique species of animals, however, females are the vessels that carry forth each subsequent generation, and it is the gender most likely to oversee the nurturing and rearing of the children. Women today must redefine and reclaim the art and science of mothering in a way that makes sense for each one of us *individually*. But the hard science of conception and gestation has shed light on some interesting hardwired elements of motherhood.

THE SIREN CRY OF THE FERTILE FEMALE

The human female's unique physiology exhibits an extremely wide range of hormone secretion responses that reflect where she is in the reproductive cycle. Researchers fascinated with these effects have looked into how these cyclical changes affectively and subjectively influence both women and men. For instance, women's gaits have been found to be more attractive to men during the period in which women are ovulating.[3] Women prefer certain facial qualities in males depending on where they are in their menstrual cycle, with a pronounced desire for strongly masculine faces exhibited at peak fertility times.[4] Body odor also changes during the menstrual cycle, with its level of intensity at its lowest and attractiveness at its highest to males when women are at their most fertile period as compared to two other points measured during the menstrual cycle.[5] Another study has shown that the level of attractiveness of a woman's voice to males is at its highest when the risk of conception is at its height; this is considered most likely due to the varying effects of different hormones on the larynx just as they influence other aspects of physiology.[6] The metaphor of the "siren call" of women to men may not be so far off base.

THE INNER GLOW OF A PREGNANT WOMAN

At the moment of conception, women's bodies begin undergoing biological adjustments to allow the fertilized egg to grow into a healthy fetus. Some feminists have suggested that these changes associated with pregnancy, birth, and nursing a child are what give shape to the female's role as nurturer.[7] Biology may be shaping destiny, but the developing embryo is definitely shaping the changes in a woman's body needed to accommodate the new person. In fact, the saying that a "pregnant woman glows" is somewhat true, as blood volume increases by as much as 50 percent during pregnancy, causing a rosy glow for expectant moms.[8] As most of us know, gender is virtually decided from the moment the sperm cell enters the egg, depending on whether the sperm brings an X chromosome for a daughter or a Y chromosome for a son. Of course, bookshelves and Internet sites are filled with advice on how to successfully conceive the gender of choice—from wives' tales to scientific evidence, there is an abundance of information available for the fertile couple on this topic.

DAUGHTER OR SON?

Once a woman learns she is expecting, the world's attention—and frequently her own—turns to guessing at the baby's gender. Some interesting correlations with the conception of one gender over the other have been explored that stretch from economic factors to emotional and physiological traits.

Looking back through history across the globe, males have always been the favored gender. Termed *gendercide*, female offspring have been sacrificed by parents for hundreds of years.[9] In fact, estimates suggest that by 2004, possibly sixty to one hundred million females were missing from the population due to the choice of parents to sacrifice their daughters as they strove for sons. Historically, sons were perceived to be a better economic investment than daughters, as males would have the strength necessary to provide the labor that would translate into increased income or decreased workload for the family. Sadly, in earlier times when medical care was even more costly and difficult to obtain, parents frequently would allow their ill and frail infant daughters to succumb to disease and death rather than waste resources to invest in treatment.[10]

Unfortunate practices carried forward from the past, from female infanticide or medical neglect coupled with today's sex-selection technology, continue to allow parents to cooperatively shift the world's gender balance. Attitude and biology may actually work in concert to influence a baby's gender.

Another interesting historical note related to conception is that in times of stress, such as during a war, more sons will be born.[11] In times when resources are few and life is stressful, women are likely to produce more testosterone in response to their environmental deficits. Thus, male embryos have a better chance of thriving. Probably related to this increase in testosterone, according to findings that have appeared in the empirical literature, is the role of maternal dominance—the more strongly a woman perceives herself as having a dominant personality, the more likely she is to conceive sons.[12] And related to a strong personality, a woman with a strong constitution (because stronger and heavier is generally synonymous with healthier) is more likely to have a son. The timing and frequency of sexual intercourse also influence a baby's gender—the more frequent the activity, the greater the likelihood a son will be conceived due to hormonal levels of the mother's womb.[13] This scientific tenet supports the finding that married, or more specifically, cohabiting mothers are more likely to have a son than a single mother.[14]

For those women who are hoping to conceive a daughter, there are other answers beyond leaving a future baby-to-be's father. Women trying to get pregnant who cut down their salt and increase their calcium may be able to increase their chances at conceiving a daughter.[15] Maybe the "sugar and spice and all things nice" of which all "little girls are made of" really references the sweet over salty? And during the first few days after conception, female embryos consume 28 percent more glucose than male embryos—the differences in diet start early.[16] Diet, overall, has been shown to play a significant role in the baby's gender; healthy diets, as opposed to the scarcity of nutrients and food, favor the conception of males. Physical attributes of the parents also influence gender according to some research findings—some results suggested that tall and strong parents have more sons.[17] And if you are looking at your daughter and thinking that she is the most beautiful creature you've ever seen, it's probably true, especially if she looks like you! Some researchers have even suggested that beautiful people have more daughters than less attractive couples.[18] Although this last tidbit of information has been debated, if you are expecting or have a daughter, then you can simply accept it as fact!

In essence, there are several assumptions we can probably make about a woman carrying a daughter. Chances are that she is not exactly a "testosterone-wealthy" woman. Her daughter's father is probably not as young and sexually active as he once was. She probably weighs in on the slender side of the scale. And she is probably not facing significant crises, such as war or famine, at the present.

Once a daughter is on her way, many mothers are picking out dresses, hair bows, and pink paint. Other mothers are choosing more gender-neutral layette items and planning to avoid placing gender stereotypes on her daughter. Even with the potential of making a "gender-oriented politically incorrect" comment, many parents will swear that "raising sons is so much easier than raising daughters." It turns out that this belief may actually have a physiological component that surfaces during the earliest days of maternal experience—the greater the intensity of a mother's morning sickness during pregnancy, the greater the likelihood she is delivering a daughter.[19] A recently released study, however, actually indicates that a daughter takes less of a toll overall on a woman.[20] Mothers of sons have shorter life expectances than mothers of daughters after giving birth, in fact.

The female body is designed to change throughout the life course depending on what is physiologically expected of it at a certain stage. As a girl moves from childhood into adolescence, she becomes increasingly conscious of her body and its development. She may notice and obsess over many of these changes, from breasts that arrive too slowly to a first period that comes too soon. Turning to our mothers for reassurance can be easier for some young women than for others, as we found in our interviews—it seems that these changes can lead to some of the most difficult conversations young women can have with their mothers, as we'll discuss further in another chapter. However, a mother may be the best place to turn for guidance and inside information, as research continues to show that a young woman's age at menarche is significantly correlated with that of her mother. Our daughters are often more like us than they ever want to acknowledge; this makes sense given that we spend many months bathing them in the amniotic fluid that our bodies produce. And although they may also protest loudly that we just don't understand them as they dive into the "tween years," research has shown that during pregnancy, mothers' and children's hearts will beat in synchrony[21] —finding a shared rhythm that may take years to ever replicate, figuratively, once a daughter is born. The process from conception to delivery is one that is best managed through proactive maternal choices.

TAKE CARE OF THE SMALL STUFF BEFORE IT BECOMES BIG STUFF

When Jennifer, a thirty-something, first-time mother-to-be who is expecting a daughter, was asked about her feelings as she prepares for her daughter's arrival, here is her response:

> Being that this is my first child, I am feeling a little bit of everything. I am nervous, anxious, excited, joyful, fearful, etc. I am the kind of person who likes to know what is going to happen and plan accordingly, and this pregnancy experience has definitely changed that. I don't know what is going to happen from day to day or what I am going to be feeling. I have constant fears of doing something wrong while I am pregnant that may cause my daughter some problems when she is born. I am also nervous about taking care of my daughter the "right way," meaning making sure I meet all of her needs. For example, I have some idea about breastfeeding but not the reality of it. I am not sure if I would end up doing it right and potentially cause my daughter not to be able to breastfeed, which I know provides numerous health, growth, and intellectual benefits. I also fear all those unknowns of what could happen such as a stillbirth or SIDS. All these thoughts keep me up at night (that and the constant peeing).

Her response probably echoes the feelings of most women expecting their first child. Pregnancy is typically characterized by a tension between hopeful anticipation of a daughter's arrival and anxiety related to her health and well-being at birth. There is a normal amount of concern that any expectant mother may experience. However, when anxiety is overwhelming or sadness turns into depression, not only does a mother-to-be suffer, so, too, does her unborn child.

Psychological distress isn't unexpected during pregnancy—there are fears of the physical pain associated with childbirth, sadness about a changing body shape, and worries about the baby's health. In fact, almost every mother we interviewed acknowledged feeling anxiety about childbirth and childrearing. A little bit of sadness about anticipated life changes was also mentioned occasionally. However, depression is the most frequently experienced emotional disorder among expectant mothers[22] ; yet within a culture that focuses on the joy associated with pregnancy, many women may be hesitant to acknowledge or address any negative feelings experienced during this time. Women feel enormous pressures to emphasize the positive aspects of the pregnancy—the excited expectations about the joy and love the child will bring, the room design, playing in the park together. But there is so much more going on—partners who lack compassion or understanding for mood swings, physical demands that extend beyond the range of healthy for pregnant women, financial concerns, pressures from in-laws, people watching what you eat, worrying how you look, looking ahead at parenting alone, and more. Depending on the study cited, prevalence rates of the "garden variety" mood disorders, depression or anxiety, during pregnancy range from 8 percent to 30 percent.[23] Factors that increase the chances of experiencing distress include a past history of depression or anxiety, stressful life events, and less partner support throughout the pregnancy. It may be hard for expectant mothers to openly admit their distress, but admitting and finding a safe way to ameliorate them can make a huge difference on a baby's safe and healthy arrival.

Studies show that when psychological stress is not handled well during pregnancy, it is likely to affect fetal development.[24] Babies born to mothers who are struggling to cope with emotional disorders are more likely to have a lower birthweight as well as run a higher risk for spontaneous preterm arrival than those born to smoother-sailing mothers. The influence of stress during pregnancy continues into childhood and is visible through child behavior, temperament, and cognitive development. Anxious moms tend to have anxious babies,[25] and it is essential that these little girls are provided with strong, consistent, and supportive caregiving. Helping your daughter feel secure can help avoid any deficits in cognitive functioning and increases in fearfulness she may be predisposed toward developing. Healthy attachment to our daughters can only help us, as mothers, feel better about our relationships, and attachment begins to develop well before our daughters physically arrive in this earthly world.[26] Feeling positive about life and the baby on the way can make a significant difference in a daughter's future. Studies show that when depressed or clinically anxious mothers seek and accept treatment, the negative outcomes for their children are substantially reduced.[27] Sometimes treatment comes in nonclinical forms, such as reaching out to friends or understanding family members to help us as we start our motherhood journey.

GETTING OUT OF THE FUNK

We have cataloged the possible consequences of a mother's compromised psychological well-being during pregnancy, but now we will share the good news about what can be done to prevent or minimize the development of depression and anxiety for expectant mothers. Looking at the variables or circumstances that might prevent a mother-to-be from experiencing excessive distress and that might help enhance her attachment to her developing daughter, researchers have determined that two factors really matter, self-confidence and social support networks.[28] [29] These two factors are both about *relationships*; one involves looking within and building a positive relationship with oneself and seeing the value you bring to the lives of others—including your daughter. The second involves reaching out to others and establishing and cementing bonds. To be a good mother to a daughter, these are especially important, as we will be modeling for her how to have a healthy relationship with herself, first and foremost, and how to create healthy relationships with others. Both of these can be addressed early in a woman's pregnancy if either area is lacking.

SELF-CONFIDENCE STARTS WITHIN

We live in a culture that sometimes seems obsessed with self-promotion and self-aggrandizement; in fact, it is often parents who unintentionally create a sense of inflated self-esteem in their children.[30] Yet a deficit of self-confidence also tends to arise as a result of overt and covert messages sent to children from their parents. It has been found that having a strong level of self-esteem is dependent on our perceptions of support from those people with whom we have significant relationships, especially our parents, and perceptions of our competence in a variety of activities in which we seek to be successful, such as friendships or academics, for instance.[31]

It has also been found that a mother's affection for her daughter is related to the development of a daughter's self-esteem.[32] The stronger the perceived affection we felt from our mothers as children, the higher our levels of self-esteem climbed. However, the inverse was shown to be true through a separate longitudinal study that also explored the level of identification we feel with our mothers.[33] For those among us who experienced a strong identification with our mothers as we moved through childhood into young adulthood, and yet felt a great deal of rejection by our mothers, we probably struggled with issues of self-esteem. Children will accept their mother's opinion of their worth as valid and true based on the esteem in which they hold her as well as the shared sense of identity in which they accept her beliefs as their own.

Self-esteem is a complicated concept, yet it is at the basis of our beliefs of self-worth and value to others and society. When we believe that we have little to offer, it is much harder for us to feel good about our ability to mother or about our child. However, building a stronger sense of self-esteem can be a huge benefit as a woman takes on the job of mothering a baby.[34] In fact, self-esteem has been shown to play a significant role in the overall mental health of new mothers,[35] and that seems to make it an excellent target for prenatal attention so that we can more easily move into the role of supportive mother to our new daughters.

It is clear that self-esteem hinges on our perceptions of what others believe about us—thus, it is challenging to try to raise our own self-esteem in a vacuum. The sheer number of self-help books, tapes, videos, and programs available to help us increase our self-esteem is overwhelming—a quick search on a popular consumer site resulted in over fifty-four thousand related products! Another method of boosting self-esteem for pregnant women, however, is through group interventions and group prenatal education. Researchers found that women who participated in group care showed higher levels of self-esteem after the birth of their children.[36] Finding ways to get involved in group activities with women who share your interests and experiences are positive first steps for building your sense of competence as a new mother, and these group activities will also help you begin to meet the second essential condition for a positive transition to motherhood—social support.

BUILD A NETWORK OF SOCIAL SUPPORT

In the early days after a new baby arrives, there is little time to devote to networking and making social connections. It is helpful to create alliances with other expectant mothers and new mothers before your new daughter arrives. It's been shown that social support is intimately connected with a new mother's well-being,[37] yet making connections can be more difficult today than it was in generations past. Neighborhoods were once hubs of activity with children playing outside in the yards and green spaces; today's neighborhoods are often silent daytime ghost towns with seemingly deserted streets as families sequester themselves inside or within fenced yards. For expectant mothers, prenatal classes focused on childbirth, child development, or parenting are great ways to plant the seeds of friendship and support prior to your daughter's arrival. The friendships that can bloom in these settings have been found to be uniquely supportive of new mothers' mental well-being, as these friends and their babies are reference points for our own transition to motherhood as well as our daughters' development. Both of these processes—our gaining confidence as mothers and the cognitive, physical, and social development of our daughters—can bring anxiety, and the need for social support is strong. By actively seeking out empathic and supportive friends early on, the anxiety of new motherhood can be significantly lessened.

When I was a first-time expectant mother, none of my inner circle of friends had yet faced this life-altering transition. I remember trying to get the lowdown on motherhood from my own mother and my mother-in-law, but I was disappointed when both used the excuses of too much time having passed and a poor memory of how it had been to welcome their first child. I realized that not even the best book on pregnancy and childbirth was a substitute for getting the scoop on what it might be like to add a new life to my life. Unfortunately, the Internet wasn't up and running as freely as it would be just a couple of years later.

After starting a new job, I kept my eyes open for women who looked to be at about the same stage of life as I was. Luckily, I did find a couple of expectant mothers and a new mom in the building, and I fought against my introverted tendencies to approach these women and start conversations about motherhood and career balancing. These early efforts at connection eventually led to new friendships, and I felt relieved knowing that I had a social support network at the place where I spent the majority of my waking hours—on the job! Friendships with other new mothers were established through interactions at the home of the babysitter who cared for my daughter and their children when I returned to work a few months after she was born. Several of my friends from my prepregnancy days eventually moved into the same life stage as they welcomed their first babies, and it felt great to be able to offer support before they realized how valuable it would be once their babies arrived.

Other avenues for friendship development include both formal and informal meeting places for new mothers. One of the largest networks for "maternal networking" is Mothers of Preschoolers, or MOPS. This is an international organization with local group meetings that are designed to help mothers find friends and a sense of community (www.mops.org). Informal meeting grounds include developing relationships with the other mothers who are dropping off their children at the Mother's Morning Out program, day care, or church nursery.

If you are a single mother, the need for support can be even more vital. Depending on family background and family values, single parenthood can be a total nonevent or a cataclysmic occurrence. Among the women we interviewed, the majority of those who had to break the news of an unplanned pregnancy to their mothers cited this moment as the most stressful period in their relationships with their own mothers. In one extreme case, a now thirty-five-year-old woman shared that she was just seventeen when she had to share this type of news with her mother, and she stated that she was "pregnant with my first child, [my mother] slapped me and attempted to attack me . . . that was very painful." Another woman, nineteen years old, described the worst interaction she had experienced with her mother as the moment she had to admit to her mother that she was pregnant during her senior year of high school. She related that after revealing the news, her mother refused to even speak to her for the week that followed the confession. However, she went on to share that after her daughter was born, her mother witnessed her transformation from unruly adolescent to committed parent, and their relationship had begun to heal.

There are also rapidly increasing numbers of independent and self-sufficient adult women who choose to have children on their own for many reasons. Without a live-in partner to assist with the care of your child, social support may be even more essential. Building relationships with other parents and nonparents will provide you with a variety of resources and understanding friends who can ease the transition to motherhood. For those women who are welcoming new daughters into their homes with a same-gender partner, a social support system is equally as valuable as for a typical heterosexual parent couple.[38] Unfortunately, many lesbian couples continue to face familial rejection in addition to cultural stigma,[39] so finding supportive friends and gay-friendly, family-centered institutions can be key to making the early days of new parenthood—and all the years that follow—a little easier.

NOTES

1. P. Nicolson, "The Myth of the Maternal Instinct: Feminism, Evolution and the Case of Postnatal Depression," *Psychology, Evolution and Gender, 1*, no. 2 (1999a): 161–81.

2. Adrienne Rich, *Of Woman Born: Motherhood as Experience and Institution* (New York: Norton, 1986).

3. Meghan P. Provost, Vernon L. Quinsey, and Nikolaus F. Troje, "Differences in Gait across the Menstrual Cycle and Their Attractiveness to Men," *Archives of Sexual Behavior, 37*, no. 4 (2008): 598–604.

4. Benedict C. Jones, Lisa M. DeBruine, David I. Perrett, Anthony C. Little, David R. Feinberg, and Miriam J. Law Smith, "Effects of Menstrual Cycle Phase on Face Preferences," *Archives of Sexual Behavior, 37* (2008): 78–84.

5. Jan Havlicek, Radka Dvorakova, Ludek Bartos, and Jaroslav Flegr, "Non-Advertized Does Not Mean Concealed: Body Odour Changes across the Human Menstrual Cycle," *Ethology, 112* (2006): 81–90.

6. R. Nathan Pipitone and Gordon G. Gallup Jr., "Women's Voice Attractiveness Varies across the Menstrual Cycle," *Evolution and Human Behavior, 29*, no. 4 (2008): 268–74.

7. Alice Rossi, "A Biosocial Perspective on Parenting," *Daedalus, 106*, no. 2 (1977): 1–31.

8. Marian C. Condon, *Women's Health: Body, Mind, Spirit: An Integrated Approach to Wellness and Illness* (Upper Saddle River, NJ: Prentice Hall, 2004), 472.

9. D. T. Courtwright, "Gender Imbalances in History: Causes, Consequences and Social Adjustment," *Ethics, Bioscience and Life, 3* (2008): 32–40.

10. Ibid., 33.

11. Ibid., 33.

12. Valerie J. Grant, "Maternal Dominance and the Conception of Sons," *British Journal of Medical Psychology, 67*, no. 4 (1994): 343–51.

13. Courtwright, "Gender Imbalances."

14. "Girl Power: Single Mothers Are More Likely to Have Daughters," *Economist, 373*, no. 8398 (2004): 79–80.

15. A. M. Noorlander, J. P. M. Geraedts, and J. B. M. Melissen, "Female Gender Pre-Selection by Maternal Diet in Combination with Timing of Sexual Intercourse—A Prospective Study," *Reproductive BioMedicine Online, 21*, no. 6 (2010): 794–802.

16. D. K. Gardner, P. L. Wale, R. Collins, and M. Lane, "Glucose Consumption of Single Post-Compaction Human Embryos Is Predictive of Embryo Sex and Live Birth Outcome," *Human Reproduction, 26*, no. 8 (2011): 1981–86.

17. Satoshi Kanazawa, "Big and Tall Parents Have More Sons: Further Generalizations of the Trivers Willard Hypothesis (hTWH)," *Journal of Theoretical Biology, 235*, no. 4 (2005): 583–90.

18. Satoshi Kanazawa, "Beautiful Parents Have More Daughters: A Further Implication of the Generalized Trivers Willard Hypothesis (gTWH)," *Journal of Theoretical Biology, 244* (2007): 133–40.

19. Johan Askling, Gunnar Erlandsson, Magnus Kaijser, Olof Akre, and Anders Ekbom, "Sickness in Pregnancy and Sex of Child," *The Lancet, 354* (1999): 2053.

20. S. Helle and V. Lummaa, "A Trade-Off between Having Many Sons and Shorter Maternal Post-Reproductive Survival in Pre-Industrial Finland," *Biology Letters, 9*, no. 2 (2013): 20130034.

21. P. C. Ivanov, Q. D. Y. Ma, and R. P. Bartsch, "Maternal-Fetal Heartbeat Phase Synchronization," *Proceedings of the National Academy of Sciences, 106*, no. 33 (2009): 13641–642.

22. V. Satyanarayana, A. Lukose, and K. Srinivasan, "Maternal Mental Health in Pregnancy and Child Behavior," *Indian Journal of Psychiatry, 53*, no. 4 (2011): 351–61.

23. Ibid., 352.

24. Ibid., 353.

25. S. Perren, A. von Wyl, D. Burgin, H. Simoni, and K. von Klitzing, "Depressive Symptoms and Psychosocial Stress across the Transition to Parenthood: Associations with Parental Psychopathology and Child Difficulty," *Journal of Psychosomatic Obstetrics and Gynaecology, 26*, no. 3 (2005): 173–83.

26. C. Corter and A. S. Fleming, "Psychobiology of Maternal Behavior in Human Beings," in M. Bornstein (ed.), *Handbook of Parenting*, 87–116 (Hillsdale, NJ: Erlbaum, 1995).

27. M. L. Gunlicks and M. M. Weissman, "Change in Child Psychopathology with Improvement in Parental Depression: A Systematic Review," *Journal of the American Academy of Child and Adolescent Psychiatry, 47*, no. 4 (2008): 379–89.

28. B. Edwards, C. Galletly, T. Semmier-Booth, and G. Dekker, "Antenatal Psychosocial Risk Factors and Depression among Women Living in Socioeconomically Disadvantaged Suburbs in Adelaide, South Australia," *Australia and New Zealand Journal of Psychiatry, 42*, no. 1 (2008): 45–50.

29. A. Yarcheski, N. E. Mahon, T. J. Yarcheski, M. M. Hanks, and B. L. Cannella, "A Meta-Analytic Study of Predictors of Maternal-Fetal Attachment," *International Journal of Nursing Studies, 46*, no. 5 (2009): 708–15.

30. A. Assor and K. Tal, "When Parents' Affection Depends on Child's Achievement: Parental Conditional Positive Regard, Self-Aggrandizement, Shame and Coping in Adolescents," *Journal of Adolescence, 35*, no. 2 (2012): 249–60.

31. S. Harter, "The Development of Self-Representations," in W. Damon and N. Eisenberg (eds.), *Handbook of Child Psychology: Social, Emotional, and Personality Development*, 5th ed., Vol. 3 (New York: Wiley, 1998), 553–617.

32. T. Ojanen and D. G. Perry, "Relationship Schemas and the Developing Self: Perceptions of Mother and of Self as Joint Predictors of Early Adolescents' Self-Esteem," *Developmental Psychology, 43*, no. 6 (2007): 1474–83.

33. K. R. Berenson, T. N. Crawford, P. Cohen, and J. Brook, "Implications of Identification with Parents and Parents' Acceptance for Adolescent and Young Adult Self-Esteem," *Self and Identity, 4*, no. 3 (2005): 289–301.

34. D. J. Terry, T. A. McHugh, and P. Noller, "Role Dissatisfaction and the Decline in Marital Quality across the Transition to Parenthood," *Australian Journal of Psychology, 43*, no. 3 (1991): 129–32.

35. O. Taubman-ben-Ari, E. Sivan, and M. Dolizki, "The Transition to Motherhood—A Time for Growth," *Journal of Social and Clinical Psychology, 28* (2008): 943–70.

36. J. R. Ickovics, E. Reed, U. Magriples, C. Westdahl, S. S. Rising, and T. S. Kershaw, "Effects of Group Prenatal Care on Psychosocial Risk in Pregnancy: Results from a Randomized Controlled Trial," *Psychology and Health, 26*, no. 2 (2011): 235–50.

37. M. L. Nolan, V. Mason, S. Snow, W. Messenger, J. Catling, and P. Upton, "Making Friends at Antenatal Classes: A Qualitative Exploration of Friendship across the Transition to Motherhood," *The Journal of Perinatal Education, 21*, no. 3 (2012): 178–85.

38. H. M. W. Bos, F. van Balen, and D. C. van den Boom, "Experience of Parenthood, Couple Relationship, Social Support, and Child-Rearing Goals in Planned Lesbian Mother Families," *Journal of Child Psychology and Psychiatry, 45*, no. 4 (2004): 755–64.

39. S. Degges-White and J. Marszalek, "An Exploration of Long-Term, Same-Sex Relationships: Benchmarks, Perceptions, and Challenges," *Journal of LGBT Issues in Counseling, 1*, no. 4 (2006/2007): 90–120.

TWO

The Social and Cultural Aspects of Motherhood

What constitutes a "good mother" is deeply and indivisibly embedded within any specific culture in any given time period. Our expectations of ourselves as mothers are affected not only by our childhood experiences with our own mothers but also by other people in our lives, the behaviors of other mothers, and by books, television shows, movies, and advertisements. Though the *Leave It to Beaver* days are over, there are many new media role models available, from the iconic mom-daughter program *Gilmore Girls* to the more modern mothering found in *Modern Family*.

THE GOOD MOTHER

Once a woman becomes a mother, she enters a kind of sisterhood. Mothers know certain things about each other without having to say a word. Mothers know the hardship when there is "no manual" with all the right answers. They quickly learn what it is like to have "your heart on the outside of your body" as described by Linda, a mom in her early thirties. In addition, they experience how children can be deliciously sweet as well as frustratingly uncivilized. In addition to this common body of knowledge, mothers also hold a spectrum of different mothering priorities and philosophies. There are ecoconscious mothers, working mothers, breast feeders and bottle feeders, soccer moms and PTA mothers, protective mothers and permissive mothers, and so on. Yet across generations and cultures, when asked for a definition of how they defined a "good mother," women consistently named similar variations on a core theme regarding the qualities that constitute the "good mother."

15

The universally agreed-upon description of good mothering high-lighted the ability to successfully care for a child, but more emphatically, women affirmed that good mothering is marked by the ability to love one's child. Some women offered a more extensive description of a moth-er's love, such as the belief that a good mother is someone who loves her child more than she loves anyone else, loves the child unconditionally, and loves the child for the longest time—from conception to eternity.

Women also expressed that "being there" for the child is an inherent part of good mothering. In some cases, "being there" was described as a consistent physical presence, but more frequently, it was described as being readily accessible in times of need. Vickie, a thirty-five-year-old mother of a five-year-old daughter, shared that being a good mother meant being "patient with my daughter and also honoring the gift that she is to my husband and me." Less common, but still prevalent, were descriptions of a good mother as one who disciplines well or sets consis-tent and clear limits for the child. Women apparently value mothers who raise their children to be independent and to contribute positively to society. Another somewhat surprising, but not infrequently noted, qual-ity was a mother's ability to "own up to mistakes and imperfections." However, women provided differing rationales as to the importance of this mothering behavior. Tammy, a mother of four children spanning twenty-five to five years old, thought it was important "so the child can accept being imperfect, too," and Nicole, a twenty-seven-year-old mother of two young children, valued "allowing the child to have a voice of her own."

For many women who valued their religious belief systems and prac-tices, instilling faith in their progeny was an integral part of being a good mother. Women shared that this might involve shared blessings at meals, prayers at bedtime, and regular church attendance. Other women re-ported deeply valuing sharing their worldview or personal values, such as the importance of an education, generosity, or the "golden rule" with their daughters, but this theme tended to be highlighted in conversations about life lessons, not necessarily as part of the definition of a good mother. It seems all mothers wanted to share their worldview with their children and raise their children to value those things that they, them-selves, value.

Thus, on a core level, women across generations and cultures tended to see the most critical aspects of motherhood in a similar way: love, patience and acceptance, being available, and transmitting values. So how and why are the actual mothering behaviors different across genera-tions, social class, race, and other cultural dimensions?

BECOMING A MOTHER

Prior to giving birth, a woman has socially constructed mental images of herself as a mother forged from her experiences being mothered, being around other mothers, and from messages about motherhood and children from her social environment. These images may be distinct and well developed from years of fantasy play as a child combined with a great deal of self-knowledge and childcare knowledge; these images may be shadowy outlines of which she is not fully cognizant and that merely begin to surface during pregnancy. She may imagine herself calmly holding her baby, gazing into her eyes just as the mother does in the diaper commercial, or frolicking in the yard with her toddler like the woman appearing on the magazine cover. The chances are very good that the happy soon-to-be-mother is not imagining herself down the road a few years, feeling tired and yelling at her child "for the hundredth time, put your dirty clothes into the laundry bin." She is envisioning herself as an idealized mother. Though a woman may be nervous of becoming a mother, women usually see themselves as offering a child the love and guidance they see as necessary to be a good mother.

Women try to embody their idealized version of a mother. Time and again, mothers in our study told of wanting to live up to a mental image they held of how mothers *should* be, sometimes much like their mothers, and other times in direct contrast to their mothers. But in the transition from fantasizing about one's self as a mother to actually living as a mother and engaging in daily mothering behaviors, women must acknowledge and integrate the unique aspects and needs of her child; shed idealized, unattainable images of herself and motherhood; all while gaining competence in caretaking tasks. Through the caretaking reality, a woman must often form a new identity that requires a different sense of herself as a mother as well as of who she is as a person. This is called *maternal role attaining* (MRA) in the literature, and it will occur with differing degrees of confidence and satisfaction depending on the unique identity of each mother and child duo. Individual factors such as child and mother temperaments as well as a host of social factors such as social stress, socioeconomic status (SES), and various forms of social and instrumental support influence the ease in attaining confidence in the maternal role.[1]

Some women ease into motherhood with relevant knowledge, confidence, support, and adequate resources, yet many women do not have this golden constellation in place. When there are large discrepancies between what a woman has imagined motherhood would be and the reality of motherhood she faces, the transition to motherhood can be a particularly difficult one. It is noteworthy that even in the best circumstances, becoming a mother is accompanied by the grief process[2] of shedding parts of the idealized identity that did not fit the reality of a woman's mothering experience as well as parts of a woman's former self that were shed in her efforts to care for a dependent infant. Women have accused other women of engaging in a "conspiracy of silence"[3] about the negative aspects of motherhood.

Although the change in identity may be greatest when a woman gives birth to her first child, it has been emphasized that a mother's life space is continually changing with each subsequent birth, the maturing of the child(ren), the aging of the mother, environmental factors, and time.[4] We can, in fact, be a different mother to our different children or even be a different person at different points in our motherhood journey. Thus, many women may spend their lifetimes trying to embody their image of the "ideal" mother. Moreover, many women shared that being a mother was more challenging than expected.

MOTHERS OF YESTERYEAR

When we asked women how they have seen motherhood change over the generations, we heard a great many consistent reports. In retrospective reports from our women who were actively mothering in the 1950s, 1960s, and 1970s, there were many sparkling homes; apparently cleaning was a mothering duty. Women in their forties, fifties, and sixties verified these reports, sharing memories of their mothers busy keeping the houses clean and meals on the table. Stay-at-home mothers typically separated their cleaning duties into daily routines, such as dusting and vacuuming on Mondays and bathrooms and bed sheets on Tuesdays. Many watched soap operas in the afternoon or spent time in personal pastimes such as gardening, reading, or volunteering. Preparing and serving meals was another daily chore, and women shared memories of many large meals shared with the family at the table. Reflecting a mother's cultural heritage, specific foods and menus were identified with their early memories. Some of the southern women spoke of classic fried chicken or other hearty meats, mashed potatoes, and rich casseroles. Women from the Midwest reminisced about homemade pierogies, while others recalled the pasta courses at a grandmother's table. Whether a woman was a first-generation American or from several generations after her forebears' arrival, food from the "homeland" was frequently mentioned. Though mothers of yesteryear did not necessarily cook healthy, they clearly cooked hearty—and they did it every day.

According to our interviewees, the family meal routine was as common in the homes of working mothers as it was for those who were able to stay at home. Much like today's cultural patterns, working mothers came home and worked the "second shift" feeding their families every day and working hard to keep their houses in order on the weekends. Even in homes where mothers stayed home, children really were "shooed" outside to play while mothers cleaned, watched soap operas, had time to themselves, socialized with other women, or viewed television with their husbands in the evening. In the words of one fifty-seven-year-old interviewee who raised a son as a single working mother, "All of us were doing a deep house cleaning every week. Everyone I knew was scrubbing, always cleaning and letting the kids be kids."

This emphasis on domestic chores was not always as straightforward for the women of yesteryear as it may have appeared to those around them. One woman, now in her seventies, shared, "I wanted my kids to have the *Father Knows Best* family, but I hated cooking and cleaning. It always felt like a role and it was a hard role for me to play." When reflecting on the changes in motherhood over the years, many women in their thirties and forties spoke with an awed tone of their own mothers' energy and domestic prowess. One woman noted that even though her mother never complained about her domestic responsibilities, she was sure that her mother had to have been exhausted at the end of every day.

There were, however, some major differences in the behaviors of women who mothered from the 1950s into the 1980s that may have been a saving grace. These women reported having had more personal time. Women were unconcerned when the kids ran around the neighborhood unsupervised, and they put the kids to bed early to enjoy the evening for themselves. Women with means hired teenage babysitters so they could enjoy adult time. Kids had down time, unscheduled and without being entertained by their adult caretakers. Not only did these mothers engage in these self-satisfying behaviors with greater frequency than women of today, but they also did so guilt free.

MY, HOW THINGS HAVE CHANGED: INTENSIVE MOTHERING

In our interviews with women across the life span, we heard distinct differences in the expectations the older generations and modern mothers hold for themselves in motherhood. It seems that the majority of mothers today do far more than simply feed, clothe, love, and shelter their children. There is an Internet joke that occasionally circulates that outlines "The Job Description of a Mother." It provides an exhaustive list of the plethora of skills motherhood demands while offering no material compensation. Women who become mothers under the contemporary Western definition[5] of a good mother find themselves expected to be skilled nurses, teachers, guidance counselors, mechanics, organizers, dieticians, chauffeurs, and so on. Mothers believe their lives should be child centered. Moreover, all these motherly duties should be completed gracefully and selflessly.

Today's relatively new paradigm of motherhood was first labeled *intensive mothering* by sociologist Sharon Hays in her book, *The Cultural Contradictions of Motherhood*.[6] She noticed that women who had been succeeding in the workplace were reviving their efforts in the home. Women were trying to have successful careers *and* be heavily involved mothers; just like the superwomen in the stories they had been told, they were trying to "have it all." However, not only were women attempting to combine a career track with mommyhood, but today's more highly educated, post-feminist-and-post-feminist-backlash mothers were seeking to attain a high level of success in both. In her observation of this shift, Hays noted, "The idea that correct child rearing requires not only large quantities of money but also professional-level skills and copious amounts of physical, mental, and emotional energy on the part of the individual mother is a relatively recent historical phenomenon."[7] Since Hays's initial foray into critiquing the institution of intensive motherhood, she has been joined by many women's advocates who have questioned the idea that motherhood has to be so labor intensive, emotionally absorbing, and financially draining.

Though intensive mothering may require different mothering activities as the children age, its central requirement is for a mother to be *fully* engaged with her child. For instance, mothers of toddlers interviewed were concerned with having enough floor time with their children, while mothers of school-age children were often heavily engaged in their children's extracurricular activities. Where children of yesteryear may have shown up for school-based after-school extracurricular activities by riding their bikes back to the school, today's intensive mothers drive their children to their expensive "challenger-level" sport and stay to watch practices—even if that means watching one hundred practices a year! Intensive mothering is composed of five general beliefs: 1) mothers are the most "essential" caregiver to the child, 2) motherhood is the "highest" calling, 3) mothers need to stimulate their children's mental and physical development, 4) motherhood is very challenging, and 5) good mothers create a life for themselves that is child centered.[8] In order to be fully child centered, intensive mothering requires a level of investment and selflessness that some people argue is counter to the best interests of our children as well as deleterious to the well-being of mothers. Moreover, due to a host of reasons, not the least of which is the fact that intensive mothering requires a large amount of resources, it is a predominantly middle- to upper-middle-class phenomenon. Yet as the dominant narrative, it affects the practices and sense of mothering success for women throughout the United States.

DOING THE "PRETZEL"

To be a good mother within the intensive mothering paradigm, one must devote an enormous amount of personal resources to raising children. Through observation of the covers of the various mother-oriented magazines, it appears that crafting with one's child and providing vegetable dishes that resemble animals or smiley faces is part and parcel of being a mother. How is the noncrafty mother to feel? Julie Stephens describes contemporary mothers as "caught in a constant process of anxiety-ridden self-improvement."[9] One young woman shared that to her "love is wanting to be better than I am," and explained that she wants to be better in every way for her child, such as better organized, more creative, and more upbeat and fun.

Guilt and the lack of time were major themes in the reports of contemporary mothers. One mom stated, "I never have a free minute," while another woman describes herself as "bending into a pretzel to get home from work to get the children to their respective sporting events on time with something healthier than a fast food kids' meal." Mothers wanted their children to have quality time and to have nice things. They were concerned that their children would fall behind other kids if young children were not read to every night or if older children did not participate in extracurricular activities.

Many of the mothers we interviewed indicated that they are clearly sensitive to the competitiveness of modern society and are doing everything in their power to help their children have an "edge on the competition." Women used terms such as *chaos, mayhem*, and *overwhelmed* to describe their family life. Judith Warner, in her review of research on the effects of intensive mothering on mothers, cited numerous studies that indicated that a mother's self-conception, sense of well-being, and mental health were degraded when they ascribed to intensive mothering ideals.[10] Yet contemporary mothers frequently shared with us a desire to be *more* involved with their children than they were already—or at least to have more time to either "do it right" or actually to savor the time together.

In our interviews, current grandmothers of today's children also noted that today's families are "far busier" and that "women are far more involved in every aspect of their children's daily lives than we used to be." They see contemporary women as far more engaged with their children, and though they didn't voice having wished to have sacrificed themselves to any greater degree, they did often lament time spent in domestic chores at the expense of tending to their children's emotional needs or just having kid-fun. It is ironic that many contemporary moms spoke with self-recrimination of their inability to meet their mother's generational standard for clean, organized homes and hearty, healthy meals, yet the older generation of women was impressed by modern moms' involvement with their kids. The older generation of mothers, many of whom where grandmothers, were using this life lesson and described themselves as far more involved with their grandchildren than they ever were with their children.

WORK IS TO BLAME

Intensive mothering is hard work 24/7. Many of the women interviewed said they fell short as a mother (and often as an employee, too, due to being torn between roles). When asked to share how they fell short, the women often felt they failed because of their inability to balance (calmly) intensive mothering demands while keeping the home clean and organized with healthy meals on the table. Gena, a working mother of two, quantified her mothering success rate at "70 percent of the time." Despite the potentially overwhelming family schedules, women often chastised themselves for a perceived lack of organizational skills or lack of boundless energy. Equally often, mothers reported that the time demands of being in the paid labor force were to blame for their emotional predicament.

Despite having professional careers, several mothers talked about their wishes for freedom from employment. Several women explicitly stated, "I hate work." These same women were quick to describe benefits to their employment beyond income, such as feelings of accomplishment, camaraderie with colleagues, and the ability to focus on an engaging task without interruption; yet the desire to be more fully involved with their children—or more fully sane while they mothered—appeared to be of higher value than careers. The aforementioned mother, Gena, stated, "I wouldn't work if I didn't have to. If I had more time, I'd be more involved with my children. I'd play checkers." When the children entered school, women suggested that part-time work was the most desirable situation for creating a better-balanced life. Only a few women noted a belief that if their husbands shared more household chores then would they have more available time to enjoy their children. Nor did many women suggest that if they refocused energies away from meeting their children's seemingly endless needs and desires they would have the desired "me time." Though family schedules were frequently critiqued, interviewees rarely directly questioned the underlying intensive parenting beliefs.

CHILDREN RUNNING MARATHONS

The definition of a "good mother" has accumulated more qualifiers and higher qualifications in direct relation to beliefs about the "preciousness" of children and the challenges of childhood. Women have changed their mothering behaviors in a host of ways that recognize this perceived increase in children's value. Psychologists and childcare experts of the mid-1900s began encouraging the recognition of children as individuals with needs and ideas of their own, not merely as extensions of their parents. In fact, several older women noted that when they were raising children, they were deeply concerned with what others thought about their children and how their children's behavior reflected upon them as parents. Contemporary women voiced not being as concerned about their neighbors' impressions as their parents had been, but instead they were completely focused on their children's needs. Thanks to Dr. Spock's bestselling book, *The Common Sense Book of Baby and Child Care*, women were encouraged to be more affectionate with their children.[11] The way women speak to their children changed in the late 1900s. The use of positive language, we were told, will build a child's self-esteem; conversely, we came to fear that an angry command could wreak havoc on children's emotional development. As women became more cognizant of their interactions with their children and the potential impact of these interactions on their children, the job requirements of motherhood grew.

Even beyond gains in the growing cultural awareness of children's emotional and psychological well-being, children's other more material needs appear to have grown. In our increasingly complex and competitive world, mothers perceive achievement in all aspects of life—athletic, social, educational, you name it—as paramount. The exorbitant and, for some, prohibitive costs of college tuition and the competitiveness of college admission inspire some parents to view their preschooler's abilities as conduits to scholarships and future success. First-graders are running alongside their parents training for the next 5K run. Mothers feel pressured to structure most moments of a child's day with enriching activities geared toward making them future leaders. In addition to achievement, contemporary mothers are concerned about their children's safety. They perceive the world as full of safety risks such as gangs, drugs, and violence. Many of the women we interviewed discussed this "high stakes" situation. One mother clearly articulated her concern that "the consequences of not being engaged in her child's life are much greater" than they used to be.

We also heard from women who voiced their secret wish that their child not be involved in organized sports and that they not need to be driven to practices and games, yet they also stated that they would never restrict these activities and, in fact, wished they had the resources to allow their children access to even more opportunities. Women fear that if they are not involved enough in their children's lives, their children will either fall prey to the evils of the world or the child will fail in life. The need to sacrifice for our children appears to have grown exponentially in the last couple of decades. For now, it seems that women are willing to "pretzel" themselves because they love their children and want to meet the cultural expectations that their children become small superachievers and, correspondingly, overwhelm themselves trying to be wonder woman mothers.

WHERE HAS THE VILLAGE GONE? CO-MOTHERING

In Robert Putnam's book, *Bowling Alone: The Collapse and Revival of the American Community*, he outlined the disengagement of individuals from their community in favor of a more solitary existence centering on the nuclear family.[12] One white woman, age sixty, remembered the days when sharing kid duty with other women was widely practiced: "We bought a pool for the neighborhood kids. We took turns watching other women's kids so they could clean their homes in peace. The kids ran around the neighborhood building forts, riding bikes, and playing hide-and-go-seek. Sometimes, my friend and I would chat and chat while the kids played." Though some modern mothers reported carpooling with a handful of other moms, some cultures within the United States continue to share broader caretaking duties either between mothers and grand-mothers, aunts or other female relatives, or among groups of women, which was a common practice for mothers of yesteryear. Women of color tended to be more communal in their daily mothering duties, readily taking on another mouth to feed akin to the role of the "othermother" as a source of social support in African American communities.[13]

Women of color also appear to approach the role of mother from a less rigid framework than the predominantly white, middle-class, intensive-mother narrative. In a sample of 1,625 low-income African American and Hispanic mothers, 80 percent believe that a woman should have children if she wants to, even if she is not married.[14] These same researchers stated that children are so deeply valued in these communities that waiting for marriage is not necessarily prudent because males are not always "suit-able" for marriage due to limited employment options and other fallout from living in a racist society. As champions of co-mothering, women of color often believe other women have much to offer their own children.

In a series of in-depth interviews with three generations of African American women, Katherine Fouquier found other themes that chal-lenged the "good mother" definition held by society at large.[15] For in-stance, mothering their children in a racist world, African American mothers emphasized that "their daughters be self-reliant, independent, and self-assured."[16] This theme was readily apparent in our research as well.

Thus, many sociocultural factors influence the priorities of a mother. Not all contemporary mothers aspire to intensive parenting. Some, espe-cially women with fewer resources, consider themselves "making it" when they are able to meet the basic physical needs of their children.[17] Yet as the dominant narrative, the theoretical underpinnings of intensive parenting affect society at large. Thus, most people hold true at least some of the tenets such as the importance of a mother's selflessness. Intensive parenting is something like the movie stars who stare at us from magazines in the grocery store checkout: an idealized image that few obtain without airbrushing and a personal assistant but that still manages to remind us of our imperfections.

FROM MOM WITH LOVE

Women who became mothers before the 1990s, women of color, contemporary mothers, and of course, intensive mothers all do what they do out of love. Society certainly shapes what moms see as necessary for their children, whether that is to protect daughters from dating the "wrong kind of boy" or pushing them to make straight A's. Mothers want to give their daughters the good things their mothers gave to them as well as compensate for the ways they felt their own mothers fell short. They lose sleep, are worn down in caring for their kids, spend too much on prom dresses, all because they want the best for their children. Women share themselves and their life lessons so their daughters will learn what they have to offer and ultimately, have a better life.

We have now addressed the biological and sociocultural aspects of motherhood. Hopefully we have provided an overarching perspective in which to view mothers and mothering behaviors. In the following chapters, we are going to move into specifically addressing the mother-daughter relationship in a variety of ways.

NOTES

1. R. T. Mercer, "Becoming a Mother versus Maternal Role Attainment," *Journal of Nursing Scholarship, 36*, no. 3 (2004): 226–32.

2. P. Nicolson, "Loss, Happiness, and Post Partum Depression: The Ultimate Paradox," *Canadian Psychology/Psychologie canadienne, 40*, no. 2 (1999b): 162–78.

3. C. McVeigh, "Motherhood Experiences from the Perspectives of First Time Mothers," *Clinical Nursing Research, 6*, no. 4 (1997): 335–48.

4. Mercer, "Becoming a Mother versus Maternal Role Attainment."

5. A. O'Reilly, "Outlaw(ing) Motherhood: A Theory and Politic of Maternal Empowerment for the Twenty-First Century," *HECATE, 36*, no. 1/2 (2010): 17–29.

6. S. Hays, *The Cultural Contradictions of Motherhood* (New Haven, CT: Yale University Press, 1996).

7. Ibid., 5.

8. J. Warner, "Is Too Much Mothering Bad for You? A Look at the New Social Science," *The Virginia Quarterly Review, 88*, no. 4 (2012): 48–53.

9. J. Stephens, "Beyond Binaries in Motherhood Research," *Family Matters, 69* (2004): 88–93.

10. Warner, "Is Too Much Mothering Bad for You?"

11. B. Spock, *The Common Sense Book of Baby and Child Care* (New York: Simon & Schuster, Inc., 1945).

12. R. D. Putnam, *Bowling Alone: The Collapse and Revival of the American Community* (New York: Simon & Schuster, 2000).

13. F. K. Fouquier, "The Concept of Motherhood among Three Generations of African American Women," *The Journal of Nursing Scholarship, 43*, no. 2 (2011): 145–53.

14. A. Cherlin, C. Cross-Barnet, L. M. Burton, and R. Garrett-Peters, "Promises They Can Keep: Low-Income Women's Attitudes toward Motherhood, Marriage, and Divorce," *Journal of Marriage and Family, 70*, no. 4 (2008): 919–33.

15. Fouquier, "The Concept of Motherhood."

16. Ibid., 149.

17. T. Wright, "'Making It' versus Satisfaction: How Women Raising Young Children in Poverty Assess How Well They Are Doing," *Journal of Social Science Research, 39*, no. 2 (2013): 269–80.

II

Mothers and Daughters over the Life Course

THREE

Predictable Mother-Daughter Challenges over the Life Course

Disagreements between mothers and daughters will ebb and flow over the course of the relationship. We assume two-year-olds will test their independence and push against the maternal reminder to "Please do . . ." with a fervent, stubborn, "No!" Adolescent stubbornness and independence can also push a positive, harmonious relationship into dangerous, battleground territory. As one woman shared, "As a young teen and preteen, I pushed my mother to her limits and was defiant." Being aware of the typical developmental trajectory of our daughters may allow us to more effectively mother them and, potentially, to predict, mitigate, or even circumvent potential conflicts. After a quick overview of developmental stage theory, we will review some of the most frequently experienced crises that can help you prepare for obstacles or, alternately, put into perspective some of the challenges you may have already faced with your own daughter or mother.

SKIPPING ALONG THE DEVELOPMENTAL PATH

Erik Erikson outlined one of the more comprehensive and enduring theories of human development.[1] He developed a map of human psychosocial development that covered the crises and touch points we experience from birth to the final days of life. Built on a framework that addressed our urge to connect and relate to others, it describes eight stages in which our relationship with others and ourselves is the center point. Erikson used opposing outcomes as the vector that represents each stage, such as *trust versus mistrust*. Following is a brief description of each stage and how the relevant conflict may play out within the mother-daughter dyad.

BIRTH TO THE FIRST BIRTHDAY

The stage in which we are thrust with our first breath is *trust versus mistrust*. This period is typically when the initial relationship between a daughter and her mother is first established and solidified. When we are able to provide our daughters with a stable bond during this period, we are letting them know that the world is a good place and we are there for them in times of distress and times of success. The successful navigation of this crisis builds our daughter's ability to hope, the basic virtue associated with this stage, according to Erikson. When our daughter cries, it is important that we soothe, and when our daughter coos, it is important that we respond. This is a period in which that first effort to connect to a social and relational world begins.

TODDLER YEARS

The next developmental stage we encounter is *autonomy versus shame and doubt*, and this is the stage through which all demanding toddlers must pass en route to a sense of independence that will carry them through later challenges. Not surprisingly, Erikson associated the basic virtues of willpower and self-control with this conflict. Our darling daughters may surprise us with their lung capacity and endurance as they stage tantrums in response to being restrained from their desired goal. However, a recent study noted that the strength and security of the attachment between mothers and their daughters, a task worked out in that first year, resulted in less conflict in three-year-olds.[2] If a strong emotional bond exists by the time the "terrible twos" arrive, our daughters' autonomy may be on its way to a secure status as well, thus creating fewer over-the-top, screaming-until-blue-in-the-face battles of will overall.

PRESCHOOL GIRLS

These years are marked by our daughters' experiencing a wider social world in which they are given opportunities to interact with a wider range of people. Encouraged to be more interactive and responsible, they face *initiative versus guilt*. Aware of the need to be their own "little person," they also begin to understand consequences for unacceptable behavior. Purpose and direction in life are the basic virtues our daughters can begin to develop during this period. Wanting to be like their mothers and please parents at this stage, little girls begin to recognize when they have disappointed or disobeyed their parents.

PRIMARY SCHOOL YEARS

As our daughters move into the elementary school years, when development has taken a normal course, they are ready to dive enthusiastically into learning in a manner that is seldom matched at any other point, and building competence is the virtue associated here. *Industry versus inferiority* is the term used to describe the lull before the puberty-anchored emotional storm begins. Our daughters enter this period hungry to increase their knowledge and understanding of the world, but they also meet up against the potential for a sense of public failure—grades grow in importance as the teacher metes out approval or disapproval in the schools via scores. Friendship groups are often the center of "in-group" and "out-group" dynamics, with the risk of being "out" hinging on others' perspectives. Parents, too, have the power to mete out positive or negative responses to a child's behavior. The risks of feeling inferior to others in the classroom, social settings, and at home are daunting. Unfortunately, our daughter's self-esteem is contingent on how she perceives others perceive her, so this period can be instrumental in building and maintaining self-confidence.

HEADING TOWARD ADULTHOOD

As puberty begins, not only are new hormones influencing your daughter's behavior, so are new developments in the socioemotional system of her brain.[3] These developments are driving behavior as adolescents seek to manage the conflict of *identity versus identity confusion*. This conflict can take the greatest toll on the mother-daughter relationship, as the goal is individuation and creating an identity separate from the family. This new allegiance to her friends is the springboard to the solidification of the virtues of fidelity and devotion. As peers grow in importance as a daughter's reference group, mothers feel a range of emotions, few of which are positive at the outset. Our daughters are biologically driven to take risks and try on new behaviors as they prepare for the ultimate leap from daughter to partner and mother, themselves. Although not every young woman will push with the same force against parental restraints, these years can generate intense battles that are reminiscent of the iconic toddler temper tantrum. Keeping a daughter too close will keep her from becoming her own person, but allowing too much freedom may provide peers with too much control over her behavior and burgeoning identity. Striking a balance between freedom and responsibility is the optimal goal.

FINDING A PARTNER AND SETTLING DOWN

This sixth stage is located in the early adulthood period in which our daughters will be struggling with *intimacy versus isolation*. The desire for long-term romance and the fear of being single and alone play out their drama in our daughters' lives during this period. Love and affiliation are the virtue rewards for successfully establishing an authentic intimate relationship. Culturally and biologically, we are programmed to find a life partner, settle down, and raise a family. Our daughters often become aware of the "biological clock" ticking down. Although neuroscience findings have stretched the outer bounds of the adolescent developmental period into the mid-twenties,[4] the hurry to get on to the "next stage" of life can be intense. During this period, your daughter may "try on" different romantic partners to see who might fit. This can be a difficult time, as mothers must sometimes walk a careful line in looking out for a daughter's welfare and recognizing that she is an adult who will need to make her own decisions about life partners. This can also be a very rewarding period in the mother-daughter relationship, as daughters are able to see their mothers in a new light. Leaving home for college or moving out as jobs bring daughters financial independence can be a bittersweet period for mothers, but the new physical distance often spurs a return or new appreciation for psychological and emotional closeness. One young college interviewee shared that one of the highlights of her life are the monthly coffee dates she has with her mother when her mom drives up to the town where her college is located. She has recognized just how much she loves her mother and how valuable the wisdom her mother brings to her life actually has become.

MATURITY AND GIVING BACK

As lives and relationships settle into place, with families underway or independence embraced, the decision of giving back to the world or retreating is faced through the conflict of *generativity versus stagnation*. This is the period in which daughters may become part of the "sandwich generation," caring for their own immediate family or professional obligations but now being needed to care for their aging parents. This period is when the need to come full circle from daughter to caregiver can require new ways of relating between a mother and daughter. The virtue that this period can build is related to care and production. Because women view relationships as primary ways of affecting change in the world, some may see caring for their mothers as an act of gratitude as well as a responsibility. Other women may feel a sense of frustration and reluctance to devote time to this new responsibility. Changing relationships can produce a wide range of emotional responses across mother-daughter dyads and within an individual dyad itself.

A TIME OF REVIEW

The older adult years are truly a time in which we measure our days—not just those we have left, but the weight and quality of those that have made up our lives. We face the final crisis of *integrity versus despair* as we work to own the values of wisdom and renunciation. By this time, daughters have taken on the role of matriarchs of their families, and their mothers are memories and photos on the mantle. This period, perhaps of all, is the most essential to having lived a good life. For it is during the self-accounting process of the value of our days that will inform us if we have made the choices along the way that can bring us peace as we take a final leaving from our worldly relationships. Deathbed confessions, long-awaited words of forgiveness, and honesty with oneself are all aspects of the process of coming to terms with one's past.

EXPECT THE WORST, BUT HOPE FOR THE BEST

Because the dynamics of every mother-daughter dyad is unique and the metaphorical *boiling point* of everyone differs, there is little chance of avoiding conflict or tempests altogether. Being aware of the natural sequence of our daughters' and our own development, however, may provide a more understanding perspective of the struggles our relationships may face. The following is a stage-by-stage summary of the potential land mines and road bumps that may be found on the path to raising a daughter based on what we know of development and the experiences of many mothers.

INFANT DAUGHTERS

As described in an earlier section of the book, this period is crucial for developing a strong attachment between mothers and daughters. In most cases, a mother's biology has kicked her maternal drives into gear by the time her daughter arrives. Her brain and body are primed to meet the needs of an infant daughter, and the ability to meet her daughter's needs successfully, typically, is a positive reinforcement for continued interaction and bonding. A mother's body knows what to do.

However, bumps in the road to a happy mom and happy baby can arise from a mother's sense of failure to meet her baby's needs. Colicky, fretful babies can frustrate a woman's sense of confidence as a mother. Infants that have a difficult time adjusting to change in routine can affect a mother's sense of competence. Separation anxiety can be especially trying, as mothers may desire a break from caregiving yet experience significant guilt as they walk away from their daughter's cries. Most mothers are in the Eriksonian stage focused on raising a family, yet the conflict of work versus mothering or caring for a difficult infant may lead them to question their effectiveness in this role. The basic conflict faced by a daughter is the need to believe that she can trust that the world is a positive place; by responding to her needs, a mother helps her avoid feelings of mistrust. A mother who works too hard to please may face a future of attending to the needs of a daughter who is unwilling to meet her own needs or self-soothe.

By understanding your needs as a mother, and how they may be influencing your feelings about your relationship with your daughter, can be enlightening. The developmental path of the two of you is important to consider as you work through relationship difficulties and seek to maximize your daughter's own development.

A ONE, AND A (TERRIBLE) TWO, AND A THREE

These years can be a delightful time in which mothers watch their daughters move from crawling and cruising to running into life headlong. Toddlers are eager to stretch their grasp of the world and meet it with enthusiasm and fervor! What a little girl does not really know, yet, is that limits are in her best interest. Thus, much of the conflict between mother and daughter now is about boundary setting and boundary pushing. This is really just a harbinger of the adolescent years, but most mothers have a much easier time regarding being heard and being respected as a rule setter by their toddlers.

Toilet training is a task associated with this period, and mothers and daughters can run into frustration in this area if daughters are pushed too hard. Preferences for one parent over another can also be a point of contention for a mother. However, it is essential that a daughter or her other parent is not punished because of a mother's jealousy. Toddlers enjoy exerting their will on the world, and the bigger the reaction from a parent, the more delight they may take in following desires that push buttons.

Autonomy is an essential element of healthy emotional functioning, and its achievement by toddlers is an important accomplishment. Mothers and daughters can benefit from a well-managed, toddler-sized power struggle when adolescence rolls around. Consistent interaction, consistent rules, and adequate opportunities for self-direction in her life can provide a strong foundation for producing a daughter who is more easily able to handle life. Toddlers are supposed to assert themselves, but mothers must step up and consistently provide rules and limits that keep their daughters safe.

PRESCHOOL PLAY DATES

By their third birthday, children have a growing awareness of limits, boundaries, and right and wrong. They are also being internally driven to develop a sense of purpose in their actions. They enjoy opportunities to engage with other children, begin cooperative play, and enjoy adventurous activities. They also may engage in activities that they know would meet with their parents' disapproval. A daughter who has been well taught about limits may feel guilt even as she crosses the boundary her mother has set. Preschoolers are able to follow rules most of the time, but a little girl's individual temperament or her need to follow her own desires (aka "taking initiative") may lead her into misbehavior. This seemingly blatant disrespect of a mother's rules may be a foretaste of a young girl's future drive, initiative, and leadership abilities.

Parenting preschoolers can provide a great deal of joy as parents witness their exposure to new activities and new situations. Play dates for this age group can provide important social opportunities as children learn how to play well with others, yet playmates may have different rules about permitted activities and mothers may meet friction with their daughters who follow the lead of a playmate into verboten behaviors. Meltdowns at the end of busy days, visits with playmates, and holiday parties may also create friction between mothers and daughters. Being aware of a daughter's rhythms and preferred routines can allow mothers to prepare for and mitigate potential stressors. Mothers who are trying hard to parent successfully should bear in mind that a preschooler meltdown is not necessarily a reflection of her parenting skills. Individual temperament plays a big role in our responses when our resources are low—and by the time a daughter is four or five, mothers can be pretty sure they will know how their daughters will respond in stressful situations.

Preschoolers are ready to try on the roles of adults, and preschool and nursery playrooms abound with the props to do just this. Dress-up clothing, high-heeled shoes, neckties, and briefcases prepare children for the roles they see modeled by their idealized parents. Mothers can model healthy relationships to their partners, their friends, their extended family, and, of course, their children. The need to be "just like mom" can spawn quite a few scenarios in which mothers may feel frustration with their daughters. Often, a little girl this age prefers her father to her mother's company. Whether or not Freud had it right that little girls are fearful of their powerful mothers and seek to be like them to avoid losing their love, most young girls enjoy spending time with their fathers. Mothers may experience jealousy as daughters beg their fathers to accompany them in whatever task their mothers are trying to accomplish. In addition, the desire to emulate a mother's behavior can result in a preschooler sneaking into closets, jewelry boxes, and makeup drawers.

One mother, Michelle, enjoyed sharing an illustrative story of when her now twelve-year-old daughter, Brooke, was three and very much wanting to be like Michelle. She recalls a day when her daughter went eagerly to her nap, partially because she was going to be napping on her mother's bed, which was a special treat. A couple of hours later, when Michelle felt that Brooke should have already been awake and making her way back into the living room, she decided to take a peek at her daughter to make sure she was all right. She found Brook sitting in the middle of the bed with her face covered in a variety of hues and types of makeup! Brooke had gotten into her mother's makeup drawer in the vanity, and she explained to her mother, "I wanna be pretty like you, Mom!" Michelle said the easiest way to handle it was with a reminder of the rules and a warm washcloth—the expression on her daughter's face clearly showed her awareness that she had broken the rules.

ON THE BUS AND OFF TO SCHOOL

This next stage takes your daughter from play dates into schoolrooms, which can be a wonderful opportunity for a mother to see her daughter blossom into an eager learner and a good citizen, ideally. Well aware of the role of parental boundaries and family rules, your school-aged daughter should be ready for success in an environment layered with new rules and expectations of behavior and performance. However, crisis points for mothers and daughters may show up in the form of coping with a daughter who feels unable to handle the schoolwork assigned. Negative self-talk or beliefs about her own ability can be reinforced by poor marks in school, which can set the pair up for a potentially lengthy, well-entrenched round of school-related conflict.

Daughters this age are taking pride in their growing independence and sense of self, so it is important that mothers provide positive feedback to their daughters' positive developments. Mothers hold a great deal of influence during these years, and it may be the last period for many years before a daughter is as captive and respectful as she is right now. Mothers should allow missteps and poor choices (whether it is choosing the wrong friend for the wrong reason, wearing the wrong clothing for the wrong situation, etc.) that have natural and logical consequences attached to them to be learning experiences without adding their own layer of condemnation too strongly. The developmental crisis she is facing now revolves around feeling competent and avoiding a feeling of inferiority. When life circumstances and unpredictable others are joined by her mother in pointing out her flaws, a young girl can begin to believe that she is a failure in life. In addition, mothers who tend toward perfectionism may have a difficult time accepting their daughter's inexpert attempts at household chores. Being able to correct your daughter gently while providing positive feedback about honest efforts may minimize conflicts during these years.

Overall, these years can provide more joy than stress as your daughter moves into the rhythm of school, well-chosen extracurricular activities, and family responsibilities. Some mothers may have a difficult time, however, if they are too personally invested in the maternal role required in earlier years. By the time daughters reach elementary school and step up on the school bus for the first time, it is normal to experience a little nostalgia for the years in which our lives were more intertwined with our daughters' lives. Their interdependence begins to morph into independence if parents have done their job well. This can be a difficult transition to witness for some mothers, and if a longing for a more dependent daughter is left unchecked, conflict between the pair can erupt or a daughter's normal development may be compromised.

PEERS TRUMP PARENTS

The years that daughters move from girlhood to womanhood are by far the most fraught with drama, disrespect, and distance of any other period. The need to find out who she is will require that a daughter temporarily sever—or at least significantly unravel—her ties with the family with whom she resides. Unable to use her mother as a reference point for whom she wants to be as an adult, a daughter seems to place her mother at the opposite end of the spectrum and views her as all she does *not* want to be. The daughter who did her chores on time, who cared about doing well in school, and being seen as a "good" daughter/student/citizen may let go of all of these prior identities in an effort to reconceptualize and reconstruct her self-defined identity. And the loss of the little girl once known so well by her mother can be the event that heralds the arrival of impassioned conflicts, unwavering declarations of separateness, and threats and demands that may go as easily unheeded as they were put forth.

Regardless of the rationale for this behavior that biology, genetics, and brain functioning all provide, clashes between mothers and daughters during this time can probably never be avoided. While you may feel that your daughter's path from birth to adolescence was on an even keel, highlighted along the way with teddy bear tea parties and quarters freely awarded for report card A's, adolescence can be a time when the dormant drive to assert oneself is awakened and given free expression.

Risk-taking behaviors have never been nor will they ever seem as appealing as they do to teens. Nor will a daughter ever have to work so hard to claim her identity. Although a thorough explanation of the difficulties inherent in individuation of young girls is provided in an earlier chapter, it is worth reemphasizing how hard a daughter must work to create her own identity. Sons are able to separate from their close identification with their mother as gender awareness develops when they are young. The shared gender identity between daughter and mother do not allow daughters an easy "jumping-off point" in their independent identity creation. Thus, a lot has to happen during the adolescent years as our daughters prepare themselves for the independent roles they will have to assume as they move into the next phase of life.

Mothers may assume that they have gotten down the parenting thing pretty well after a dozen or more years, but their own identities as mothers may be shaken by the shift in the relationship with their teen-aged daughters. For mothers who had their daughters in their early twenties, they may be going through their own identity crisis as they see their fortieth birthday quickly approaching. For mothers who had their daughters later in life, their daughter's quest for identity and her sexual development may be especially challenging, as she may feel her own gender and sexually located identity shift as menopause looms. Being aware of the ways in which our own identities as women and mothers interplay with our adolescent daughters' developing identity as a woman and sexual being can provide us with a new perspective. However well we understand, though, it may do nothing to quell the conflicts that some mother-daughter dyads will face.

SPEED DATE, MOVE IN, BUILD A FAMILY

By the time a daughter has reached her early or mid-twenties, she probably has moved past the need to define herself in juxtaposition to her mother and in alignment with her peers. She is now focused on defining the future and the style of life she wants to lead as she seeks to blend her own identity with that of a primary partner. While daughters are less likely to bring home a "bad boy boyfriend" for shock value, as they might have when they were a few years younger, they may bring home romantic partners that mothers perceive as less than ideal. This time, though, the stakes may be higher, as a daughter is typically hoping to find the partner with whom she can build a life. A mother's desire to influence her daughter's choices may be understandable, but it is important that a mother be able to withhold judgments and comments that she may forever regret. Honoring your daughter's feelings and choices is necessary, but if her safety or well-being is genuinely at stake, this must be communicated in such a way that she can hear the risks you have detected without feeling as if she must move into defensiveness or minimize a partner's behaviors.

Another potential disruption in the mother-daughter relationship may actually be a physical disruption if a daughter is planning a geographical location out of easy driving distance of her parents. Supporting our children as they make their way in the world seems so much easier when they are nearby. However, the world grows smaller every day, and mothers may need to rely on communication technology and air travel to keep them close to their daughters. Mothers may have to weigh the benefit of harboring their own emotional discomfort against their daughter's happiness and success in the world.

During this stage, mothers will need to be able to support their adult daughter's choices as best they can. Negative emotions beyond disapproval can possibly include jealousy, as a daughter reaches professional, personal, or financial goals that a mother may have been unable to achieve. If a mother expresses persistent and unchanging disapproval of a partner, a job, or a home choice, resentment of her mother's feelings by a daughter can permanently mar the relationship. Financial relationships can also be sources of conflict if a daughter requires financial assistance from her parents.

By the time our daughters are settling down and building families, most mothers are entering into their own developmental crisis of midlife—avoiding stagnation through increased generativity. Letting a child independently move forward in her life can be a wonderful means to express generative power. Moreover, with the potential for grandchildren, a mother may find a brand new way of influencing the future as she moves into the grandmother role.

FACING END-OF-LIFE WITH PRIDE

Only infrequently does a mother witness a daughter's transition into this role, but not infrequently, our adult daughters will play a significant part of our lives as we enter this stage. This is the period in which virtually all of us are left to feel somewhat helpless and in need of others' care. Spending our adulthood as caregivers of our daughters, this period finds us requiring that our daughters give back to us. With a focus on finding integrity in our lived histories, the ways in which our daughters respond to our frailty and needs often gives testament to the integrity of our mothering.

Areas of conflict during these years are frequently related to a mother's reluctance to give up her independence. Adult daughters may see the clear need for a mother to move in with her or a sibling or accept assistance in the form of nursing care or increasing assistance from children. Mothers may see a clearly interfering daughter who does not recognize the value of her mother's continued independence. Some disagreements may begin as innocuous disagreements over in whose home a holiday meal will be held or whose recipe for stuffing will be followed. As mothers begin to see their roles usurped by the subsequent generation, some may be gratified to see how well their daughters have matured into strong women. Other mothers may seek to maintain control over family events in order to continue to feel valued and relevant, and their daughters may respond by either fighting for their cause or submitting to their mothers' wishes, "at least, for this year."

CONCLUSION

As we look at the lifelong development trajectory, as outlined by Erikson's theory based on our social and emotional expressions, we can see how that as we strive for independence and interdependence or individuation balanced with affiliation that our connections to parents will need to shift to make room for our new lives. Mothers and daughters experience an intimate connection born from early caregiving and shared gender, yet it is this relationship that must undergo the greatest shift as daughters redefine their identities as they mature. We have provided a summary of the predictable flash points for mother-daughter clashes, and in the following chapters we will provide a more detailed exploration of the relationship over time.

NOTES

1. E. Erikson, *Identity: Youth and Crisis* (New York: W. W. Norton, 1968).

2. T. M. Panfile, D. J. Laible, and J. L. Eye, "Conflict Frequency within Mother-Child Dyads across Contexts: Links with Attachment and Security," *Early Childhood Research Quarterly, 27* (2012): 147–55.

3. L. Steinberg, "A Social Neuroscience Perspective on Adolescent Risk-Taking," *Developmental Review, 28* (2008): 78–106.

4. Ibid.

FOUR

Learning to Be a Mother

The Early Years

Although the expectation of someday becoming a mother is planted early in the minds of little girls, many women are unprepared for the seismic shift in identity and priorities that accompany the arrival of their first child. As is increasingly common among significant life events, pregnancy and childbirth are glorified and commercialized by the popular media and consumer products manufacturers. Baby showers, couples' showers, lingerie showers, and a liberal dose of folk wisdom and medical science typically accompany our transition into motherhood. Although there are experienced mothers who may warn expectant mothers of the significant changes in store for them, this is something no woman is able to appreciate fully until her newborn child makes her way into her waiting arms.

DELIVERY DAY AND NEUROCHEMICAL DEVELOPMENTS

Much is said about the importance of bonding with your infant immediately after birth. I can all too easily recall the terror I felt as the nurse placed my sticky, screaming daughter on my chest in the delivery room before the obstetrician had begun sewing up the episiotomy site. I felt so unsure of what I was supposed to do with my newborn as the nurse encouraged me to "go ahead and nurse her." I was a brand new mother, but I had never been the type of woman who would "ooh and ahh" over babies or children. As I wrapped my arms around my daughter, I felt as if I had received the keys to the kingdom, but I was not sure that I was fully ready to enter! I do know that I had fallen in love with my daughter during my pregnancy somewhere along the line, probably around the twentieth or twenty-fourth week of gestation, according to the research.[1,2] I had been thrilled when I learned that I was expecting a daughter, as this was exactly the gender both her father and I had hoped we would conceive the first time around. Yet this naked, squirming, red creature clearly knew more about what she needed than her own mother did at the outset.

When a newborn is placed upon her mother's chest, a very important learning and healing environment for the baby and her mother is created. A daughter is already learning the scent of her mother and her mother's milk, and she will be able to discriminate the scent of her mother's breast from others in a very short time.[3] In addition, her sucking and squirming on her mother's chest may be nature's way of massaging the uterus and expelling the placenta.[4] The mother-daughter dyad instinctively moves into a dance of interdependence. When one woman, Kim, was asked about her first interactions with her now twenty-three-year-old daughter, she said, "I fell in love with her the moment I first held her in my arms. I was thrilled she was a girl!" This feeling of connection is helped along by our body's neurochemistry system.

As the baby girl nurses, her mother's body releases oxytocin, which has been called the bonding hormone or the hormone of love. As a mother cradles her suckling baby at her breast, oxytocin circulates and affects a number of processes. It causes the uterus to contract, helping mom's body return to its prepregnant state; it stimulates lactation; it aids in the mom's face-recognition process, making sure she is able to recognize her own daughter; and it creates a warm, fuzzy feeling between the pair. We are falling even more deeply in love as the chemicals of social affiliation swim throughout our bodies. And as an aside, oxytocin is not only a positive force in social behaviors, but also a dysfunction has been found to be related to the appearance of some very challenging conditions,[5] including obsessive compulsive disorder, eating disorders, addictions, and even autism.[6] Some researchers believe that it may hold the key to finding solutions for behavioral and psychological problems related to social connections.

History shows that we humans are social creatures—building villages and communities from earliest times—and our need to connect and define our relationships is rooted in our genes. Building a newborn daughter's first relationship through just twenty-five minutes of skin-to-skin contact with her mother will have a long-lasting positive effect on their interactions months and years later.[7] These little girls will cry less as babies and experience a more secure attachment to their mothers. Although the effect may be a little less powerful in the tween/teen years, anything that might make that transition easier is worth the investment, according to most mothers of young adult daughters with whom we spoke. Researchers have also found that daughters who had been told their birth stories by their mothers more frequently growing up had higher levels of self-esteem and stronger attachment to their mothers as adults.[8]

As is true in most things, practice improves performance, and we get better at responding to our newborns. However, first-time moms especially benefit from a couple of neurochemicals beyond oxytocin that reinforce good mothering. Estradiol and cortisol are two such hormones[9]; when mothers' bodies maintain strong levels of estradiol prior to and after birth, they show higher levels of attachment to their newborns. Researchers found that cortisol, the stress hormone mentioned as potentially having a negative influence on child development, plays a positive role in early maternal behavior. Higher cortisol levels in new moms were correlated with more active caregiving toward newborns as well as a greater attraction to their newborns' scent and a keener ability to discriminate their own son or daughter's scent from that of other babies. Mothering well is a continuous challenge, and it is essential that we soak up all of the assistance we receive—whether biological or environmental in nature—and oxytocin is an essential chemical in promoting love and connection.

As I look back at photographs taken almost two and a half decades ago in the delivery room, I do not just see a frightened mother and a squalling newborn; I am able to see the beautiful face of the beautiful young woman who made me a mother. I see the blue eyes that have been looking back at me for all these years—sometimes with curiosity, sometimes confusion, sometimes anger, and sometimes tenderness. Nevertheless, the bond that formed in the early days—whether helped by oxytocin or the other birth-synched neurochemicals of estradiol or cortisol—has withstood a barrage of developmental assaults over time. Those photos also remind me that the mother-daughter dyad is comprised of two connected, but separate, individuals, and no matter how much I would like to have my daughter not have to suffer any pain or hurt in life, I am only a part of her story and not the author.

That period from your daughter's birth to your return to a somewhat normal lifestyle, albeit with a new routine, can vary depending on your culture, your circumstances, and your needs. While some women are eager to get back up to speed as soon after birth as possible, some women enjoy taking their time to get to know their daughters before returning to the pace of their prebaby life. Even the Christian Bible provides many reminders and guidelines regarding the treatment of women during the various stages of the lifelong reproductive course. Even mothers of the furry or feathered kind should be treated with respect.[10] Individual and religious preferences aside, long-standing cultural traditions may influence your own path during what may be perceived as a potentially vulnerable[11] period for you and your daughter.

"DOING THE MONTH" EASTERN STYLE

When a mother gives birth in China, her mother and mother-in-law may swoop in and provide instrumental assistance to the pair as they support the new mother in the traditional custom of "doing the month."[12] During this period, her activities, diet, and emotional state are all the focus of regulation with a goal of helping the mother and child get off to a healthy start.[13] Although the intentions are good, contemporary research suggests that the result may not be as beneficial as new grandmothers may envision, as many new mothers feel that the month of supervision can be stifling. Conflicting results, however, show up in the literature, with some researchers finding that the month-long coddling results in fewer instances of postnatal depression,[14] while others have found no beneficial effects to a mother's well-being.[15] One interesting note is that adding a regular dose of physical exercise to the postpartum "doing the month" routine did decrease new mothers' fatigue.[16] This, in itself, may be encouragement to all new mothers to find gentle ways to add physical activity to their newly busy schedules.

Traveling just a little further around the globe, there is a somewhat similar practice followed in Japan. Called *satogaeri childbirth*,[17] the practice involves the return of the new mother and her child to her parents' home. Here, her own mother looks after the needs of the new mother, and she passes along the skills of infant care. Those of us who have returned home from the hospital with a new daughter and next to no childrearing experience may fantasize about how marvelous it might be to be taken care of for a few weeks with our only responsibility being the mothering of our new baby. In addition, although many new mothers have affirmed that this can be beneficial, many feel that it is a sacrifice to give up privacy as they seek to establish their own new family. Whether a new mom returns to her childhood home or her mother takes up temporary residence at the new mom's home, there are still likely to be some conflicts as new mothers feel the urge to exert their independence and ability to look after themselves and their infants.

"LYING-IN" AT HOME

In Western countries, the time surrounding the labor and delivery period historically was termed the "lying-in" period and traditionally has been a time in which the mother is restricted to little beyond bed rest and remaining isolated with her newborn from the external world. Although originally conceived as a method of keeping the vulnerable mother and newborn safe from infection and illness, one medical professional noted that by sealing out the external world, germs and contaminants were sealed *inside* the new mother's room. As hospital births became the norm and insurance reimbursements have shrunk, there is little time built into a modern world for "lying-in" or gently easing into the role of mother.[18] Even a slew of assistants—mothers, mothers-in-law, fathers, partners, or nannies—do not guarantee easy achievement of the art of becoming a mother.

THE "BABY BLUES"

While the definition of "baby blues" is pretty much self-explanatory, there are still no solid explanations for why some new mothers go from experiencing the blues to full-blown postpartum depression (PPD). According to the American College of Obstetricians and Gynecologists, PPD is "likely to result from body, mind, and lifestyle factors combined."[19] Over half of new mothers will get at least a slight case of the baby blues,[20] which is characterized by feelings of anxiety, irritability, and bouts of unexpected tears. These usually hit by about the fourth or fifth day after you have delivered your baby, and symptoms take a relatively quick course to resolution.[21] Mothers of daughters, however, are pretty fortunate, as they are less likely to experience even this little dip in the road after childbirth.[22, 23] Unfortunately, our daughters will not offer any protection against the development of full-on PPD, although one recent study of new mothers in France did provide some interesting results. For this group, bearing a son, as opposed to a daughter, negatively influenced a woman's quality of life in three different areas—her physical role, her emotional role, and her vitality.[24] Daughters bring their own special challenges, but many of these remain unrevealed until girls reach their tween years when their own version of emotional fickleness emerges in full force.

The baby blues have been attributed to drops in estrogen production in the body,[25] but a recent study revealed that postnatal depression might actually be located in the brain, where affective processing was found to be compromised.[26] What the researchers found was that women with PPD did not register emotional cues and emotional responses in the same manner as nondepressed mothers. Their inability to notice their babies' signals and messages probably accounts for their inability to build strong emotional bonds with their children. As one young mother of a four-year-old shared when asked about difficult experiences with her daughter, "Well, hopefully she will not remember this, but I experienced postpartum depression for one year." With about 15 percent to 29 percent of mothers estimated to suffer from this disorder, a goodly number of daughters are affected by their mothers' PPD, even if they carry no actual memory of their mother's distress.[27]

In their attempts to determine why hormonal changes have a stronger impact on some women and less on others, studies have found numerous psychosocial factors contribute to the development of postpartum depression.[28, 29, 30] For instance, women with infants may become isolated, physically and emotionally overburdened with infant care, and have inadequate support. In addition, new mothers suffer numerous forms of loss, such as the loss of occupational status and identity and the loss of prepregnancy physical appearance and sexuality in addition to the losses of autonomy, time, and the sense of a separate self. There are so many losses that women suffer when they give birth that some researchers consider postpartum depression to be a bereavement or grief process.

The greater the discrepancy between the expectations and the reality of life with the new addition to the family, the more likely a woman is to experience depression. Some of this discrepancy stems from the marital relationship. In fact, a poor relationship between the mother and her male partner has been found to be one of the most consistent contributors to PPD.[31, 32] Women are often surprised and dismayed at the limited emotional and practical contributions of the father of their child. Despite the new century and even in relationships that were relatively egalitarian prior to the birth, childcare-related activities fall primarily on women. Another aspect of this discrepancy is the conflict between an idealized vision of motherhood and the reality of being the mother.

Faced with this conflict, women often struggle within themselves and by themselves. We often find it difficult to talk about how we feel about ourselves as mothers, particularly regarding the areas in which we are disappointed by this transition. This silent struggle is, unfortunately, frequently reinforced by reluctance among many to hear these difficulties, though the difficulties usually stem from unrealistic expectations of motherhood offered to us from the society we live in.

Some women are able to "let go" of these unrealistic standards. This is often dependent upon the ability to accept their feelings and discuss these within responsive and nonjudgmental personal and professional relationships. Though well intentioned, support systems (friends, family, professionals) who want the woman suffering from PPD to focus on the gains and joys of motherhood, this approach may actually intensify the problem because it prevents the losses from being validated and increases the confusion and self-doubt. It is most important that the *losses and their magnitude* are recognized and acknowledged first and with great care.

A daughter is naturally more emotionally aware and socially oriented than a son, and a mother's PPD will affect each gender differently. Research shows that daughters living with depressed mothers will show an increase in emotional sensitivity,[33] perhaps reflecting an attempt to step into the caregiver role for their moms. Sons, however, seem to block the negative emotional displays by their mothers, which may reflect the male brain's proclivity to avoid emotional conflicts. These differences are visible as early as eight weeks of age. All of the long-term effects a mother's depression bears on her offspring are not yet known, but researchers found that it can also result in compromised cognitive development, including language development.[34]

When a mother is depressed, she may show little response or interest in her daughter, or she may be hypervigilant with her infant. And when an infant's cries do not draw the attention or care of her mother, she may retreat into a withdrawn state, as well.[35] Our newborn daughters rely on us for social cues, emotional learning, and responsive interactions to grow into healthy, responsive adults. Depression is treatable at this stage of life, just as it is at other stages. Unfortunately, as we noted in an earlier chapter, motherhood is perceived as a time of joy and fulfillment. If a new mother is feeling less than overjoyed and less than "normal," she may be ashamed to ask for assistance. If you or a friend or a partner are feeling blues that just won't fade and a daughter is heading toward her one-month benchmark, it is important to contact a health professional to ensure that the little girl receives the best mothering possible.

Other suggestions for new mothers suffering from PPD:

- Seek professional help for marital difficulties
- Find supportive people—do not isolate yourself even if it is what you feel like doing
- Ask for help—emotional and practical to the new mother
- Read books that offer an honest, balanced perspective about motherhood, such as Naomi Wolf's *Misconceptions: Truth, Lies, and the Unexpected Journey to Motherhood.*
- Treat yourself as well as you can, including eating right, exercise, and *sleep*
- Seek professional help to increase the likelihood you will feel better sooner
- Seek professional help *immediately* if

    1. You are unable to function normally; can't cope with everyday situations
    2. Have thoughts of harming yourself or the baby
    3. Feeling extremely anxious, scared, and panicked most of the day

Depression puts a wedge between a mother and her daughter, but treatment can remove that obstacle to a healthy relationship. Unfortunately, the divide may actually arise from medically necessary separations.

MOTHERING FROM AFAR: WHEN MEDICAL NECESSITY SEPARATES MOTHERS AND NEWBORN DAUGHTERS

Unfortunately, not every birth is easy—some mothers' lives may be at risk as delivery approaches; some infants may arrive too soon to be able to function self-sufficiently; and unfortunate and distressing medical problems may arise for mother or child. It is not within the scope of this book to explore the multitude of things that may go wrong, but we do want to focus on the distress that can arise when your daughter's delivery is fraught with difficulty and the need for emergency medical interventions.

Research shows that when newborns are in need of intensive medical care, mothers are likely to be in need of psychological care, as well. In fact, if your daughter is in need of intensive medical care, you are about three times more likely to suffer from postnatal depression.[36] And, not surprisingly, the younger your baby was at birth, the longer the duration of hospitalization, and the lower the birth weight were all correlated with the level of depression a mother experienced. Beyond depression, acute stress disorder and posttraumatic stress disorder are likely to arise. In one study,[37] over a third of mothers and about a quarter of the fathers met the diagnostic criteria for acute stress disorder between three and five days after their babies had been admitted to the neonatal intensive care unit (NICU).

When we queried one mother about the most difficult conversation she had held with her daughter, the twenty-eight-year-old mother replied, "I talked to my daughter in the NICU, she was born ten weeks premature, on the day I was discharged and I had to leave her behind. I told her I was sorry for not taking care of myself and I thought it was my fault she was born early." She described how she was emotionally affected by what she thought she might have done wrong—self-blame can take a toll on a mother's mental health.

Another mother who had delivered her daughter too early shared a moving story regarding her own feelings of inadequacy and responsibility for her daughter's early delivery:

> I think the most important thing that has happened to me while raising my daughter happened when she was four months old. You will need a little background on my pregnancy/her birth to understand my feelings. To begin, I lost my first child at twenty-two weeks. I was utterly devastated and became obsessed with getting pregnant again. I did, and at thirty-one weeks, I was admitted to the hospital with pre-eclampsia. I was terrified that this baby would also die because in my mind, I knew what my body did to babies in my stomach. For three weeks, I was in the hospital praying that my baby would not die. The walls felt like they were closing in, and I truly wanted my daughter to be out of my body because I feared she would die. At thirty-four weeks, she was born with a few complications, stayed in the NICU (neonatal intensive care unit) for twenty days, and then we brought her home! I was suffering from postpartum depression very badly . . . the hospital stay, the birth, the NICU . . . it all took a toll on me. I felt absolutely no bond whatsoever with Zoey. I loved her more than I

could explain, but I could not connect with her. At four months, we had her on the table in her bouncy seat (stupid mistake made by too many new parents), and she tipped off the table and fell to the floor, hitting her head on the wooden chair, before we could catch her. There was no blood, no mark, the crying stopped, but we decided to take her to the emergency room anyway. It was discovered that she had a fractured skull and blood on her brain. My world stopped. Now, at this point, I need to explain a little about my own relationship with my mom. My mom still likes taking care of my brother and I, and while I was having trouble with the postpartum, she was helping me get through it, she was helping with Zoey, and I became VERY dependent on her. So when Zoey fell and we found out how critical her situation was, I immediately called my mom; however, she was out of town. I realized that I was all on my own with my husband. Zoey was airlifted to the PICU (pediatric intensive care unit) at a hospital in Chicago. What was I going to do? I needed my mom. But I then realized that Zoey needed her mom, too. We ended up having a horrible thirty-six hours at this hospital, and I had to be the one to advocate for my baby. I was her mother. I could not allow this hospital care for her in the terrible way they were. When she was finally released, I found that I had bonded with Zoey in a way I could not explain. All of my fears were gone, and momma bear had finally kicked in. They say that something good always comes from something bad, and I had never noticed experiencing that until this whole ordeal. I was finally bonded with my baby girl in the way I had always imagined.

LaToya, a thirty-year-old mother of a two-year-old NICU "graduate," shared that she had a strong support system that allowed her to make multiple daily trips to the NICU to breastfeed her tiny daughter and that she was able to pump enough milk to feed many other of her daughter's NICU pals. She describes her daughter today as a "fighter" who knows what she wants and who is always trying to best her five-year-old brother in any competition. As LaToya shared photos of her tiny daughter just a few hours old, she only saw the strength and spirit of her little girl, never the potential for an unhappy outcome. The ability to step up to motherhood, as in LaToya's example, is essential to creating a bond with your infant daughter, especially if you and she were separated early after birth. If you do feel that you are suffering from something more significant than just the blues, let your physician know what is happening so that proper treatment can begin. Fortunately, depression associated with a daughter's stay in the NICU is likely to get better with time—one study of over four hundred parents of NICU babies showed that after nine months, increased depression and anxiety symptoms were no longer evident for the majority of parents.[38] For mothers, the ameliorating factors turned out to be the higher level of early distress and the quality of the relationship between parents. Therefore, it looks like the more caring and invested a mother is in her child's well-being and the better her relationship with her coparent, the more effectively she will handle the stress of a baby in distress.

BONDING THROUGH THE FIRST YEAR'S TEARS

The first year can be difficult for some mothers and daughters as they struggle to find a shared rhythm and routine. Fussy newborn daughters will put their mothers to the test through their neediness the first few months. This is evidenced by an account from a mother of a now four-year-old daughter, "I would say the most difficult period in our relationship would be when my daughter was an infant because she cried every day, and I didn't always know why she was crying."

Stephanie, the mother of a now ten-year-old girl, describing her first few months as a mother to her daughter, shared, "My relationship with my daughter started out as a rocky one! I wanted a baby so much. After a year of trying, I was worried when we didn't become pregnant. After two years of infertility treatment, countless disappointments and thousands of dollars, we were finally pregnant . . . so, when I delivered this beautiful, healthy baby girl, I was blissfully happy. However, that was short-lived. She suffered from "colic" (whatever that really is) and cried for the first four months of her life. I found it hard to bond with her between lack of sleep and frustration over the insane amount of crying (both her and me). Luckily, that ended, and we were able to finally start bonding. I nursed her and that was our bonding time! I love every minute of it. Being a mom is so awesome!"

What can be especially frustrating about the early fussiness is that doctors cannot pinpoint the cause or cure for colic.[39] We do know that it does indeed exist, that the crying of our colicky daughters is quantitatively different from that of noncolicky little girls,[40] and that colicky babies often take a toll on their caregivers! With a colicky daughter, we are more likely to show symptoms of depression[41] even six months after our daughters are born. Although Stephanie mentioned the bonding time she enjoyed while breastfeeding, it is disheartening that many mothers are actually more likely to end breastfeeding if their daughters experience colicky bouts of distress.[42] Yet we know that breast milk is actually helpful in enhancing your daughter's night sleeping patterns due to the melatonin you pass on through your milk.[43]

While about 75 percent of new mothers do start out breastfeeding their newborns, only about 20 percent keep it up to the recommended year mark.[44] While many hospitals do not make it easy for new mothers to begin the breastfeeding routine, if you are physically able to nurse your daughter, you and your daughter will reap an assortment of health benefits. Not only does it help your daughter sleep better, it also makes you stronger—breastfeeding mothers have bigger, stronger bones later in life.[45] Your daughter is also likely to show higher cognitive ability and more advanced educational achievement later on, as well.[46] Women who breastfeed their babies exclusively during the early months also report higher levels of self-concept according to recent studies,[47] and they are typically less anxious about their childrearing practices and enjoy more positive feelings about their child.[48]

It should go without saying that the care and feeding of your daughter is a very personal choice. Mothers and daughters who share a gaze over a bottle filled with formula can be just as close and connected as any mother-daughter duo. One mother, whose daughter is now twenty-one, shared that she had "tried and tried the breastfeeding thing, but it just never seemed to get easier. I think my fears about what people would say if I didn't breastfeed were actually a big part of my anxiety over the whole issue. And I think those fears made me even less likely to succeed." She and her daughter are actually a very close pair, and they have a strong bond that many mothers might envy—at twenty-one, most daughters are fighting for independence, but watching this pair together shows a joyful interdependence that shows that breast or bottle, it is the relationship between mother and daughter that matters.

ROUNDING THE BEND INTO AND OUT OF THE TERRIBLE TWOS

Once a mother and daughter make it through the first year, the crying and fretting—of both mother and daughter—has quieted and new challenges appear on the horizon. As little girls rush to get their balance and learn to walk, mothers are often behind them looking out for their safety every step of the way. When several researchers analyzed the playground interactions of parents and their daughters and sons as the children were being taught to slide down a pole, parents treated their kids differently based on gender.[49] We are quick to encourage our sons to try out the task on their own, providing directions and encouragement. For daughters, parents tend to be very "hands on" and physically help them master the trick. Sons are raised to be independent risk takers, but daughters are encouraged to rely on others for support from even their earliest learning experiences.

Mothers and daughters may be working through significant individuation and separation issues together. Raised to engage in mutually reciprocal relationships, according to Nancy Chodorow, women self-define in terms of relationships with others.[50] Sons can be encouraged to be independent and grow into strong men, the opposite of a mother. Daughters, however, experience identification with their mother and must find a way to individuate, yet they are bound to the shared gender identity and might struggle more than young males to exert independence while remaining connected during the toddler and later adolescent years. Perhaps mothers can see a daughter's future too clearly and may rush in to protect her while she is young enough to actually be protected from the world. Toddler girls decked out in "mini-mommy" outfits or pink sneakers may look like adorable dolls, but it may be a mother's way of clinging tight to a daughter who will soon be fighting to be let go. Some mothers, though, recognize the value of helping a little girl to be bravely adventurous; a mother reminisced about an interaction she'd had two decades ago with her older daughter, Rachel, when Rachel was about eighteen months old, "We lived in Alaska and I'll never forget the first big snow we had when she had just recently learned to walk. I was holding her outside in the yard, and I put her down in the snow in her little snow boots and snowsuit. She looked up at me as if to ask me what was going on, then I encouraged her to start walking! I wanted to let her experience new things from when she was little—I didn't want her to be afraid."

The mother in the story above was eager to encourage her daughter to move forward in life, literally and figuratively, without fear. And she probably already sensed the circumstances or things that raised fear in her toddler. Mothers can provide much more accurate predictions of how their little girls will react in the face of potentially fearful circumstances than their sons.[51] We, as mothers, have a greater sensitivity to the needs of our daughters[52] and probably have a deep empathy with them borne of shared gender and shared experience. Mothers should intentionally encourage their daughters to strike out on their own and work toward autonomy in these early years, while being ready to provide support if true risk appears. In an interesting review of his cases, a psychoanalyst noted that several clients who had not managed to successfully develop a healthy separation and interdependence with their mothers shared the pattern of choosing a husband but retaining a long-term lover as a result of their inability to successfully navigate this important developmental milestone that is rooted in our toddler years.[53] Clearly, it is important to help our daughters learn to move through life with courage and confidence.

NOTES

1. C. Corter and A. S. Fleming, "Psychobiology of Maternal Behavior in Human Beings," in M. Bornstein (ed.), *Handbook of Parenting*, 87–116 (Hillsdale, NJ: Erlbaum, 1995).

2. Dario Maestripieri, "Biological Bases of Maternal Attachment," *Current Directions in Psychological Science, 10*, no. 3 (2001): 79–83.

3. K. Mizuno, N. Mizuno, T. Shinohara, and M. Noda, "Mother-Infant Skin-to-Skin Contact after Delivery Results in Early Recognition of Own Mother's Milk Odour," *Acta Paediatrica, 93*, no. 12 (2004): 1640–45.

4. R. H. Porter, "The Biological Significance of Skin-to-Skin Contact and Maternal Odours," *Acta Paediatrica, 93*, no. 12 (2004): 1560–62.

5. D. Marazziti and M. C. Dell'osso, "The Role of Oxytocin in Neuropsychiatric Disorders," *Current Medical Chemistry, 15* (2008): 698–704.

6. E. A. Hammock and L. J. Young, "Oxytocin, Vasopressin and Pair Bonding: Implications for Autism," *Philosophical Transcripts Royal Society London B Biological Sciences, 361,* no. 1476 (2006): 2187–98.

7. K. Bystrova, V. Ivanova, M. Edhborg, A. S. Matthiesen, A. Ransjo-Arvidson, R. Mukhamedrakhimov et al., "Early Contact versus Separation: Effects on Mother-Infant Interaction One Year Later," *Birth, 36,* no. 2 (2009): 97–109.

8. J. M. Hayden, J. A. Singer, and J. C. Chrisler, "The Transmission of Birth Stories from Mother to Daughter: Self-Esteem and Mother-Daughter Attachment," *Sex Roles, 55* (2006): 373–83.

9. Maestripieri, "Biological Bases of Maternal Attachment."

10. A. Lichtenstein, "The Maternal Instinct in Scripture: Toward a Literary Understanding," *Journal of Evolutionary Psychology, 5,* no. 3–4 (1984): 147–48.

11. L. C. Callister, "Doing the Month: Chinese Postpartum Practices," *MCN American Journal of Maternal and Child Nursing, 31,* no. 6 (2006): 309.

12. E. Holroyd, V. Lopez, and S. W. Chan, "Negotiating 'Doing the Month': An Ethnographic Study Examining the Postnatal Practices of Two Generations of Chinese Women," *Nursing and Health Sciences, 13* (2011): 47–52.

13. S. S. K. Leung, D. Arthur, and I. M. Martinson, "Perceived Stress and Support of the Chinese Postpartum Ritual 'Doing the Month,'" *Health Care for Women International, 26,* no. 3 (2005): 212–24.

14. L. Chien, C. Tai, Y. Ko, C. Huang, and S. Sheu, "Adherence to 'Doing the Month' Practices Is Associated with Fewer Physical and Depressive Symptoms among Postpartum Women in Taiwan," *Research in Nursing and Health, 29,* no. 5 (2006): 374–83.

15. Leung et al., "Perceived Stress and Support of the Chinese Postpartum Ritual 'Doing the Month.'"

16. Y. Ko, C. Yang, and L. C. Chiang, "Effects of Postpartum Exercise Program on Fatigue and Depression during 'Doing the Month' Period," *Journal of Nursing Research, 16,* no. 3 (2008): 177–85.

17. Y. Kobayashi, "Assistance Received from Parturients' Own Mothers during 'Satogaeri' (Their Perinatal Visit and Stay with Their Parents) and Development of the Mother-Infant Relationship and Maternal Identity," *Journal of Japan Academy of Midwifery, 1* (2010): 28–39.

18. B. Lynch, "Postpartum Culture: The Loss of the Lying-In Time," speech given at Doulas of North America (DONA) Annual Conference in New Orleans, July 2004.

19. American College of Obstetricians and Gynecologists, Frequently Asked Questions: Labor, Delivery, and Postpartum Care, 2011, www.acog.org/~/media/For%20Patients/faq091.pdf?dmc=1&ts=20130616T0852124419.

20. A. De Magistris, E. Coni, M. Puddu, M. Zonza, and V. Fanos, "Screening of Postpartum Depression: Comparison between Mothers in the Neonatal Intensive Care Unit and in the Neonatal Section," *The Journal of Maternal-Fetal and Neonatal Medicine,* 23(S3) (2010): 101–3.

21. Harvard Mental Health Letter, "Beyond the 'Baby Blues,'" 28, no. 3 (September 2011).

22. S. M. Sylven, F. C. Papadopoulos, V. Mpazakidis, L. Ekselius, I. Sundstrom-Poromaa, and A. Skalkidou, "Newborn Gender as a Predictor of Postpartum Mood Disturbances in a Sample of Swedish Women," *Archives of Women's Mental Health, 14,* no. 3 (2001): 195–201.

23. D. Lagerberg and M. Magnusson, "Infant Gender and Postpartum Sadness in the Light of Region of Birth and Some Other Factors: A Contribution to the Knowledge of Postpartum Depression," *Archives of Women's Mental Health, 15,* no. 2 (2012): 121–30.

24. C. de Tychey, S. Briancon, J. Lighezzolo, E. Spitz, B. Kabuth, V. de Luigi, C. Messembourg, F. Girvan, A. Rosati, A. Thockler, and S. Vincent, "Quality of Life, Postnatal Depression and Baby Gender," *Journal of Clinical Nursing, 17,* no. 3 (2008): 312–22.

25. De Magistris et al., "Screening of Postpartum Depression."

26. E. L. Moses-Kolko, S. B. Perlman, K. L. Wisner, J. James, A. T. Saul, and M. L. Phillips, "Abnormally Reduced Dorsomedial Prefrontal Cortical Activity and Effective Connectivity with Amygdala in Response to Negative Emotional Faces in Postpartum Depression," *American Journal of Psychiatry, 167* (2010): 1373–80.

27. P. Gremigni, L. Mariani, V. Marracino, A. Tranquilli, and A. Turi, "Partner Support and Postpartum Depressive Symptoms," *Journal of Psychosomatic Obstetrics & Gynecology, 32,* no. 3 (2011): 135–40.

28. M. W. O'Hara, "Postpartum Depression: What We Know," *Journal of Clinical Psychology, 65,* no. 12 (2009): 1258–69.

29. P. Boyce and A. Hickey, "Psychosocial Risk Factors to Major Depression after Childbirth," *Social Psychiatry Pyschiatric Epidemiology, 40,* no. 8 (2005): 605–12.

30. C. T. Beck, "Postpartum Depression: A Metasynthesis," *Qualitative Health Research, 12,* no. 4 (2002): 453–72.

31. N. Mauthner, "Re-assessing the Importance and Role of the Marital Relationship in Postnatal Depression: Methodological and Theoretical Implications," *Journal of Reproductive & Infant Psychology, 16,* no. 2 (1998): 157–76.

32. Beck, "Postpartum Depression: A Metasynthesis."

33. K. Hatzinikolaou and L. Murray, "Infant Sensitivity to Negative Maternal Emotional Shifts: Effects of Infant Sex, Maternal Postnatal Depression, and Interactive Style," *Infant Mental Health Journal, 31,* no. 5 (2010): 591–610.

34. M. Zajicek-Farber, "The Contributions of Parenting and Postnatal Depression on Emergent Language of Children in Low-Income Families," *Journal of Child & Family Studies, 19* (2010): 257–69.

35. C. Puckering, E. McIntosh, A. Hickey, and J. Longford, "Mellow Babies: A Group Intervention for Infants and Mothers Experiencing Postnatal Depression," *Counselling Psychology Review, 25,* 28–40.

36. De Magistris et al., "Screening of Postpartum Depression."

37. D. S. Lefkowitz, C. Baxt, and J. R. Evans, "Prevalence and Correlates of Posttraumatic Stress and Postpartum Depression in Parents of Infants in the Neonatal Intensive Care Unit (NICU)," *Journal of Clinical Psychology in Medical Settings, 17,* no. 3 (2010): 230–37.

38. J. D. Carter, R. T. Mulder, C. M. A. Frampton, and B. A. Darlow, "Infants Admitted to a Neonatal Intensive Care Unit: Parental Psychological Status at 9 Months," *Acta Paediatrica, 96,* no. 9 (2007): 1286–89.

39. B. G. Kvitvaer, J. Miller, and D. Newell, "Improving our Understanding of the Colicky Infant: A Prospective Observational Study," *Journal of Clinical Nursing, 21* (2012): 63–69.

40. P. S. Zeskind and R. G. Barr, "Acoustic Characteristics of Naturally Occurring Cries of Infants with 'Colic,'" *Child Development, 68,* no. 3 (1997): 394–403.

41. T. Vik, V. Grote, J. Escribano, J. Socha, E. Verduci, M. Fristsch, C. Carlier, R. von Kries, and B. Koletzko, "Infantile Colic, Prolonged Crying and Maternal Depression," *Acta Paediatrica, 98,* no 8 (2009): 1344–48.

42. C. R. Howard, N. Lanphear, B. P. Lanphear, S. Eberly, and R. A. Lawrence, "Parental Responses to Infant Crying and Colic: The Effect on Breastfeeding Duration," *Breastfeeding Medicine, 1,* no. 3 (2006): 146–55.

43. A. Cohen Engler, A. Hadash, N. Shehadeh, and G. Pillar, "Breastfeeding May Improve Nocturnal Sleep and Reduce Infantile Colic: Potential Role of Breast Milk Melatonin," *European Journal of Pediatrics, 171,* no. 4 (2012): 729–32.

44. N. Bakalar, "Despite Advice, Many Fail to Breast-Feed, *New York Times,* April 19, 2010, 7.

45. D. J. Chapman, "Longer Cumulative Breastfeeding Duration Associated with Improved Bone Strength," *Journal of Human Lactation, 28,* no. 18 (2012): 18–19.

46. A. Reynolds, "Breastfeeding and Brain Development," *Pediatrics Clinics of North America, 48* (2011): 159–71.

47. J. R. Britton and H. L. Britton, "Maternal Self-Concept and Breastfeeding," *Journal of Human Lactation, 24*, no. 4 (2008): 431–38.

48. S. Takemoto and S. Nakamura, "How Infant Feeding Methods Relate to Anxiety Over Child-Rearing and Feelings toward the Child," *Journal of Japan Academy of Midwifery, 25*, no. 2 (2011): 225–32.

49. B. Morrongiello and T. Dawber, "Parental Influence on Toddlers' Injury-Risk Behaviors: Are Sons and Daughters Socialized Differently?" *Journal of Applied Developmental Psychology, 20*, no. 2 (1999): 227–51.

50. N. Chodorow, *Feminism and Psychoanalytic Theory* (New Haven, CT: Yale University Press, 1991).

51. E. J. Kiel and K. A. Buss, "Maternal Accuracy in Predicting Toddlers' Behaviors and Associations with Toddlers' Fearful Temperament," *Child Development, 77*, no. 2 (2006): 355–70.

52. S. J. Schoppe-Sullivan, M. I. Diener, S. C. Mangelsdorf, G. L. Brown, J. L. McHale, and C. A. Frosch, "Attachment and Sensitivity in Family Context: The Roles of Parent and Infant Gender," *Infant and Child Development, 15*, no. 4 (2006): 367–85.

53. D. Mendell, "The Impact of the Mother-Daughter Relationship on Women's Relationships with Me: The Two-Man Phenomenon," *Issues in Psychoanalytic Psychology, 19* (1997): 213–23.

FIVE

The Honeymoon Years

Daughters in Early Childhood

With a few distinct exceptions, most of the women we interviewed reported that they felt close to their mothers while they were young. The easy connection of youthful relationships was experienced even within mother-daughter relationships that disintegrated in subsequent years. Mothers of young daughters frequently shared that their favorite part of this time is the easy expression of mutual, unconditional love. One mother, when asked what she enjoyed most in her relationships with her young daughter, shared, "She loves me, and I love her. I never knew that I could love someone as much as I love her. Her laughter is contagious. She is very independent and outgoing. She is a daredevil." By hearing this mother talk about her daughter, it is easy to imagine this woman finding delight in her daughter's company.

When my own children were young, my mother would tell me "the days may be long but the years are so short." Even though other parts of my life might have been a mess, when my youngest had learned to potty independently and the oldest was young, sweet, and did not talk back, my relationship with my kids was like a honeymoon.

DOING GIRLY THINGS

Mothers of little girls say they adore spending time with their daughters. They tell each other "I love you" and cuddle on the couch. These mothers described many universally shared and mutually enjoyable activities such as one mother catalogued: "We paint our nails together, she helps me cook, we go shopping together, and I love rocking her to sleep." With an overabundance of adorable little girl fashion items, it can be such a pleasure putting together darling outfits with matching hair bows. For some women, having a little girl is like playing dress up with the most beautiful doll in the world! When asked to share a memory of her childhood relationship with her mother, Ginny, now twenty-five, said that while she could not exactly come up with a single event, she did recall an ongoing routine that developed during her years in dance. Ginny shared, "I have fond memories of mom doing my hair and makeup for every dance recital, competition, and costume photo shoot. No one else could do my makeup or hair prettier! She always used this one gel that she would glob on my hair and it was not going ANYWHERE until I washed it! It had a funny name . . . goo something. I know! Dippity Doo!"

THE WORLD ACCORDING TO MOM

Not only do moms pick out their daughters' outfits and fix their daughters' hair but also they make most of the major decisions for their children. They make the play dates until their daughters are further along in elementary school, as a rule, so they have only themselves to blame if their daughters' friends are not up to snuff. Often, kids today enjoy opportunities to make choices that their parents may not have had the opportunity to make. Yet parents still pose the questions and provide the range of options. One interviewee remembers that her mother would give her a small amount of freedom to choose her clothing for school, but it was more like, "Yes, you may wear pants today to school. But you must choose between the red or yellow pair, but you may not choose jeans." Some children have more demanding temperaments as they grow older; but all girls will want to make increasingly more of their own decisions. Although elementary-age girls may pout and shout about their mothers' chosen dinner menu, as long as mom is in charge, women reported their daughters did not make the kind of choices they found hard to forgive.

Perhaps mom as the ultimate decision maker coupled with a general lack of a lengthy history of animosity between mothers and daughters, women with elementary-age girls frequently reported open communication with their young daughters as just another pleasurable aspect of their relationship. However, many mothers have traditionally hidden aspects of their identities that were more fun loving and youthful than they believed the motherhood role should entail. One woman with whom we spoke, Vickie, who is now in her early sixties, shared a story that typifies the metamorphosis that can occur during a daughter's early childhood years and forever shifts her perspective and understanding of who her mother really is:

> My mother was always at home, taking care of my brother, my father, and me. She would have a full breakfast cooked and ready at 6:00 a.m.,

a full supper all freshly cooked and ready at 5:00 p.m. After work, school, and supper, the four of us went outside and worked in the vegetable gardens or took care of other outside chores until dark. Then we returned inside for homework and a little TV watching before bedtime. My mother was always busy with her hands even when she was relaxing at the end of the day—crocheting afghans, doilies, flowers. She was a whirlwind of activity, but often silent.

When we went to visit her mother and father, my grandmother and grandfather, and all the family came over for Sunday dinner (lunch), my mother met up with her three sisters and one brother, and they would begin talking nonstop, laughing and teasing, while preparing dinner. Kids were in and out of the kitchen, back porch, dining area, living room, everywhere! But the sisters did not pay us any attention. This was their time together, and they enjoyed it. All of her siblings called my mother Mut. I was astonished when I first heard her called that and when I heard her laughter! Her name was Annie Mae Christopher Frye, and she much preferred just Mae. However, when she got together with her family, they just called her Mut and they did not even remember why. Neither did she! She was the middle child, with two older sisters, Mary and Frances, a younger sister, Bobbie, and a younger brother, L. E. Jr. They called him Bud. The sisters had their very distinct styles of dressing, but their purses were almost always the same—even well into adulthood.

The realization that my mother was so much more than just my mom was one of those early milestones in growing up. To see her laughing and happy made me happy for her and us as a family. Ever after, to me, she was an exotic, adventurous mom called Mut in affection. On the way home from these Sunday visits, I would ask her questions about her family when she was growing up. She had so many stories about the land, the river, the mountains, walking miles to school, going to work early as a young adult, and all the fun times the young people had. I treasure her stories still.

However, not every daughter takes away such a tender insight into her mother's unique, individual identity.

EVEN THE YOUNG ONES BRING CHALLENGES

The young childhood years are not without challenges for the mother-daughter relationship. Studies indicate that women find motherhood in the young years to be a stressful endeavor, but the "negative was usually ascribed to the practical aspects of motherhood whilst the emotional aspects were likely to be described positively."[1] Mothers occasionally reported that they were confused, frustrated, and exhausted by their daughters' mood swings, drama, or other disturbing behaviors. Nevertheless, in the long run, these behaviors were not the most damaging to the mother-daughter relationship.

As children enter elementary school and grow more independent, their personalities start to crystallize. Many daughters also experience growing awareness of the importance of their mothers' roles in their lives. One young woman, twenty-four, was able to recall easily a moment in her early childhood when she realized how much her mother meant to her as well as just how much her welfare meant to her mother:

> On a hot August morning in 1993, I had the first truly terrifying moment of my short, short life: My mother made me go to kindergarten.
>
> I cannot recall what time she made me get out of bed, but to four-year-old me, it may as well have been 3 a.m. She had my first-day-of-school dress picked out (I am pretty sure it was blue). I do not remember what I had for breakfast (most likely oatmeal as I remember it was my favorite breakfast meal at that age) or if my younger brothers were still asleep or awake.
>
> She had my bus number written on an index card. It was displayed through one of the plastic windows on my first book bag. She walked me outside and waited with me at the bus stop, telling me to have a great day, that everything would be fine, that she would be thinking of me all day, and that she would be here when I got home. All of a sudden, there was an awful roar coming up the street and this huge, ugly, and bright yellow machine was stopping in front of my house and was waiting to eat me right up. My mom hugged me and told me she loved me and to have a great day.
>
> Once the yellow beast spit me out at my elementary school, I became completely and utterly self-conscious and wanted to go home right then and there. A nice teacher or TA helped me find Mrs. Gunther's kindergarten class, I sat at the seat the teacher put me at, and the rest of the day is a blur until the end.
>
> I checked, double-checked, and triple-checked the handwriting on my mother's note card to make sure I got on the correct bus. I sat and waited and waited and waited for the bus to take me home. Finally Iris, the bus driver I would come to know and love over the years, told me this was my stop and that my mom was waiting for me to get off the bus. I grabbed my book bag, clamored out of the too-big seat, practically threw myself out of the bus, and ran as fast as my little legs could take me across the road and into my mother's open arms. I clung to her for what felt like forever (at least long enough for the bus to turn around in the cul-de-sac down the road and leave my neighborhood).
>
> She took me by the hand, led me inside, sat me down at the kitchen table for my first ever after-school snack, and asked me how my day was. I cannot remember what I said or what she said in return, but I remember the feeling I got of complete love and concern. After that, I knew I could return to school the next day because I knew that at the end of the day, no matter how scary or terrifying (or maybe one day it could be truly fun), that my mom would make everything okay.

Some moms reported having a very hard time adapting to differences between either the daughter's personality in comparison to her own or how she would have liked her daughter to be. These mothers were often quite concerned that the attributes they saw developing in their young daughter might hinder her future success. For instance, one middle-aged, particularly ambitious mom was concerned that her daughter who "just wanted to play, play, play" would underachieve in life. Another mother reported feeling jealous of her daughter's relationship with her husband, stating, "The two of them are like birds of a feather and I had always thought my daughter would be like me!" Fully accepting one's daughter (and, eventually, one's mother) may be a lifelong adventure that can bring joy or hardship depending on which way the acceptance pendulum swings.

The mother of two very-close-in-age daughters, Erin, shared the joy she felt just watching her daughters' unique personalities develop:

> I have the two most amazing daughters in the world. Of course, I am also very biased. Paige is four, Bailey is three, and my life did not feel complete until they were both in it. I look at them every day and wonder what they will be when they grow up. They are two such completely different individuals, but at the same time so much the same. Paige is very outgoing and friendly to everyone she meets. Bailey is very shy but extremely inquisitive and humorous. Both of them are so caring and considerate of others, it is awesome to watch them play with other children.
>
> My favorite moments with my girls are when we are being silly and carefree. They love to turn the music up and dance around the house with me. Whenever I look at either of them, I feel so proud to be able to call them my daughters. When I see them helping each other with a puzzle or comforting one another when they are scared or not feeling well, it is then that I know I am doing something right.

It seems that during this period, the good outweighs the struggles for many mothers. However, there can also be significant challenges that shape the future relationship between a mother and her daughter.

EARLY DAMAGE

Some women shared with us family situations that were so difficult that the mother-daughter relationship suffered deep wounds at an early age. Mothers who abused substances, mothers who abused their children, mothers involved with men who were toxic to the family system . . . these are some of the stories told where mothers did the most pronounced damage to the mother-daughter bond.

Some women shared that they had felt abandoned by their mothers when they were little girls. One mother with whom we spoke, Dorothy, felt that younger siblings with greater needs had usurped her place in the family and the affection hierarchy. As she related, "My relationship with my mother shifted when I was around nine because my mother had two kids (brothers eight and nine years younger) after me that took her attention away from me. As a result, I lived with my grandmother and aunt for the majority of my life from age ten up to eighteen."

Another woman, now forty-four, told her ongoing story of a volatile, up-and-down relationship with her mom: "During my childhood, my mother was always busy working, so I was often left to my own devices and caring for my younger sister. At one point, I felt totally abandoned by my mother but did not know the circumstances that facilitated it. It was not until my teen years that I got closer to my mother. I think she went overboard in trying to make up for the loss of time and hurt feelings. Yet as a young adult, I was still the one who had to make decisions regarding my younger sibling's care. I also felt abandoned again when my mother wasn't there for the birth of my first child or the later custody battle."

Donna told about her relationship with her mom starting from a young age that remained troubled for almost thirty years. "My mom had me when she was seventeen and was still in high school. I was mad at her all the time. She was not doing what other mothers were doing. She was smart but not nurturing. My father was not around. She worked and worked; she worked the swing shift and worked the farm. I had to grow up too fast. I was taking care of my little brothers, skipping school, dressing trampy. She was nowhere to be found." Yet early damage did not always destroy the mother-daughter relationship. Donna, now at forty-six, sees her mother differently; she describes the relationship as close because "I know that Mother did what she had to." Akin to the experience of Donna's mother, research has shown that a teen mother has much to navigate between managing her own adolescence and raising a young child.[2] For the most part, however, the mother-daughter relationship during childhood is a relatively peaceful period—the calm before the adolescent storm.

SMELLING THE FLOWERS

When life circumstances are reasonably good and mom is able to be a stable presence in her daughter's life, the mother–young daughter relationship yields security and love. It can be a joy to watch your daughter grow from an infant, blossoming into a young girl. The fact that it is a time during which mothers often feel important and loved in return is an excellent plus. We invited a mom and daughter duo to share a few words describing what made their relationship special. The newly turned twelve-year-old daughter's mother responded, "[My daughter] wanted to share how special it is to her that I still tuck her in at night even though she's twelve years old. That is still a special thing for her." When mothers and daughters get it right during these early years, it may take some of the sting out of the adolescent rebellion that most every young girl has to experience. In the following chapter, we will explore the highs and lows that mark this period in life.

NOTES

1. J. J. Weaver and J. M. Ussher, "How Motherhood Changes Life: A Discourse Analytic Study with Mothers of Young Children," *Journal of Reproductive & Infant Psychology, 15*, no. 1 (1997): 51–69.

2. P. Trautmann-Villalba, M. Gerhold, M. Laucht, and M. H. Schmidt, "Early Motherhood and Disruptive Behavior in School-Age Child," *Acta Paediatrica, 93*, 120–25.

SIX

Living in the Hood

Teenagehood

Mothering a teen-aged daughter is a path filled with contradictions and conundrums. As much as we would like to have our daughters find their own identities and forge their own paths, we still want to be consulted or at least serve as the role model they use. However, the need to please their mothers is a behavior motivation pretty much lost by the time young women reach adolescence. Yet for all of the frustrations we may feel at our daughters' choices, there is still a strong need to protect them and "make it all better." As one of the authors recalls,

I have a memory of one of those contradictory moments when I was feeling two distinct and opposite reactions regarding my daughter's choices and experiences. She was deep in the midst of her Goth phase, and her clothing was always some shade of black or gray, her lipstick a blackish red, her eyes fiercely lined in black kohl, and her jewelry a bracelet and choker of black leather and enough spikes to rival her typically sarcastic dialogue. At this particular moment in memory, we were standing in the line at the airport security checkpoint. It was October 2002, just a little over twenty-four months after 9/11. As we finally reached the security conveyer belt, we hoisted up our carry-on luggage and purses. As Gigi walked through the security scanner, the security guard immediately stopped her in her tracks and asked her to remove her bracelet and choker. He told her that they were going to be confiscated, as they were potential weapons and were not allowed on board the plane.

As a mother who loathed the whole "Goth ensemble," I felt vindication that my daughter's unappealing fashion choices were "officially" unacceptable. Joy welled up into my heart! Within milliseconds, however, the joy transformed into heartbreak and grief that my daughter's prized and independently purchased jewelry was being tossed into a bin from which they would be unrecoverable. Through that universally experienced and almost preternatural deep maternal instinct and maternal intuition, I knew immediately the pain that this incident caused my daughter; but being the adolescent that she had recently become, she could not acknowledge hurt, only cool nonchalance and disinterest in the whole event. I wanted to comfort her, but knew that this would be far from cool in the airport. I did quietly whisper that I would cover the expense of replacement jewelry, if that was what she wanted. "Whatever!" was her airport response, and at that moment, I realized then that mothering a teen daughter was probably going to be the most unpredictable and difficult journey I would ever experience.

ENJOYING THE RIDE

For some lucky women, their mother-daughter relationships remain close and communicative all their lives, with no notable years of hiatus or lapses. Gwen, a middle school teacher with two teenage girls aged fifteen and nineteen, shared this:

> I love the teenage stage. Teens are easy. You can hang out with them. We like the same things. Shopping, hair, nails. I talk with them about anything they want to talk about—sex, you name it. I think it is important they hear about it from me, not just their friends at school. I'm close with my girls. I love to spend a lot time with them.

Other moms shared that they, too, found the conversations more engaging than during the early years of motherhood, such as Nancy, who said that now she is able to have the kind of philosophical discussions she naturally prefers. There are few things she finds more enjoyable than sitting on the patio in the evening with her daughter and her daughter's friends talking about SCC football, love, and the meaning of life.

Open communication seems to be a key component to a happy mother-daughter dyad in the teen years. In fact, one woman who believes her relationship with her daughter to be "far more open than most" has encouraged her daughter to be highly discriminating about who she shares her secrets, "since your friends will have looser lips than your mother." This mother, like several other mothers of teens we interviewed, tries very hard to be her daughter's best confidant. In addition, many women do in fact report that once they are mature enough to appreciate it, mom is definitely the best person to tell one's innermost secrets.

BUMPS IN THE ROAD

Like any relationship, the mother-daughter relationship is affected by a wide variety of factors. Even in relatively satisfying relationships, moms can have a difficult time keeping a level head when daughters "get an attitude." Stated quite strongly by one mother of a teenage girl, "She really pisses me off. Typical teenage stuff—she thinks she knows it all and she only really cares about herself." As noted by Jenny, "It hurts when my daughter that I love so much throws her hand in the air [motions like a stop signal] and tells me, 'Like, what do you think you're doing?' She talks to me like one of those obnoxious teens in movies. I thought my girl would never be like that!"

In the words of a daughter, "Sometimes, I wanted to do things my way, and my mother did not tolerate it. I also had a smart mouth, so there would be arguments." Maintaining a clear perspective when a daughter transforms into a barely recognizable young woman can be quite a feat. A mother of three said she used to get upset when her eldest was a young teen, but with both her second and her third child, when they copped "an attitude," she reminded herself it is a developmentally appropriate behavior—and moreover, she recognized that it was just a temporary stage that all adolescents passed through.

Haughty attitudes are not the only communication hurdles mothers of adolescent daughters must surmount. Losing the cherished talk time can be tough on the heart when a previously chatty daughter "hibernates" in her room for a weekend. Lisa joked that if her daughter did not show up and hang around the family room for a lengthy time, a quick logon to Facebook would let her see her daughter's latest update and would allow Lisa to check up her without risking an argument. It may be even more disheartening when a daughter consistently turns away from her mother in the midst of a conversation. Daughters can make it painfully clear when they do not want to hear a mother's input or viewpoints without saying a word. Most adolescent daughters quickly master the fine art of "disdainful body language." Whether it is the look in her eyes, the toss of her head, or the heavy sighing as she leaves the room, daughters frequently treat their mothers to this "louder than words silent treatment." For many teens, part of the individuation process means no longer inviting or listening to mom's well-intended advice and guidance. Yet there are difficult conversations that must take place.

When we inquired about their most challenging conversations with their teens, our interviewees bravely shared some very tough topics. Sadly, some mothers found themselves in situations that necessitated discussions on domestic violence or sexual assault—either in regard to her own life or to her daughter's circumstances. Ongoing conversations with one's mom are an integral part of healing from these traumatic events; thus, it is highly important for mothers to face these issues with their daughters' needs in mind. When a mother feels a conversation is almost too painful for her to address, she should recognize how important the topic may be to her daughter's well-being. Good mothering requires a willingness to model inner strength and unconditional love, and these require the ability to place a daughter's needs above her own.

Divorce, separation, and wayward fathers were also among the more difficult conversations. A daughter remembers her mother telling her about her parents' separation over lunch at McDonalds—after which, she never wanted to eat there again. Moreover, she recalled how she hated her parents for at least a year following that day. Despite a study indicating that the companionship levels of mother-daughter dyads does not vary by the mother's marital relationship status (divorced, living with a nonbiological father, remarried to a nonbiological father, and so on),[1] many of our interviewees reported that divorce caused a relationship shift. It appears that many factors come into play in how children handle the separation of their parents. It seems that the degree to which mom is still available to her daughter is possibly the most important.

The most frequently mentioned difficult conversations, however, were those pertaining to sex. Whether it was sexual orientation, the menstrual cycle, the "birds and the bees," or the decision to engage in sexual activity, these were the topics that made many mothers (and daughters) get sweaty hands and pounding hearts.

TRUST, PROTECTIVENESS, AND THE DATING SCENE

While teens are seeking to explore their world, their own identities, and dabble in romantic encounters, their mothers simultaneously perceive adolescence as a time of increased vulnerability. Many of our interviewees did engage in high-risk behaviors as teens, such as borrowing a parent's car prior to any driver training, consuming unknown illicit substances, and engaging in sex with questionable partners. However, since adolescents do not have a fully developed prefrontal cortex, they tend to have difficulty accurately judging the degree of risk in a situation. So even though it may be wise for a mother to seek to protect her teenage girl, it may often be poorly received and runs counter to the adolescent drive to individuate, which involves risk taking and identity formation.

A woman who is now forty-two and has a sixteen-year-old daughter herself perceived her mother's trust in her shift quite dramatically when she was a teenager: "My mother really took on multiple personalities. She went from being a loving mother all the time to being a drill sergeant, policeman, counselor, teacher, and many others, yet in retrospect, I know it was all because she loved me and was protecting me." Wrestling free from mom's watchful eye is a typical teen goal. Some teens are more upfront about their rebellious ways, while others are completely (and successfully) covert. The covertness was often a means of not disappointing mom or avoiding mom's wrath.

Some mothers have an easy time remembering what they were like as teens. They remember engaging in activities without their mothers' approval. These memories certainly affect how they parent a teen. Rebecca described her own teen years:

> I was *too* wild. I'm lucky to have survived those years. Now I'm very involved with my own daughter's life—she doesn't have the distance from me to get into the kind of trouble I got into. And there are a lot of benefits from being this way. I know her friends—and their families. Her friends think I am funny. I know her interests and daily activities so I can offer guidance when needed. In some ways I am having the good clean teen fun I never had before.

Conversely, owing to a very different personal history, another mother shared that she does not really worry about what her daughter does to which she is not privy; this mother imagines it to be fairly harmless and believes everyone needs privacy and space.

According to many interviewees, their mothers became intensely protective when the teenage daughter attempted to enter the dating scene. At a minimum, mothers would apparently like to have some degree of influence over their daughter's choice in partner. One teen's mom shared that "if she must date, I wish she would date someone respectful, smart, and responsible, but that doesn't seem to be the type of criteria she cares about. Not only is it disappointing, it has me worried for her." Not only does the choice of who to date seem to be idiosyncratic, part of a teen achieving an adaptive individuation from her family includes her mother's acceptance of the teen's emerging independence and the decisions associated with it.[2] Another woman easily recalled her mother's interference in her love life. She described how it had made her feel disrespected, "like she didn't think I was mature enough or smart enough to make intelligent decisions, especially pertaining to men."

However, hands down, time and again, mother after mother reported that the most personally challenging of her daughter's decisions was the decision to have sex. A deep chasm can be created by a daughter's teenage sexual behavior. As one woman shared:

> When I was younger, my mother and I were very close. I was her little baby and everywhere she went, I was right by her side. She couldn't ever get rid of me. As I got older, she and I grew even closer. My mother never cared about me talking to boys, because I was her baby, and she knew that I knew better not to do anything wrong. I told my mother everything, and when I say everything, I mean everything. But two days before my sixteenth birthday I told my mother that I had sex. I felt that this was something that she needed to know, and I felt that it would be better if I told her rather than her hear it from someone else. Our relationship changed completely. She didn't trust me very much,

and I tried to gain it back by staying home and not asking to go places. I also went as far as breaking up with the guy to make her more at ease about me ever going out and doing anything again. I did everything in my power to show my mother that I knew I had done something that I should not have and that it wouldn't happen again. As time has passed we aren't as close, but we do have our talks like the old times.

In this case, her adolescent sexual encounter ended with the trust damage to her relationship with her mother, but for other women, sexual intercourse sometimes engendered teenage pregnancy—an even more difficult conversation.

BODY IMAGE

One of the especially challenging aspects of adolescence is the physical changes of puberty. For instance, a teen has to navigate breast development, menses, and new sexual feelings, as well as the associated changes in her social and familial environment. The social world highly influenced by the media offers a host of messages about the young female body, from how to look and act to the "best" size of every body part such as breasts, thighs, and even toes. In addition to experiencing physical changes of her own due to aging, Mom, concurrently, has feelings about her own body. It is no surprise that teens pick up on these messages loud and clear.

Some young women develop body image problems due in part to criticism experienced at home. Clara, a small-framed blonde and particularly beautiful young woman, discussed her mom's painful critique of her developing body, stating that her mother would examine how fat her clothes made her look before she left the house every day. These examination sessions were devastating to Clara, and ultimately, she began sneaking out of the house—especially if she was going swimming—in order to avoid her mother's critical eye. Despite the fact that Clara is fit and trim and no longer lives at home, she has internalized her mother's critique of her body; she continues to wrestle with a highly distorted body image.

More frequently, women who shared that their mothers had negative impacts on their self-image did not report that their mothers were destructively or overtly critical of their appearances. In fact, many mothers are making a point intentionally to tell their daughters of their beauty. Yet from a young age, women see and hear their mothers critique themselves, worry about weight, and sanction food choices according to calorie content. Robin identified precisely this process of body image transmission: "Because she felt ugly and I look like her, I had to be ugly, too." Mothers are only human and may be just as influenced by societal expectations and possibly just as grieved by their bodies as adolescents may be.

There have been an increasing number of breast augmentation surgeries for adolescent women in the last few years. Many of these surgeries are given by parents to their daughters in honor of high school graduation, eighteenth birthdays, and so on. In fact, an investigation of the rationale for gifting breast implants for high school graduation revealed that these mothers and daughters tended to literally buy into the sociocultural beliefs about physical appearance and femininity, perceiving small breasts as "inadequate." Five out of ten of these mothers had breast implants themselves, and all were happy to support the surgery for their daughters to access the self-confidence that augmented breasts were perceived to supply.[3]

But daughters do not always inherit a mother's insecurities and issues. A middle-aged mom shared that her sixth-grade daughter surpassed her in height—at twelve years old her daughter is 5′8″ and growing. However, her mother is delightfully surprised by her daughter's unflappable love of being so tall. An avid basketball player with a great attitude, she tells her mom she wants to reach six feet tall and that she knows she won't have any trouble meeting a man—after all her brothers are 6′3″ and 6′4″!

LETTING GO: HOT AND COLD

Due to the process of individuation and pubertal mood swings of teens coupled with the biopsychosocial stages of their mothers' in life, many intense personal narratives are created during the teen years. As a teen focuses her energy on her peers and creates distance between herself and her family, she is better able and more willing to see the imperfections in her family—and her mother. Many women report having mistakenly believed as teens that their mothers were lacking in intelligence ("dumb") about anything that mattered, such as friends or boys. Other women developed a more striking personal critique, such as Julia, who, as a teen, resented her mother for "her dependency on men and never fulfilling her own dreams." For women who had to mother their mothers or mother their siblings due to a lack of competency on their mother's part, the teen years armed them with the knowledge of the wrongness of their life circumstances. Not all of these mother-daughter relationships recover.

The letting-go process that is inherent in the individuation process of adolescence can be quite formidable for both the mother and the daughter. Some mothers are better able to cope with change than others are. Anne described the recent changes in her relationship with her fifteen-year-old daughter: "When my daughter turned thirteen, she was no longer a mini-me. Now she has her own views, likes, opinions, and so on. Sometimes, it adds to our time together, but other times, I feel like I have lost someone special and I'd really like to have that someone back." Although one young woman is now twenty-five, she still expresses her frustration with the dynamic of being held back by her mother: "I feel that my mother and I had a 'typical' mother-daughter relationship as a teenager. I felt she was an authority figure who often prevented me from the choices I wanted to make. It would be safe to say that we did not see eye to eye." Another young woman, twenty-two, and still technically in adolescence, shared an extreme example of a mother who was unable easily to let go: "My mother has always treated me like I'm five years old. I'm used to it now, but when I was a teen, it used to really burn me up. I once wrote in my English journal that she was the worst mother ever and I hated her. Still to this day she has not loosened up, but I'm not mad about it anymore." Nevertheless, most women, however unwillingly, do loosen up and allow their daughters to become the individuals they are destined to be.

REMEMBER WHEN

When the teen years become a memory, many women reflected that they were "the least close time" in their mother-daughter relationship. An abundance of favorite teenhood memories were based around shopping together or receiving a considerate gift from mom. Whether it was a beautiful patent leather purse or a highly desired prom dress, many women recall the special purchase, making them feel loved. Sometimes, contrary to the self-absorbed teen stereotype, these women recognized that purchasing the gift represented a sacrifice by their mothers. Therefore, if you are currently a mother of a teen, there is hope that your daughter will someday recognize the many small or large sacrifices you are making for her. The really good news is that a very large percentage of mother-daughter relationships experience rejuvenation as the daughter moves into young adulthood and moves out of the house!

NOTES

1. G. L. Fox and J. K. Inazu, "The Influence of Mother's Marital History on the Mother-Daughter Relationship in Black and White Households," *Journal of Marriage and the Family, 44,* 143–53.

2. P. V. Trad, "Adolescent Girls and Their Mothers Realigning the Relationship," *The American Journal of Family Therapy, 23* (1995): 11–24.

3. L. A. Fowler and A. R. Moore, "Breast Implants for Graduation: A Sociological Examination of Daughter and Mother Narratives," *Sociology Mind, 2* (2012): 109–15.

SEVEN

Mothering Adult Daughters

The Gift of Friendship

After speaking with daughters of all ages from toddler to older adult, it was gratifying to realize how many of us are increasingly able to appreciate and cherish our mothers, perhaps even when the journey is rocky or when she is not all that we wanted or needed her to be. Many women indicated that their own journey into adulthood provided them with the chance to deepen and transform their relationships with their mothers. As one woman shared, the mother-daughter relationship is "a work in progress." Moreover, because the relationship overlaps two generations, it is destined to arouse its fair share of ambivalence[1] in mothers and daughters, as well as entail a fair amount of work to keep it healthy. Luckily, research suggests that the relationship does begin to even out and roll more smoothly over the years as daughters move into adulthood.[2]

ANCIENT MOTHER-DAUGHTER INDIVIDUATION STRUGGLES

One of the most enduring and archetypal tales describing the mother-daughter relationship as a daughter grows into adulthood is the Greek myth of Demeter, the mother-goddess, and Persephone, her virginal daughter. Demeter loses her daughter to Hades, the underworld god, who steals Persephone away and tricks her into being tied to him and his realm. When Demeter, also goddess of the harvest, loses her daughter, she brings barrenness and drought to the land until she can be reunited with Persephone. Unfortunately, the circumstances of her abduction require Persephone to spend a portion of each year in the underworld, a period during during which the earth is dormant. When Persephone is allowed to return to the world above and to her mother, her arrival is heralded by the new growth of vegetation of spring. This story illustrates the loss that occurs for mothers when their daughters grow up, move out into the world, and develop the new identity of life partner and mate to another.

A woman in her mid-thirties, Mickey, described the moment when she realized just how powerful her relationship and connection to her mother actually was in comparison to her commitment to the man whom she termed her "practice husband." The story has undertones of the Demeter-Persephone relationship in her own unwillingness to cleave to her husband and risk losing connection to her mother:

> My first marriage was my "practice marriage" that ended because he and I started growing in different directions—the things that were important to me and the things that were important to him were two completely different things! In a marriage counseling session, I had said to the counselor that I thought he was spending too much time with his friends. My husband-at-the-time could only counter with "and she spends too much time with her mom." What?!
> So the marriage counselor asked him if he was willing to put his friends on the back burner in order work on our marriage. He said yes. The marriage counselor asked me if I was willing to put my mom on the back burner in order to work on our marriage. I replied, "My mother bent over backwards for twenty-five years raising my brother and I and doing everything she could do for us to get us through school and college and life in general. If working on my marriage means putting my mom on the back burner, then no. I am NOT willing to work on my marriage." And that was the end of marriage counseling! (This only turned out for the best because of the fantastic husband I have now!)

Many mothers hope that the sacrifices they make for their daughters will be acknowledged so surely at some point in their daughters' lives, if not necessarily in the counselor's office. Launching a daughter into adulthood opens up avenues for new paradigms of relating as well as new possibilities for cracks and fissures to develop. No longer simply their mothers' daughters, young women face the most daunting task of individuation yet—creating a separate identity and taking on a new adult status that can create a new level of connection and *competition* with their mothers.

THE PUSH-PULL OF HEALTHY DEVELOPMENT

As we have noted throughout the book, the mother-daughter relationship is possibly the most significant, influential relationships that a female will ever experience. Its power is felt from a daughter's first breath until her last; we might carry guilt and hopes related to this integral relationship throughout every subsequent relationship and choice we make. In fact, each choice daughters make (relational, career, or social) is influenced by, and influences, this relationship.[3] An adult woman may believe that her feelings about her mother and their relationship are intricately woven into her trajectory through chronological milestones, choosing when and whom to marry/partner, whether or not to have children, her career ambitions and decisions, as well as the development and playing out of her friendships and other relationships. Three specific milestone/lifestyle events are intimately woven through this essential relationship: marital status, parenthood status, and employment status.[4] As a woman moves through these varied realms of action, she is stepping from behind the shadow and influence of her mother as she adds new layers of identity to her story. We will focus most on the influence of marriage/partnership decisions as separate chapters explore the realms of parenthood and career.

Just as adolescents push for their own independent identity, adult women also struggle with the desire to be both different and independent from their mothers in spite of the inescapable emotional and biological connection to their mothers. The events that shaped the childhood and adolescent relationship between mother and daughter can create festering wounds and discord that endure well into adulthood. Asked about the most difficult period of her relationship with her mother, a forty-six-year-old shared an example of unresolved hurt that continued to affect her relationship with her mother: "My mother is still very abrasive. She feels she is allowed to say anything she wants to me because she is my mother, regardless of my feelings. . . . We hardly talk at all now." Several other women have noted that sibling rivalry has continued to create difficulties in their relationships with their mothers. It can be difficult to grow into an independent woman when the emotional baggage from early family experiences is weighting down a burgeoning adult. This weight can include childhood inequities, adolescent turmoil, and the hopes and dreams of the prior generation.

Not only are daughters carrying their own expectations and hopes about their future accomplishments into their adult lives, they are also carrying those of their mothers. As noted in earlier chapters, the identification between a mother and her daughter can be uniquely intense, just as the competition between them also might be. This can create a dynamic in which daughters feel driven to achieve a life shaped by that of their mothers or shaped around the unfulfilled dreams of their mothers. Either way, they will likely be unfulfilled themselves until they are supported in the opportunity to identify their *own* dreams and pursue these in lieu of their mother-identified aspirations. It has been noted that the development of both a successful romantic partnership and career path symbolically can provide a daughter with proof that she is now a woman in her own right.[5] It is through the taking on of external roles that she is able to create the strongest sense of internal identity.

FINDING A MATE AND LONG-TERM RELATIONSHIPS

Romantic love is the overarching theme and focus of so much of the activities in our lives—we are bombarded with the importance of finding our true love and, if the first one does not work out, finding the next candidate. Most of us grew up on fairy tales that illustrated just how important a good man can be—from rescuing Rapunzel from the castle, awakening Snow White from her deathlike sleep, to helping a mermaid get her legs! The hope and promise of "happily ever after" brings eager anticipation and hope to young girls as they begin to chase the boys in the schoolyard in elementary school and long for attention from their crushes in middle and high school.

Mothers are relegated to the sidelines as their daughters grow into sexually mature women who are valued for their worth as potential mates and mothers. However, even from the sidelines, mothers are strongly invested in the outcome of their daughters' courtships and love affairs. Even—or especially?—wedding planning can invite discord between mothers and daughters, as one young woman noted. Describing the difficulties she and her mother had been having, a twenty-five-year-old woman shared that the worst moments she had experienced in her relationship to her mother were "during the planning of my wedding. My mother and I had several tiffs. It can be difficult having two strongly opinionated women making financial decisions." From her perspective, she might have seen financial issues as the central points of contention; however, this may have just served as a safe place for disagreement as her mother worked through the issues of loss and transition that come from the marriage and departure of a daughter from the nuclear family.

Taking the Bad with the Good

Mothers would like their daughters to find perfect mates, and it can be painful to see them enter into relationships that offer them less than the best. Witnessing their daughters grow up to be lovers is a tall order for many mothers, and it can be difficult to accept the potential irrevocable changes this might bring to the mother-daughter relationship. Even more difficult to accept can be partners that mothers perceive to be less-than-ideal choices. When a person or relationship is believed to be harmful for a daughter, it is hard not to speak out. This, however, can damage the mother-daughter relationship, whether or not the mother was "right." As a woman in her late twenties shared:

I dated a guy my mother was not too fond of, however, the love I had for him would not allow that to interfere with the relationship he and I had. We ended up dating seven years; that entire seven years, my mother and I never saw eye-to-eye on that relationship. At times, this had us writing letters to one another because we were not speaking to one another even though we were living under the same roof. Eventually we broke up, but on my terms.

Stories of ways in which a woman's mother might try to warn her away from a poor choice for a long-term relationship were frequently shared with us by our interviewees. One twenty-year-old related this story: "The worst time [in our relationship] was when I wanted to date someone from a different racial group. My mom was raised in the South and does not believe in that. We have worked out our differences, but she would still not approve to this day if I did." Another woman shared that when she broke away from expectations about the religious faith of a boyfriend, she and her mother experienced a low point in their relationship.

For some mothers, it is the fear of what others might say or of a daughter's heart being broken that fuel the debate about the romantic relationship. For another mother, it was the actuality of a literal bone break: "In August 2004, my ex-husband and I had a motorcycle wreck. I fractured my hand and knee, but he wasn't hurt. My mom tried to tell me then that he did not love me and that he would not be there for me when I needed him. It turned out that she was right—I was hurt, he was fine, and he was not willing to care for me as I healed. Looking back, she was right, but at that moment I did not want to listen to her." Sometimes, it is still hard for her to acknowledge this.

We can all too easily be blinded by love, especially when we are trying to avoid the signs of a poor partner choice. A twenty-nine-year-old shared that "the worst time for our relationship was when I was married to my ex-husband. He was very controlling, and I could not see that at first. I thought she just wanted me to come back home, but she was just looking out for me." After she divorced her husband, she shared that this brought about the most significant shift in her relationship with her mother. She revealed, "My mom is my best friend, and I would not take anything for her. As a teenager, I could not stand her. As I got older, I realized that she was only trying to help and do what was best for me. She goes above and beyond her call of duty to help me to this day. I can call her any time day or night and she will be there, no questions asked. I can depend on her no matter what. I love her like no other."

Being able to move beyond a mother's disappointment in her daughter's romantic relationship choices is indeed possible, although it might require concessions or commitment on both sides.

Geographical Growth Trajectories

For many of the young women coming of age today, the concept of staying close to home throughout adulthood is not considered a realistic option. The desire for autonomy and control over their own lives can encourage geographical "comings of age" for young women. In addition, geographical distance between mother and daughter can sometimes be healthy and supportive of individuation for young women who may have grown too comfortable close to home. However beneficial it may be in the long run, a daughter's decision to uproot and launch herself a thousand miles out of the family nest can create distress for her mother. As one woman recalled, "When I moved to New York with my boyfriend immediately after college, my mother was very upset. She said that she would never give me her blessing." Another woman shared, "When I moved to Mississippi in 1997, Momma was not very happy with it, nor did she approve of my new marriage. We didn't talk for a few months. It was during that time that she was diagnosed with diabetes and became ill." Reminiscent of a story shared in another chapter of an adult daughter who came out as a lesbian to a mother who responded by immediately taking ill, it seems that a daughter's forward growth away from where she was raised (geographically and philosophically) can wreak havoc on the well-being of her mother. Mothers cannot help but see themselves in their daughters as they watch them grow from infancy to adulthood, but when a daughter is ready to "rebirth" her life in a manner quite different than motherly expectations devise, it can be traumatic for both women involved.

A Daughter Is a Daughter for All Her Life?

When we grow into a new relationship in the role of partner, necessary shifts should occur in most other relationships. There is a need to breathe life and shape into new connections apart from the relationships that have been developing since birth. To find room for a partner in our lives, we may have to draw back from our parents, especially our mothers. In fact, in the case of wives who are childless and show excessive neediness toward their mothers or express excessive concern/caregiving to their mothers, they may actually suffer from compromised psychological well-being! A little bit of space needs to be injected into the mother-daughter relationship once a woman has chosen a partner. However, this newly organized relationship does not have to result in a long-term estrangement or permanent distancing between the women. One woman described how the reorganization happened so naturally for her:

> Our relationships shifted a few months after I was married. My mother, father, and I have a very close relationship. However, after I got married, I realized that I didn't have to call and tell them every time my

husband and I traveled out of town. My mother and I stopped calling each other so much, and it was strange at first. However, we have both let go and have become closer from that.

Many women have commented on the positive influence that marriage and motherhood had on their relationships with their mothers. Some women believe that their decision to marry has fulfilled their mother's most basic expectation for them and that having a child is further affirmation of their successful accomplishment of a woman's most important roles, wife and mother.

One woman noted, "I feel like our relationship shifted for the good after I got married. She didn't treat me like a child anymore. I guess she figured I had grown up." Another woman was more concrete in her estimation of how marriage shifted her relationship with her mother: "When I got married, my mother and I seemed to have more in common and more to talk about." Shared interests and experiences are the building blocks of friendships, so it makes sense that these new commonalities would draw mother and daughter closer. A fifty-year-old recalled, "Once I was married, my relationship changed to more of a friend than a mother and daughter relationship." This new entrée into the friendship circle, however, may be affected by shifts and faults that appear in the romantic relationships of mothers or daughters.

WHEN ROMANTIC RELATIONSHIPS FAIL

Sometimes, it is helpful for a mother to examine closely her own significant romantic relationships for clues to her daughter's perspectives and choices. Research shows that it is within our own nuclear family, as children, that our values and patterns for interacting with others are first shaped.[6] The relationship a mother has with her daughter's father or coparent provides the initial model for how a romantic relationship can be. The messages that we send to our daughters or that our daughters take with them from their childhood can often be longer lasting and more potent that we might want to imagine. While it is well documented that mothers create the first impression and lasting template for a child's adult attachment styles and relationships,[7, 8] we may not be as aware of the lessons that our own primary romantic relationships are teaching our daughters. As daughters, we might not be aware of the inextricable intersection of our romantic relationships with our mother-daughter relationships.

A Mother's Divorce

Since divorce became as common as long-term marriage, researchers have created two opposing camps—those who believe that divorce harms children irrevocably and those who see no more danger in being a child of divorce than a child whose parents celebrate their golden anniversary. While there seems to be no terribly calamitous harm done to children of divorce that is universally realized in all families, the jury is still out on the effect divorce has on daughters' long-term romantic success or pursuits. Some studies have shown that these women may be less likely to marry or marry at a later age; other studies suggest these young women are more likely to be sexually active earlier and more pervasively. There also appears to be a need to explore the experiences of women whose mothers divorced after their daughters had found their life partners.

The natural balance of life can be upset when a mother is dealing with a broken heart, needing the same kind of support that she might have at sixteen but trying to find this comfort in the nearest "mother figure" she might have in her life at the moment—her daughter.

> A most recent shift that has also occurred would be in within the last year to year and a half now that I have been married for three years and on my own for the last five to six years. I am 100 percent not dependent upon her and working full time and being in school full time and balancing that with time with my husband and friends [that] she has become, I feel, more needy and clingy and looking for a closeness that we hadn't had in a few years while she is getting her life together.

This was shared by a twenty-five-year-old daughter whose mother was in the midst of a painful divorce. Another woman who saw her parents move from separation into divorce pinpoints this period as having been the most negatively influential in her relationship with her mother. As she described,

> The time our relationship was strained the most was probably when she and my dad were going through their separation and divorce. My mom completely changed during those five years, and I felt like she was not there for me when I needed her to be and the focus was always on her. I felt like she was not interested in me or my accomplishments or my day-to-day activities, and it made it more difficult because I did not live at home during those years and so there was physical distance between us as well. More and more separation occurred, and walls were put up as protective barriers.

When the "fairytale romance" falls apart for a young woman's parents, she can feel as if her own self-authored story is at risk of crumbling. Accepting that no relationship is "break-up proof" can be an important educational experience, in the best-case scenario. Being supportive of parents and siblings can help model and build resiliency for the family members, although the loss felt may be as permanent as a loss due to death.

A Daughter's Divorce

When love and relationships fail, regardless of the harm she may have suffered, some women may be fearful of their mothers' reactions to their breakup. In fact, some of women's most difficult conversations with their mothers involved the revelation of a daughter's failing relationship. After noting the strong family-oriented background from which she came, one woman shared that the most difficult conversation with her mother as an adult was "when I announced I was getting a divorce." Although they are close again, she and her mother had to rely on time to help heal the rift. Another woman provided a point-counterpoint description of how her relationship with her mother had shifted over the years. She shared that when her children were born, she felt a significant shift in her relationship with her mother as she moved onto a more level playing field. The worst moment of her relationship, however, was found in the period in which she was divorcing her husband. Her mother was opposed to the divorce and did not provide the empathy or support needed by her daughter.

There is a lot to be gained, however, when a mother is able to put the needs of a daughter ahead of the worries of what others might say or a mother's own personal investment in a daughter's marriage. As a very young divorcee recalled, "I recently went through a much unexpected divorce. Everyone around me was trying to tell me what to do and how to live my life, giving unwarranted advice. My mother stepped back and let me vent to her about my hurt and frustrations while never once offering advice . . . other than doing what makes me happy. She never degraded my ex-spouse, but she simply listened and was a friend. She has always gone out of her way to make sure my needs—physical, emotional, and mental—are met to the best of her ability."

The strength that it takes for a mother to be present for a daughter as she is facing the disintegration of a marriage is significant. It can be the easier route for a mother to shame her daughter about her decision to leave the marriage or join her in berating the spouse. Yet as the young woman above noted, it is the presence and support of a mother that is the most valued contribution to the healing process. A sixty-three-year-old mother described the painful experience of first learning about her own thirty-four-year-old daughter's failed marriage a few hours earlier:

> I just returned from having lunch with my thirty-five-year-old (and eldest) daughter who has decided to divorce her husband of ten years. Listening to her talk about her decision and watching the shift in her emotions from anger to guilt to hurt to sadness to determination almost brought me to tears. But I fought back the tears, feeling that I had to remain calm and composed so that my own anger and sadness would not cause her to worry about me. She does that—worries about my reactions to the situations and feelings she experiences. Whether she

does this to protect me or to protect herself, I am not sure. It's not
something about which we can easily talk.

The gift of being present and putting a daughter's needs above a mother's own needs embody a mother's ability to let her daughter grow into her own selfhood, without the need to "stamp" her development with a mother's branding.

Being present for our daughters—and allowing our mothers to be present for us—can be a significant step in refining this bond that shifts and stretches over the life course. Beyond romantic relationships, which allow a daughter to define herself in relation to her partner, are the opportunities a daughter has to define herself as an individual via career identity.

CAREER WOMEN

From what we learned through our interviews, it is clear that the majority of mothers today are wholeheartedly supporting their daughters' forays into the professional world. A more detailed exploration of this topic is found in a subsequent chapter. Education, too, is valued across generations, and mothers help their daughters find a way to pursue higher education through any means possible. As one early thirties woman described with a laugh, "College was not an option—it was a requirement. By the time I was a senior in high school, my mother had already applied to several colleges on my behalf." Mothers should encourage their daughters to plan big and bold, if that is how they envision their professional careers taking shape. One fifty-seven-year-old woman, though, shared a few regrets about her career path in relation to how her life took a different course than her mother's life had:

> I was career-oriented and willing to take risks and expand my horizons
> to fulfill goals. I think I took this to the extreme that was unconsciously
> a rebellious attitude toward my mother. I am different from her in that
> way, but wish I had not been so extremely different and could not
> incorporate the family life that she had along with a career.

Trying to balance career and marriage along with relationships with parents and others can be challenging; in fact, married daughters who were unemployed feel closer to their mothers than those who are working.[9]

Some women may try to pin their own unfulfilled career aspirations on their daughters, but this tactic seldom succeeds. As mothers begin to see their own days shorten and as menopause arrives, they may find themselves feeling a bit of envy as they gaze upon their youthful daughters whose lives are so full of potential and fertility.[10] Maintaining a supportive, nondirective stance as a daughter weighs professional fields or even the decision to work or not will be freeing to the younger woman and can be gratifying to her mother as she watches her daughter make sound choices. Letting go of the need to direct a daughter can be difficult. As a woman of three adult daughters reflected, "I loved playing with dolls as a child. . . . What I failed to realize as a child playing with dolls was that children are not dolls. They have wills and personalities of their own and do not easily conform to the roles we, as mothers, would have them play."

While some women we interviewed regretted that they had not been as content to stay at home with children as their mothers might have hoped, others longed for having had careers as exciting and satisfying as their entrepreneurial mothers modeled. Recognizing that every adult must be encouraged on the path that they believe to be right for themselves can be challenging, but it is essential in helping daughters become the women they are meant to be.

POSITIVE GROWTH WITH MATURITY

What do we need from our mothers as we become adults ourselves? Very much the same things we needed as children—unconditional love, emotional support, and understanding. A welcome shift in the tone of the relationship may also accompany a daughter's development as an adult. As a woman's daughter gains more equal footing in life experiences and maturity, a flavor of friendship is frequently added to the mother-daughter relationship. One seventy-one-year-old interviewee shared:

> I am fortunate still to have my wonderful mother. We have always had an almost perfect relationship as I have had with my daughters. I don't know what magic we have been blessed with, but we sure have it. Amy and Sally, my daughters, are so much alike and so different, but the love is the same. I will be going against all the rules in saying that I am good friends with my kids. I know the books say that you have to be a parent and not a friend. NOT true in my case. I have always been best friends with my mom and I am great friends with my girls. We have always been honest and open with each other . . . even when it was hard to be open.

A proud mother of two daughters and a son, she has had to accept not only two thousand miles of geographical distance between herself and one of her daughters but also the distance between heterosexual expectations of this daughter and the lesbian reality. However, she embraces her daughter with the unconditional love that all of us hope for from our mothers. "Always listen" is her admonition to other mothers whose adult daughters are making choices that they might not prefer, "even when it isn't easy to do."

Another mother of adult daughters, thirty-five- and thirty-six-years-old, was asked what she appreciated most in her daughters today, and she enthusiastically responded,

> Most everything! I love their humor, their smarts, their love for each other, and their love of family. They are young women who are making a difference in the world . . . and I know if I said we needed them, they would be here in a heartbeat.

She recalled that the teenage years had presented significant challenges for her as they tested boundaries, showed typical rebellious attitudes, and experienced mood swings. She said she was shocked that "these adorable, wonderful, loving little girls turned into something unrecognizable." She used the word *scary* to describe how it had been watching them make decisions that led to unfortunate consequences, but she affirmed again how proud she was of how they had matured into smart and accomplished women who were both on paths to make the world a better place.

Some daughters, however, were not raised by mothers nearly as supportive and accepting as the two described above. Many mothers are ill equipped to offer much beyond the very basics to their daughters, and it leaves their daughters longing for a warm, maternal embrace—literally and figuratively. Daughters may try to enhance the relationship they do have but be unable to let go of the past wrongs due to the significance of the past damage done. As one woman shared, she still has a strained relationship with her mother, although she noted, "after several years of counseling I learned her behaviors were influenced by her being raised by an alcoholic father." She continues to make efforts to keep in touch, but she feels that there is too much of the past still between them: "We do write letters and talk on the phone once a month. . . . I can only visit for a few days because she is so controlling." Unfortunately, both women are missing a potentially rich and rewarding relationship, even though both are apparently trying to create something more than they had in the daughter's early years. Learning new responses and new roles in relation to an adult daughter can provide mothers with a relationship that is unlike any either woman has experienced before. Through the combination of shared life history, familial bonds, and the respect and acceptance found in strong adult friendships, adult daughters can find and offer great joy to their mothers through an evolved relationship.

FRIENDSHIP AT ITS SWEETEST

Women often begin to see significant positive shifts in their relationships as they leave for college, during their early twenties, when they marry, when they become mothers, and when they become caregivers for their mothers. Each of these life events propels young women further into increasing responsibility for themselves and to others. This modified understanding of a woman's life can allow her to see her mother through new eyes that no longer only look for faults and shortcomings. Able to recognize her mother's struggles and more clearly understand her mother's sacrifices made for her daughter's sake allow her to appreciate her mother in a way never before possible.

In her mid-twenties, one young woman shared her understanding of how her relationship with her mother had changed over the past few years. She affirmed that she and her mom "have become more peers and friends now that I am an adult." The growing empathy between a daughter and her mother allows them both to take their relationship to a different space in which shared female knowledge is a bridge, not a site of competition. Another woman reflected that once she left for college, "my mother finally began to see me as an adult." And now, fifteen years later, her mother calls her every day and they just chat about the day's events, what is going on in their lives, and "nothing in particular," just as if they were "best buddies," as she described it. Another woman, now forty-two-years-old, who had experienced a great deal of conflict over the years with her mother, recognized the need for a relationship shift. She was able to make this happen, she said, "when I allowed myself to give my mom another chance to be not only a loving mom, but my friend as well."

When able to build strong relationships with their mothers, adult daughters are not only facilitating happier times at family get-togethers, research showed that they are facilitating their own psychological and emotional well-being, too.[11] Self-esteem, anxiety, and depression are all affected by a woman's relationship with her mother—so there is a big payoff when the relationship is carefully tended and maintained throughout adulthood. For many women, the relationship blossoms into "best friends" as they grow closer as adults. One woman shared, "My mother and I have a great relationship. My mother is my best friend. When it comes to trusting someone she will be the one no matter what the situation may be." Sometimes, daughters may be surprised—and unsettled—by the trust their mothers now extend to them, as one young woman explained, "My mother and I are best friends. Sometimes that is not a good thing because she tells me about things that I really should not know about, like financial burdens and other things, but I know she tells me these things because we are so close. We talk a lot and express our feelings about things to each other a lot." One woman recalled that when she had been a teenager, her mother had colluded with her to keep her father from finding out about an unfortunate experience into which she had found her way. She laughs now, thirty years later, at how this proved her mother's love then and, today, they are best friends, "who both know where the bodies are buried!" she humorously added.

Best friends accept one another unconditionally as well as allow the other to grow. They also allow one another's voice to be heard, as a forty-two-year-old noted about her relationship with her mother: "The best aspect of our relationship is that we can talk. No matter what it is, we can talk about the good, the bad, and the ugly. Our communication with one another is like mother-daughter/sisters/best friends." While many women described the openness of their conversations with their mothers, we want to share a humorous confession of a thirty-nine-year-old daughter as she describes how "free" her mother now was in the "girl talks" they share today: "We are becoming the best of friends so much so that she shared a sexual exploit between her and my father. I was not ready, and she shared before she really thought about it. And when I called the next day, she was like . . . .'Well, I didn't know if I'd ever hear from you again.'"

CONCLUSION

Successfully raising a daughter to maturity is not an easy task, and it requires an unfathomable measure of energy on the part of her mother—and the daughter, as well. Individuation is not easy work for mothers or daughters. As one twenty-five-year-old noted when asked how she was different from her mother, "I'm not unhappy about my differences. . . . I feel that I worked hard growing up!" Another woman shared her own experiences in trying to be seen as an adult by her mother and recounted how she had seen herself change in the past couple of years: "I remember being fearless until about twenty-four or twenty-five. And, then, I started to shift to getting worried about things. My mom will not even buy me a chef's knife because she says I need a knife safety class and I am almost thirty! I laughed about this until my boyfriend pointed out that I always say, 'Is that safe?' I wish I could let loose a little bit more." For this young woman, she still has a way to go before she feels she will be "grown up" in her own and her mother's eyes. She may believe her mother is over-protective, but she acknowledged that we cannot choose our mothers, just as mothers cannot choose or control the development of their daughters.

Returning to the wisdom of B. R., who has raised three daughters to their mid-thirties, she shared her realization that for our daughters, "the mother they desire to have may not be the mother we want or need to be." She noted that perhaps she seemed to have been focusing on disappointments in her mother-daughter relationships in the interview, and she explained that she was not disappointed in her daughters, rather that

> the disappointment lies in the expectations that I set for myself as a mother and I suspect that many mothers have set similar expectations of themselves; the expectation that we have the power to mold and

shape our daughters into our likeness or any other likeness of our choosing and to be the perfect mother to that likeness.

What I have discovered, and continue to remind myself, is that my daughters are not extensions of me. They did not choose to come into this world solely to fulfill my wish to be a mother. They do not necessarily see life as I see it, and the hopes, dreams, and ambitions I have for them may not be what they have for themselves. Although they may have experiences similar to mine, their responses to them will likely be very different from mine. . . . I want my daughters to know that I love, accept, and respect each of them for the person that she is with no other expectations on my part.

By learning to accept that she is imperfect, but perfectly willing to be present for her daughter, a mother will be able to model unconditional love and full acceptance of her daughter, no matter how imperfect her daughter may feel herself to be. Letting go of expectations of how a daughter "should have" turned out or how a mother "should have" been will allow for the development of what the adult relationship can be.

NOTES

1. L. K. Fowler, *Family Life Month Packet, Ohio State University*, 1999. Retrieved from http://www.hec.ohio.state.edul/famlife/.

2. S. A. Mottram and N. Hortacsu, "Adult Daughter Aging Mother Relationship over the Life Cycle: The Turkish Case," *Journal of Aging Studies, 19*, no. 4 (2005): 471–88.

3. M. T. Notman, "Mothers and Daughters as Adults," *Psychoanalytic Inquiry: A Topical Journal for Mental Health Professionals, 26* (2006): 137–53.

4. K. Kitamura and T. Muto, "The Influence of Adult Mother-Daughter Relationships on Daughters' Psychological Well-Being: Life Events of Marriage and Childbearing," *Japanese Journal of Developmental Psychology, 12* (2001): 46–57.

5. Ibid.

6. P. L. Berger and T. Luckmann, *The Social Construction of Reality: A Treatise in the Sociology of Knowledge* (New York: Doubleday, 1966).

7. J. Bowlby, "The Making and Breaking of Affectional Bonds," *British Journal of Psychiatry, 130* (1977): 201–10.

8. D. W. Winnicott, *Babies and Their Mothers* (London: Free Association Books, 1988).

9. Kitamura and Muto, "The Influence of Adult Mother-Daughter Relationships on Daughters' Psychological Well-Being."

10. Notman, "Mothers and Daughters as Adults."

11. G. Baruch and R. C. Barnett, "Adult Daughters' Relationships with Their Mothers," *Journal of Marriage and the Family, 45*, no. 3 (1983): 601–6.

EIGHT

The Cycle Begins Again

Daughters Becoming Mothers

Becoming a mother is a highly desired goal for the majority of little girls; we encourage mothering instincts and desires from the first gift of a stuffed animal or soft doll to our newborn daughters. Our drive for survival of the species is clearly evidenced in our desire to see our female young practice mothering behaviors from their earliest days. Newborn boys are gifted with baseball mitts and models of cars and trucks that invite agentic behaviors, while newborn girls are given toys that invite caregiving, nurturing, and communal behaviors. Moreover, whether it is nature, nurture, or a combination of both, as babies turn into young children, little girls seem to prefer these "feminine" toys while boys prefer toys that are more "masculine." Researchers have sought to make sense of these choices and look to social learning theories, cognitive development theories, and biologically based hormone-related conditions.[1] We may come into this world interested in both stereotypically masculine and feminine toys, but our socialization supports a consistently narrowed focus on more gender-specific toys as we grow up. More girls may be receiving more gender-neutral options—with pink plastic power tools and workbenches now available for preschoolers—but we still encourage gender-differentiated play, overall, regardless of our daughters' interests. One mother we interviewed recalled the short-lived shelf life of a relatively pricey dollhouse for her daughter. The thrill of playing with the pretend family was gone before Easter, and the house and its inhabitants were gathering dust by summer.

Yet for many of us who might have fought the mold to be "little mothers" to dolls, stuffed animals, or siblings, the drive to become a mother ourselves is often too strong to resist once we grow into adulthood. Moreover, many of us promise ourselves that we are going to avoid the mistakes that our own mothers made with us as children and "get it right" this time around. For many of us, our identity as a mother is tied up inextricably with our identity as a daughter. There is an often-quoted saying that "children learn what they live," and when it comes to mothering, we often have just one model on which to pattern our own identity. Becoming a mother ourselves is a lightning rod for revisiting the primary relationship and its assorted emotional baggage with our own mother figures.

TRYING TO FALL FURTHER FROM THE TREE

Many of the women interviewed recalled affirming as adolescents that when they became mothers, they would never treat their daughters the way they were being treated. The need to revise the role and refashion the identity of *mother* seems to be well ingrained across all demographic sectors. In order to separate from our mothers and individuate as young women, we must turn against our mothers to make ourselves "not like" them. This can be a difficult transition, as noted in our earlier chapter on mothering adolescent daughters. We spend a dozen years being groomed into our roles as females and potential mothers, yet we are then spurred on by hormones and biology to begin the transition from being primarily a daughter to our mothers to being a potential mate for a yet unknown other. Yet this role of mate or partner to another is frequently upstaged when we become mothers ourselves.

ENTERING THE "MOTHERHOOD CONSTELLATION"

Daniel Stern has termed the period in which we shift attention and priorities of cognitive concern as the *motherhood constellation*.[2] He has recognized how a psychic shift occurs for women as they move into the new, all-consuming role of mother. No longer focused on the male/partner-female roles in her life, pregnancy and motherhood bring on a new triadic focus for women made up of three players—her mother, herself, and her baby. Making up the motherhood constellation are four themes that surround this triumvirate: life growth, or the concern for her baby's development; primary relatedness, referring to a mother's connection to her child; supporting matrix, including the support systems necessary for her to successfully raise her child; and identity reorganization, which refers to a mother's ability to shift her focus and priorities and self-image to meet the needs of her motherhood responsibilities.[3] He went on to note that new mothers need a maternal figure, ideally their own mother, to validate their parenting abilities and successes as mothers. Thus, this can underscore how satisfying it can be for mothers to receive positive feedback about their parenting abilities from their own mothers. When asked about the most important periods of transition in their relationships with their mothers, becoming a mother themselves stood out across generations and cultural identities. One woman described the experience of "coming of age" as a mother as having shifted her relationship with her own mother from "mother to best friend." Like many women, joining the ranks of experienced mother brought new credibility to their worth and a new sense of connection to their mothers.

One woman noted that it was when she was pregnant with her second child and very ill that she felt closest to her mother. As she shared:

> I went, with my oldest daughter, to stay with my parents, as I needed care and help. My mother had experienced the same difficulty when she was pregnant with me, so she totally understood what I was going through. That was a time I felt that we really connected, and she took very good care of both my daughter and me.

Becoming a mother, for many women, is the ultimate achievement of their lives—born to propagate the species, desiring to earn the approval of their own mothers, and feeling the need to conform to society's expectations of motherhood, when a woman chooses to give birth and raise a child, she is gratifying the desires of others both known and unknown to her. Optimally, she is also satisfying her own desire to raise a child. However, there are times when the imminent "bundle of joy" creates a bunch of anxiety.

UNPLANNED PREGNANCY AND THE MOTHER-DAUGHTER RELATIONSHIP

Although many women are eager to share with their mothers the results of a positive pregnancy test, there are many young women for whom the news of an impending birth is an unwelcome fact, not a message of joy. For these young women, entering into motherhood is a transition that is out of sync with their expected developmental trajectory. Adding additional fuel to the potential fire is that research has shown that there is a connection between already troubled family relations and the likelihood of an earlier age at menarche and first pregnancy.[4] When asked about the most difficult conversations they had experienced with their mothers as teenagers, unplanned pregnancy definitely was at the top of the list.

A thirty-nine-year-old clearly recalled the difficulty she had breaking the news of her pregnancy to her mother, even though she was twenty-one years old at the time. The daughter's lack of a spouse was the problematic situation. In addition, it can be very hard on the young women's mothers, as well. When this woman recounted the most difficult conversation she has experienced with her own thirteen-year-old daughter, in sad irony, it was when her daughter had recently revealed that she was not only sexually active but pregnant as well.

Although most of us believe that unintended pregnancies only happen to "those families," meaning poorer or less educated, it is certainly sobering to realize that by the age of forty-five, over half of all U.S. women will have experienced an unplanned pregnancy.[5] In addition, research does confirm that the likelihood increases for poor, low income, cohabiting, and minority women.[6] We gathered the stories of a diverse group of adult women and heard an overabundance of stories of ill-timed pregnancies. Because this issue is a public health issue and affects every one of us, we want to share a few of these individual's recollections of their difficulties related to this issue.

Challenging Consequences

When a "baby has a baby," it can affect everyone in the family. While some "grandmothers-to-be" may swoop in to provide emotional support—and material support—to their daughters, others may be less willing to do so. In a recent research study,[7] the presence of a pregnant adolescent daughter predicted that there would be less affection overall between mothers and all of their children than in homes where teen daughters were not facing pregnancy. Not only that, but the mothers of these pregnant girls were more likely to put aside any dreams for their pregnant daughters in that the mothers' hopes for a brighter future were wholly transferred to the nonpregnant girls in the family as well as treating the "good girls" in the family more favorably.

Some of the women we interviewed shared sobering and heartbreaking stories of their experiences of revealing their pregnancy to their mothers. A forty-five-year-old woman clearly remembers the most difficult conversation she had with her mother on a day twenty-five years in the past in which she had to admit to her mother that she was expecting a child:

> [The most difficult time in my relationship was] when I got pregnant with my oldest and was not married. I was twenty. My stepfather is a preacher. Oh, the name-calling he did and threats he made to my boyfriend, now husband! [My mother] left town the night we were coming home and left me to face him. I never heard her say he was wrong. She takes "stand by your man" to another level.

This woman learned about more than one type of relationship loyalty that evening. Not surprisingly, the "absent mother" had given birth to her daughter when she was only sixteen years old. Unready and unable to care for her daughter, she had allowed her parents to shoulder the responsibility of raising her child. When further questioned about the state of their mother-daughter relationship today, she reiterated, "My feelings were distanced more after I had my son at twenty and left my parents' home to live with my aunt . . . [today], we talk once a week on the phone. We are not close, but respectful." In many cases, that is as best as it might be hoped.

When another adolescent, then sixteen, now fifty-one, had to break the news of her pregnancy to her mother, she recalled that "it was very difficult, and she did not want to deal with it." A nineteen-year-old interviewee remembers very well the most painful moment in her relationship with her mother, as it had happened only a year or so ago, "when I had to tell my mother that I was pregnant." This young woman's story does not end with mother and daughter reconciling as they begin joyous preparations for a new addition to the family. Here is the story she shared that can provide insight into the layers of complexity that teenagers must sort through as they are asked to make critical life decisions:

> My senior year, I slipped and had sex with a guy who I had been talking to for five years. At the time, it felt like the right thing to do. He always talked about it and told me that he would always be there. I thought that he loved and cared about me. I was head over hills for him, and I was so "for sure" that he and I were going to get married and live happily ever after.
>
> It was time for my period, but it didn't start. It hadn't crossed my mind that I could be pregnant, but I was. My mother and I had a long talk about what was the next move, should I keep the baby or not . . . we came to an agreement. I had an abortion. When I walked from the back of the center, my mother sat there waiting for me. When we got back in the car I cried and apologized and thanked my mother, because although she could have made me have the baby, she gave me a second chance to make better decisions and I promised myself that I would never put myself through anything like that again. I think this was the moment me and my mother's relationship reached its peak, and she was my backbone.

Down the Road—The Voice of an Adult Daughter of a Young, Unwed Mother

Generations of young women are growing up being nurtured by single mothers who are making it on their own, as best they can. Oftentimes, it is indeed the love of grandmothers and extended families or fictive kin (which refers to teachers, coaches, and other adults that play significant roles in the lives of youth) that allows these young girls to feel nurtured, loved, and cared for. We provide a broader look at what mothers teach their daughters about social support in a later chapter, but it is clear that the availability of a blood or fictive kin network enhances our well-being, especially in stressful families-of-origin.[8]

Being born into a stress-filled family can bring about significant, lifelong negative repercussions as noted earlier in this chapter, including the occurrence of the first pregnancy. The stress between mother and grandmother that accompanied one twenty-eight-year-old's conception is a part of her story that shaped her identity today: "My mother and her mother had a difficult relationship. She became pregnant with me in college, and her mother wanted her to have an abortion. She told my mother that she wasn't taking care of that damn chap." The antagonism between the original mother-daughter pair was replicated in the next generation, although this young woman has been able to build a relationship with her grandmother: "I was taught how to love by my grandmother and aunt. My mother taught me how *not* to treat a child. [The relationship with my mother is] better because I have truly forgiven her. I can pick up the phone and call her—even if she denies the call. I try to reach out and invite her to spend time with her grandchildren. She often refuses. I hope she changes one day." Although this woman has not been able to fully soften her mother's heart, she has become more able to let go of some of the animosity she, herself, had carried so long toward her mother that had weighted her down.

Acceptance in Place of Rejection

Not every mother-daughter relationship is sorely tested by an untimely, too early pregnancy. For many mothers, their love for their daughter and the joy a baby can bring will overshadow any disappointment or sense of unfulfilled dreams. As a twenty-four-year-old mother of a five-year-old recalled, "When I told my mother that I was pregnant, she told me that it was okay. People make mistakes, but we have to learn from them and keep living." She went on to share that giving birth to her daughter caused the greatest shift in her relationship with her mother, and in a good way. Asked about the state of their relationship, she replied that it was "stronger than ever!" Accepting our daughters, faults and all, can be difficult, but it can pay off in terms of long-term benefits— through our roles as mothers and, potentially, grandmothers.

THE TIMING IS RIGHT: A WELCOME ADDITION

We would like to revisit the concepts of the "motherhood constellation" and a woman's need for validation of her ability to mother another.[9] The intensity of this need and the satisfaction felt when met can provide a uniquely tender mother-daughter connection. Regardless of maternal age and marital status, the impending arrival of a member of the next generation offers the opportunity for a mother to validate her pregnant daughter's worth. As one woman recalled:

> When I found out that I was pregnant with my first child, I was scared and kind of unsure how my mother would react due to the fact that I was not married. After I told my mother, she reassured me that there

was nothing so bad that I could do that would change the unconditional love she had for me. That is always how my mother has made me feel. She always lets me know when I am wrong, but at the same time, she still lets me know that she loves me no matter what.

Being able to provide unconditional love is what good mothering is all about, and being able to validate a daughter's adequacy as a mother matters greatly to her success in this role. This woman's appreciation of her mother goes deep as she reflects on her relationship with her own daughters: "Like my mother, I make my daughters feel that they are able to discuss anything with me. I like that about my relationship with my mom and like that I have the same kind of relationship with my daughters." Giving birth to her first child, even though it was not on the preferred timeline, was an integral, strengthening moment in their relationship.

CHANGING NEEDS WITHIN THE RELATIONSHIP

When a woman discovers she is pregnant, she is likely to feel a growing preoccupation with her own mother and their relationship, even if her mother is no longer alive.[10] The longing for approval, as noted earlier, can create anxiety and helplessness as mothers worry about their babies' health and their maternal skills. Researchers have noted that new mothers who are far from their own mothers may even look to health professionals or "surrogate mothers," such as nannies, for approval of their mothering behaviors. For women who have easy access to their mothers, sharing news and updates throughout pregnancy is a prevalent activity. As doctor visits grow more frequent, so does contact between daughters and their mothers. Childbearing is the most significant and archetypally feminine activity that women can exhibit, and the shared power between mother and daughter creates a deeply intense connection.

Although women are not consciously aware of the depth of their need to relate to their mothers, their actions illustrate the heightened desire to strengthen their bond. As a twenty-four-year-old brand-new mother shared:

> I recently was diagnosed with IUGR [intrauterine growth restriction] in my pregnancy, my mom was the first person I called after my husband, and I left the doctor's office. They told us that we would have to go to the checkups twice a week, and they may take our child at any moment because he has a better chance outside the womb.
>
> After that phone call with mom, I felt at peace. . . . She gave me just the scripture I needed from the Bible and such encouragement.
>
> She called me every day and came to see me every week until our son was born. She is my rock and is always there when I need her.

When a mother is able to provide her daughter with emotional support at such a critical moment in her development, it can fill a mother with a corresponding amount of satisfaction and joy. Born to bring to adulthood the next generation safely, being present to ease a daughter's transition into the maternal role can be especially gratifying for a mother.

We asked a very pregnant twenty-five-year-old about a time in which her relationship with her mother had shifted through the years. She quickly responded, "I am currently pregnant with my first child (was due yesterday!). This has altered my already-strong relationship with my mom as we have bonded over my pregnancy and the impending birth of her first grandson." Invited to share a story that might illustrate the best aspects of their relationship, she shared, "We are super close and always have been. We've always been open with each other, but now that I'm pregnant, any modesty is out the window—she knows every detail of my cervix right now! But we are open and honest with each other, and I've been able to be that way with her because she never judges me." Many interviewees echoed this all-embracing love that is shared by this pair.

Another woman recounted the large role her mother played in terms of instrumental support at the actual arrival of her first born. She shared, "When I delivered my first child at twenty-seven, my mother was right there. She saw my son's head first; she cut the cord; she gave him his first bath; and she taught me how to breastfeed. She has been there every step of the way." Providing support and helping her daughter gain competence in maternal responsibilities is perhaps one of the greatest gifts a mother can give her daughter. In a case in which a new mother was gravely ill, this gift could be even more welcome, as this mother recalled: "When I had my first child, my mother moved in with me because I was really sick. She got up with the baby at night until I was able to do so. She taught me how to take care of my baby, how to sooth her when she was cranky, and how to show love as she has always shown me." Even for mothers and daughters who have poor relationships, a new life on its way can be a pathway to healing.

A BABY'S CRY CAN BRIDGE THE GAP

As we have mentioned in prior chapters, many women have a very difficult time sharing the difficult and painful stories of their relationships with their mothers. This hesitance speaks to the huge emotional investment we have in our mother-daughter connections—and when they are damaged, it can take significant transformations to heal wounds. However, for some women, the arrival of a child can turn around a relationship rapidly. When asked about a special moment in her relationship with her mother, a twenty-four-year-old recalled, "I am not sure if I have any stories because our relationship was so strained for many years. If I had to think of one story, it would be when we went shopping together while I was pregnant. This was the first time where I could see that we had anything in common as we agreed upon clothing and shoes. It was a nice bonding experience, especially since I was expecting a baby, myself."

Another young mother had also experienced a surprisingly pleasant moment with her mother from whom she had been virtually estranged since infancy. Grateful that her mother had given up custody to her father, she related that the one positive story she could share about her relationship occurred in relation to her own transition to motherhood: "I remember at the birth of my first child, she brought a big thirty-gallon bag of goodies and Tylenol for me, just in case." Clearly, the transition from "maiden to mother" changes not only a daughter's perspective on her connection to her mother but also her mother's connection to her daughter.

For some families, it can seem as if young motherhood is written into the DNA as successive generations begin earlier than expected. One woman recalled how difficult her teenage years were as she rebelled so hard against her parents' rules. Eager to be independent and viewed as an adult, she took action that many similar young women do—they marry and start a family of their own:

> I married young at eighteen and had my first child four months before I turned twenty. I lived far away from my family; they were seven hundred miles away. Somehow, motherhood was instinctual to me. I took my responsibility of being a mother seriously; it forced me to grow up overnight but I was okay with that. It wasn't long, though, before I was a single mother trying to fend for my small child and myself. My mom stepped in to help when needed but stayed back far enough to let me maintain my independence. She now respected me as an adult, albeit, young.
>
> As my daughter grew, I, too, encountered speed bumps with her. She has certainly given us a run for our money. When my daughter was seventeen, she became pregnant. I remember dreading calling my family members to let them know what was going on with our family. I particularly dreaded calling my mom. I thought about the disappointment she would feel in my daughter and myself. I thought I would get a barrage of questions and "I told you" and "I can't believe it!" There were questions but there was also a lot of compassion and empathy that was unexpected. Over the following months, my mom was a source of comfort and support. Although I came to terms with the fact that my child was having a child, I still had many dark moments. Looking back, I don't know how I would have got through that without my mom. She was always there, trying to comfort me; trying to assure me that everything would be okay.

Her relationship with her mother was able to grow stronger as each of them stepped up to a new level—from mother to grandmother and grandmother to great grandmother.

"GRANDMOTHER = EXPERT" ON CARING FOR NEWBORNS

A brand new grandmother, "Mimi" to her grandbaby, recently shared her joy at being called upon as the "expert" in infant care. In the hospital room just a few hours after the birth of a granddaughter, Mimi had given newborn Kyleigh a bottle and passed her back to the new mother, suggesting that she change the baby's diaper. Never having done anything beyond "diaper practice" in the childbirth class, the new mother peppered the "expert grandma" with "more questions about diapers, wipes, and babies' bottoms than I'd ever imagined anyone could ask!" She went on to share that she was pleased to "have all the answers," since it had been a long time since any of her children had felt that way about her. Mimi also shared that just looking at baby Kyleigh brought ineffable joy to her heart and that she could not stop smiling since the new life appeared in her family. Asked to share more about the joy she felt, Mimi just shook her head and said that she did not know how to describe it, but that it just filled her heart completely and spilled over onto the whole family.

Another woman, Pam, who is in her late forties, shared a story about her daughter's entry into mothering a daughter of her own. She shared that her most cherished moment in her relationship with her daughter actually was found during these first few days of her granddaughter's life. Her daughter was frequently calling her to ask how to do this or do that for the baby. Trying to build her confidence, the grandmother complimented her daughter on her ability to mother the little baby, and her daughter responded, "Mom, it is only because you have been able to teach me so well! You are an amazing mom!" For all three generations in this family, the mother-daughter relationship is clearly going to be a positive aspect of their lives for a long, long time.

READY TO BE A GRANDMOTHER?

While many mothers of daughters firmly in their peak "reproductive years" may long to hear news of a new pregnancy, some are not nearly as eager. Research suggests that the psychological transition to grandparenthood occurs in "expectant grandmothers" rather than after the arrival of the first grandchild.[11] For many women today, this transition does not represent taking on just a new special social status worthy of reverence but rather crossing into the state of "being old," so to speak.[12] Being able to move into that role, however, can pay off big dividends for all three generations. When a grandmother is able to spend quality time with her grandkids, not only do the kids win out but also her own mental well-being is enhanced, even when we take into consideration the costs of time and energy invested in the effort to get together.[13] Research also has shown that for children of divorced parents, the active presence of maternal grandmothers in the children's life positively influences their psychological adjustment.[14]

However, some women worry that their mothers may be embracing the grandmother role a little too enthusiastically. While many women are grateful at how much support their mothers offer them, the sense of "ownership" of the new grandchild that some women display can potentially signal problems for the growing family.

WHOSE BABY IS IT?

For some new mothers, caring for a baby can seem like tackling a new job for which they are untrained and unprepared. Women frequently call on their own mothers for instrumental support as they get up to speed on the care and feeding of the new arrival, which often is perceived as a great compliment to a grandmother. However, some women may feel as if their new babies are being "taken over" by their mothers. As a thirty-seven-year-old related,

> When my daughter was born, my mother was so overprotective of her. She was scared when other people would hold her. She didn't even trust my husband to hold his own daughter in fear that he would be too rough with her.

Trying to learn the role of mother while being a go-between for two very important support people is undoubtedly stressful: "She also felt that my husband was not letting her have enough time with my daughter since she was just visiting us. I was put in the middle of them, which was very frustrating." However, three months after the birth of her first child, she has a little more perspective as she describes the overall relationship with her mother: "We have a great relationship. We argue, we forgive, and then we are fine again. My relationship with her is more of a friend-ship. I don't know what I would do without her. She drives me crazy sometimes, but I love her." Although they have been through significantly challenging times in their earlier years, including dealing with mental illness and abuse, she feels that they are on track with their relationship in a way that was not conceivable years ago.

Another new mother shared that it was bearing her mother's grandchild that has bridged a gap between the women. She explained that their mother-daughter relationship is "at it's best when we share moments with my son. He has become the connection between us that we have when there seems to be no other connection." Babies have a way of bringing together the most disconnected mothers and daughters.

CONCLUSION

There are four sacred moments, according to Navajo tradition, during which a spirit enters a baby's human form. These are conception, when an expectant mother first feels the baby move, when the baby takes her first breath after delivery, and when a baby first laughs. When we asked women what events in life significantly shifted their relationships with their mothers, three events stood out—finding a life partner/getting married, having a child, and witnessing the health of a mother fail. Of these three, stepping into the role of mother herself resonated most powerfully for our interviewees. And each of the moments at which "spirit" enters an infant's physical body can propel a new mother ever closer to her own mother or a "stand-in" mother, if need be. As women, we are aware of the significant power we hold to bring life and form to our generation's hope for the future, and this recognition—at a level deeper than simple cognitive awareness—heightens the desire we feel to connect with the generations before us.

NOTES

1. V. Jadva, M. Hines, and S. Golombok, "Infants' Preferences for Toys, Colors, and Shapes: Sex Differences and Similarities," *Archives of Sexual Behavior, 39*, no. 6 (2010): 1261–73.

2. D. N. Stern, *The Motherhood Constellation: A Unified View of Parent-Infant Psychotherapy* (New York: Basic Books, 1995).

3. Ibid., 173.

4. J. S. Chisholm, J. A. Quinlivan, R. W. Petersen, and D. A. Coall, "Early Stress Predicts Age at Menarche and First Birth, Adult Attachment, and Expected Lifespan," *Human Nature, 16*, no. 3 (2005): 233–65.

5. L. B. Finer and M. R. Zolna, "Unintended Pregnancy in the United States: Incidence and Disparities," *Contraception, 84*, no. 5 (2011): 478–85.

6. Ibid.

7. P. L. East and L. J. Jacobson, "Mothers' Differential Treatment of Their Adolescent Childbearing and Nonchildbearing Children: Contrasts between and within Families," *Journal of Family Psychology, 17*, no. 3 (2003): 384–96.

8. J. C. Hall, "The Impact of Kin and Fictive Kin Relationships on the Mental Health of Black Adult Children of Alcoholics," *Health & Social Work, 33*, no. 4 (2008): 259–66.

9. D. N. Stern, *The Motherhood Constellation: A Unified View of Parent-Infant Psychotherapy* (New York: Basic Books, 1995).

10. L. Hoffman, "When Daughter becomes Mother: Inferences from Multiple Dyadic Parent-Child Groups," *Psychoanalytic Inquiry, 24*, no. 5 (2004): 629–56.

11. S. B. Shlomo, O. Taubman-Ben-Ari, L. Findler, E. Sivan, and M. Dolizki, "Becoming a Grandmother: Maternal Grandmothers' Mental Health, Perceived Costs, and Personal Growth," *Social Work Research, 34* (2010): 45–57.

12. M. J. Armstrong, "Is Being a Grandmother Being Old? Cross-Ethnic Perspectives from New Zealand," *Journal of Cross-Cultural Gerontology, 18,* no. 3 (2003): 185–202.

13. Ibid.

14. C. E. Henderson, B. Hayslip, L. M. Sanders, and L. Louden, "Grandmother-Grandchild Relationship Quality Predicts Psychological Adjustment among Youth from Divorced Families," *Journal of Family Issues, 30,* no. 9 (2009): 1254–64.

NINE

And the Cycle Recycles

Daughters Becoming Caregivers

Although we tend to think of growing older as a personal assault to our ego or our pride, it is the much better choice than the alternative, as my own mother used to remind me. Moreover, according to the statistics, close to 20 percent of our citizens will be over age sixty-five by 2030.[1] This is a sizable number, and whether it is through healthy living or medical miracles, the size of the older adult population is definitely growing ahead of other age groups. This suggests that an increasing number of adult and mid-adult daughters will be transitioning into care-giving roles for the preceding generation, even though they may still be caring for their own children. In addition, this role of looking after the women who first looked after us can bring out a wide variety of personal responses to the situation, just as the eventual loss of one's mother can produce. There is an old saying that "motherless children see hard times," and this is painfully clear for women at many steps in life's journey. Losing a mother at any age can be an inestimable loss, as some of the stories in this chapter will address.

REALIZING THAT MOTHERS ARE MORTAL

What does that moment feel like when you first realize that your mother is not going to be in your life forever? For many women, it happens in a painful instant, even if you have seen your mother's health decline and her physical being become more fragile. In fact, author Catherine Racine has described the experience as the "zenith" of the relationship.[2] In exploring the transition of her mother's health into critical and final illness, she described the ways in which her love for her mother blossoms through the intimacy of caring for her in this final opportunity of bonding. Racine also recounts one of her final conversations with her mother,[3] in which the two openly acknowledge and reflect on the transformation of the "mother cares for daughter" relationship into "daughter cares for mother," as she recounted that her mother poignantly queried Racine about the point at which their roles had shifted.

The roles do shift for many of us, although not all of us are as cognizant of the transition as some may be. We may also attempt to stem the tide of aging—at least for a moment—to allow our relationship with our mother to fit into the frame that it once did. As Lynn, a woman of *a certain age* that was invited to recount a memory of "daughtering her mother," recounted: "Even when my mom was in her eighties and I was in my fifties, I would occasionally sit on her lap (gently) to remind us who we were and what we meant to each other." As we move further into adulthood, if we happen to hear Elton John crooning to our children and grandchildren about "the circle of life," the words may resonate with us in a far more personal and poignant manner than they once did. The circle of life moves each new generation into the roles once held by their elders, and as we age, the wheel of time moves at what seems to be an increasingly rapid pace. Taking the time to pause and take stock of where you are in the eternal circle may provide you with an opportunity to share a moment of tenderness and reminiscence for an earlier stop in time, as it did for this daughter, Beth, and her mother:

> When I was little and then, later, when my children were little, my mother would take us to the downtown Chicago Marshall Fields store to look at the windows, see Santa, purchase ornaments, and to eat under the big Christmas tree. Now it is Macy's. The line is no longer one, but three. I invited my mom to come with me this year and gave up trying to get my daughter and grandkids to come with me. Although I love my daughter and grandchildren wholeheartedly, I am so fortunate, honored, and glad to have been able to share the train ride to Chicago and back in the sole company of my mother. She is a wonderful woman who has supported me throughout all of my challenges and triumphs and the wonderful woman who has become one of my dearest and most loyal friends.
>
> This year, unfortunately, my mom had such difficulty moving around after the overdoing of the Christmas Eve festivities she had planned for all of her family, but she was such a trooper! Nothing was going to keep her from allowing us the chance to experience this tradition together this year. Although we did not get to eat under the tree this year, we ate next to a window, and together we "made the magic," as we always seem to do together. My mother always says that she wants to give her children and her grandchildren "good memories." This trip to the city is a new one now in my heart. On the way home on the train, my mother told me that she thinks this will be her final time going to

"eat under the Christmas tree," and, be this the case, I am so blessed that this last time was with me.

Although Beth has recently celebrated her fifty-second birthday and has grandchildren of her own, she still needs to experience herself as the child and her mother as the "maker of magic" from time to time. Returning to that place in which we can be perceived as still young and full of possibility—even as we have taken on the grandmother role ourselves—gives us a place where we know who we are. As many aging women lament, there comes a time when no one in our lives remembers who we were as a child. By continuing to enjoy that special connection with one's mother for as long as possible, women are able to maintain that initial identity as part of their mothers. All too soon, many daughters must step out of the role of the *cared for* and become the caregiver.

THE PASSING OF THE REINS FROM ONE GENERATION TO THE NEXT

Most women are conscious of the "pecking order" in family systems. A matriarch frequently reigns supreme over family events throughout the year. Whether it is the home at which the traditional holiday dinner is served or the woman whose recipe is always followed for family birthday cakes, the younger generation honors her wishes. The matriarch of the family is revered and, often, feared by those who are following in her footsteps. Passing the carving knife from father to son is often perceived as a badge of honor and a mark of manhood for the son; for women, passing the treasured recipes from mother to daughter may speak more about the diminishment of the mother's role than her daughter's growing competence.

The passing of the role and the reins a mother holds can be a significant event, but is not typically perceived as a celebrated "coming-of-age" for a daughter. Whereas males are brought up in a world in which they frequently rely on others to see that their needs are met—from an infant being held and fed in his mother's arms to a husband sitting down to a meal prepared by a partner, women are raised to see to the needs of others. One forty-three-year-old noted that the most difficult conversations she has had with her own mother have been, "Conversations about death and the thought that she would no longer be here with me are tough as an adult." As a matriarch steps down, it can bring a pang to the hearts of those who have followed her lead all those years. When she is stepping down due to frailty or illness, it can be especially difficult when the next "big event" rolls round and she is no longer presiding over the family. Women are raised to nurture, tend, and see to the needs of others, but when a woman is no longer able to fill this role, her sense of identity may shift inalterably. Yet for many women, the opportunity to provide

care and tending to their mothers is seen as an honor, not just an obligation.

RETURNING THE FAVOR OF TAKING CARE

When a daughter becomes the caregiver who opens her home to her ill or
aging mother, she may do so for a variety of different reasons. Some
women may do so out of guilt and a need to atone for past wrongdoings
against their mothers. Sometimes, it is the most financially sound choice
for the family for the moment. Ideally, it is done so out of love and honor
for the mother who raised her. Lisa, fifty-one, and the mother of a young
adult daughter, shared the story of her mother's battle with illness:

> My mom was absolutely my best friend. She was always there with
> honesty and encouraging words. I am thankful that as a child, teenag-
> er, and young adult, I took the time to make my mom a big part of my
> life. We went to concerts, shopped, and laughed (a lot)! When she was
> sick, I made every effort to be there for her. While doing chemo, I
> would sit with her and we would talk for hours. She always apologized
> because that wasn't what she wanted. She felt it was a burden. Howev-
> er, I assured her it was okay because no matter what we were doing,
> we were together! That's all we needed! I am lucky enough to have a
> girl of my own who has the heart and spirit of my mom. Life just works
> out that way! How blessed am I?

Another woman shared a similar story about using the hours spent
caregiving as a place to reconnect and just enjoy one another's company,
"My relationship shifted with my mother during a period recently when
she was sick for a period of months and was dependent upon me for care.
Our relationship grew stronger because we had time to talk about things,
just things—nothing important." Being able to provide needed instrumental and emotional support to her mother brought her a sense of deep
satisfaction, not a sense of sacrifice. Having the time to connect over the
everyday things is a gift; some women, however, lose their mothers before they are even women themselves.

CARING FOR AND LOSING A MOTHER IN ADOLESCENCE

When we invited women to speak about experiences in which they and
their mothers' relationships were at their best, most stories addressed the
love and tenderness that a mother had shown a daughter. However, one
woman shared a story quite different than most as she described a time
when she was able to focus on caring for her mother:

When I went off to college, my mother became very ill and was unable to care for herself. I moved back home from college to care for my mother. We became very close. I had to cook, clean, and care for the house. I helped my mother got back on her feet by caring for her health and making sure she recovered with her strength to the fullest before returning to work. She was surprised I moved back home because I was so ready to go to college.

Her love and devotion to her mother are clear, and her deep bond suggests that her mother knew well how to raise a loving daughter.

Several of the women we interviewed shared stories of having lost their mothers in adolescence well before they reached their twentieth birthday. This period of development provides the backdrop for a young woman's first efforts at individuation as a woman, and rebelliousness against mothers is a common theme. Losing a mother during this time can present young women with even more complicated and confusing feelings as their point of gender reference, the nurturer of their development, is taken from their lives, and identity development can be significantly affected by this loss.[4] This can create difficulties in the many realms in which a young woman functions—academically, socially, emotionally, and behaviorally.[5] Faced with such a critical situation at a young age, daughters may not fully understand or feel adequate to cope with their mother's illness. As a thirty-six-year-old woman recalled:

I felt my relationship shift with my mom when I found out she was diagnosed with lung cancer. I was only fourteen, and I became her caretaker. All I wanted was for her to get better! It was hard seeing my mom in so much constant pain. But even when my mother was sick with cancer, she was determined to make sure my youngest sister had a Christmas. She could not drive, so we walked in the cold to Wal-Mart to make sure this happened that year. Throughout everything, my mother persevered. She was a hard worker, and she often went without to make sure her three daughters had.

Things were so hard when my mother became sick, and I really did not know how to help her. I'm embarrassed to share that I mistook her for acting stubborn when it was really her being sick. Sometimes when she would not eat, I would think she was being stubborn, when actually she was sick. I would get so upset because I wanted her to eat, get her strength, and move us back home out of my aunt's home. I was blessed fourteen years to have my mother, and before she passed, I would say I had a good relationship with my mom. We had a strong relationship. I believed she saw me as her "strong" daughter. My oldest sister could not stand to see my mom ill and she really didn't know how to adjust, and my youngest sister was only nine, so I'm not sure if she really knew much. During that time, I would go to school, go to the hospital, go to school, and go to the hospital . . . that was my cycle. Toward the end, I just wanted to be there, in her presence, and let her know she was not alone. And I was there, at the hospital, holding her hand when God called her home.

Spiritual faith can provide much needed comfort for many women when they lose their mothers. Trying to make sense of how short a time a mother was present in a daughter's life can be challenging, especially when a daughter loses her mother so young. Some young women are able consciously to find a positive outcome of some sort when they lose their mothers so early. A thirty-year-old recalls the loss of her mother fourteen years ago:

> My mom died from breast cancer when I was sixteen, but before leaving this earth, she taught me that there were great gifts on the inside of me and that my future was unlimited. She really believed that I could be anything. That gave me confidence to excel academically, socially, and even athletically. More importantly, she taught me about Christ. I know that He is my Lord and Savior. I knew how to pray, which is what got me through her dying when I was at the stage of transition in my life. Prayer truly saved me, and so did singing. If she had never exposed me to Christianity, who knows where I would be right now? Last but not least, my mother taught me that I can handle anything. To watch her, at the age of thirty-two, battle cancer . . . losing her hair, being constantly sick, being put on oxygen at age thirty-four, and being fed with a tube feeder are just a few things I watched her endure. She had always had a problem with fear, but when this diagnosis came, she overcame her fears. She fought hard! That is why when I am faced with things that make me want to "throw in the towel," God used her to pass on to me long suffering and courage; I would not trade it for the world.

She summed up the sense of security and permanence that a mother-daughter relationship can provide:

> All in all, even though I only had her in my world for sixteen years, our relationship was irreplaceable and deep. Most people live their whole lives not being sure if this person or that person loves them, but I am confident that, although God loves me best, my mother's love for me was pure, and I know she gave me her best. So our relationship was really all that a daughter could ask for.

Having time to say good-bye might take place in the hospital or in the home of a mother or her daughter. Regardless of where it occurs, this opportunity can provide the surviving daughter with a settled heart and a deep sense of emotional closure that can carry her throughout the remaining days of her own life.

TENDING THE LIFE THAT GAVE YOU YOURS

The love a mother feels for a daughter can be so strong that she would be willing to put her daughter's well-being easily above her own. One daughter realized just how deep her own mother's love ran a few months after she had been critically ill. As this daughter recalled,

> When my mom was diagnosed with cancer, I was crushed. Naturally, I was in tears as she told me the news. But my mom told me not to be sad, because she had prayed for this to happen. I didn't understand what she meant! She then told me that when I had been diagnosed with cancer months earlier, that she prayed daily for God to take it from me and give it to her. She told me that she had lived her life and that it was now my time to live.

When our mothers' health begins to critically fail, many of us may need to do more than become overseers of medical appointments and medication management; we may move back in with our mothers or invite our mothers to move in with us. This decision can be a difficult juncture in a daughter's life, as this is the point at which she may never again truly see herself as "her mother's child." To lose your parents, no matter what your age, is to become an orphan, and the resulting grief is not necessarily mediated by chronological age. Losing your mother can be particularly painful as the bond involves a sense of deep identification that is shared only between mothers and daughters. If you are able to share your mother's final days living under the same roof, however, this may actually offer some protection from the intensity of grief that women experience at the loss of our mothers.[6] Unfortunately, researchers found that this same situation might result in even greater despair for a daughter than if her mother died in a hospital. Perhaps this is due to the sense of guilt we may carry with us about not being able to prolong our mother's life or allay her suffering at the end. The need to care for the one who cared most for us throughout our lives can be strong.

In a prior chapter, we mentioned the story of the woman who had left her home to go to New York City with her boyfriend right out of college. Promised that she would never have her mother's blessings, this young woman actually atoned for that wrong she had done her mother in a heartrending manner. Her mother became ill with cancer—after the New York flame had burned out and she had returned home—and she took on the role of caregiver for her mother. Allowing the past to remain in the past, she and her mother developed a united front as they fought against the disease's inevitable toll:

> My mother and I oftentimes used humor to take the sting out of things that had the capacity to be very upsetting. My mother never went to the beauty shop and came home happy, so when she was diagnosed with cancer, I made the comment that she could no longer "bitch"

about her bad haircuts. She thought that was hilarious. She also had to remind me often that lots of people didn't share the same kind of twisted humor that we did and to be careful of whom I joked around. People were too serious, she said.

We had a good relationship; however, there were times that it was difficult. We were very close, and she taught me a lot of things. Through taking care of her, I have learned a lot about myself, and I am thankful for that. She was my best friend, and I miss her every day.

For Sharon, a woman in her mid-forties, the loss of her own mother occurred in two stages; the first was the onset of bipolar disorder, a disease that irrevocably took away much of her mother from her before she lost her mother to cancer. She has grieved twice now for the relationship that so many of us may take for granted—and one that may never have developed due to the factors beyond one's own or one's mother's control:

> I was thirty when my mom died. She had cancer, and I took care of her through it all. She also struggled with bipolar disorder, so in some ways, I felt like parts of me lost her even before her death. After she died, while I felt a bit of a sense of relief, I was definitely pretty sad. And I am not so sure I was sad for myself, as I was for her . . . or actually, what she had to endure. I would think, "What a shame she won't be able to spend time with her grandchild" (at the time, there was just one). Or I would think back and wonder why she had to have such a hard life . . . I felt bad that things could not have been more "normal" for her.
>
> I think I miss her most when I hear others talking about their own moms . . . knowing they can pick up the phone or drop by for a visit. Even when they complain about them, I still think, "I don't have that." I may be stereotyping a bit, but my siblings are all brothers, and they are not the best communicators. While there are friends to talk with, no one knows you like your mom . . . sometimes I think, "I won't share this with my friend because they've got stuff of their own" . . . but your mom loves you unconditionally and would listen, console, etc., without hesitation.

She feels fortunate that she was able to be present with her mother at the final moment of her life, and this comforts Sharon, knowing that she gave back to her mother all that she could possibly could:

> As hard as it was to see her take her last breath, it was also the best thing, and I am so glad I was there. Not everyone has that privilege. It was very hard to lose my mom, but I can lay my head down every night and know I did my very best to have helped her and been by her side.

Another woman, Stephanie, had to watch her mother, just forty years old, suffer from the disease and treatment of cancer when she, herself, was a daughter of twenty. As she described it:

She fought it with all she had. I basically cared for her during the year she took treatments. This gave us a lot of quiet quality time driving to and from the treatment center and also all day during treatments. She always apologized; but for me, I was glad to be able to care for her. Although it was tough seeing her so sick, she fought valiantly and won her battle with cancer. What a relief because I still needed her so much in my life.

Unfortunately, several years later, her mother was again diagnosed with cancer that resulted in Stephanie losing her mother when she was just thirty:

When I was around twenty-eight, my mom was again diagnosed with cancer. This time, it was really bad. She had metastatic, stage IV lung cancer, a death sentence in our eyes. We had very little hope of her surviving more than a month. While we were planning her funeral (in our minds), she was pleading with the Lord to give her the strength she needed to fight this cancer. While the treatments were almost intolerable, she managed to live her life to the fullest and never, ever give up. She lived nearly two years after being diagnosed. During this time she got to spend time with my daughter, Lauren, and help me through the difficult pregnancy, birth, and hospitalization of my son, Brayden, who was born ten weeks premature. She died almost three months after he was born and two weeks after his actual due date. I believe she held on just to see me through that. That was the kind of mother/woman she was.

When another woman, thirty-nine years old, realized one day that she and her mother were often staying up into the wee hours of the morning just "talking and sharing," she realized that their relationship had grown to include deep friendship in the bond. This newly evolved friendship was not as long-lived as either woman would have wanted it to be, as the daughter recounted:

Momma later came to my home to live and die in my care. I took care of her for thirty days and was beside her when she died. We became extremely close. And she left it to me to make the decision not to have any more chemotherapy. Our relationship was amazing. Momma was my best friend. I became her caretaker. I loved every minute of it. I felt blessed that she would allow me to be the one to see her through her last days on Earth. I miss our closeness and daily conversations.

Not every mother and daughter's relationship is as harmonious throughout life as others might be. While there are predictably difficult periods in this relationship, sometimes the hurt caused during earlier days can linger throughout a woman's lifetime.

THE (SOMETIMES) BITTER END

The teenaged years can be especially stressful for mothers and daughters, as described at length in an earlier chapter. Daughters may be motivated to say hurtful things to their mothers at that period in time that they would never say at any other point. One woman, now fifty-seven, shared how the memory of those trauma-filled years were still so fresh in her own mind as her mother reached the latter stages of her life when she felt they should still have so many years left together:

> I fulfilled a caregiver role and was with her throughout her illness to the end of her life. I loved her, but I also was angry and sad that she died when I felt I was so young at the time—early adulthood. Telling her how sorry I was when she was very sick and dying. It was emotionally painful for me at a profound level because I had so much regret about having been critical and angry toward her during my adolescence. I am glad I had the opportunity to tell her, but it was difficult.

Another woman, thirty-nine years old, had worked hard to let go of expectations about her mother, a woman who had abused her physically and emotionally throughout her childhood. As her mother's illness reached a crisis point, she was foisted into the caregiving role, which was not a role she wanted to assume. However, she shared that "in the caretaker role, I felt morally obligated to take care of my mother although I have two older sisters," and a very surprising—and perhaps gratifying—event happened shortly before her mother's last moments: "Before she passed she wrote on a piece of paper 'my protector' and pointed to me." Sometimes it can be too late to right the wrongs that have been done over the course of a lifetime, but a mother's acknowledgement such as this one can go a long way in challenging, not repairing, our past mistakes.

DISTANCE MAKES IT THAT MUCH HARDER—IN BOTH COGNITIVE AND GEOGRAPHICAL FORMS

When we were addressing the ways in which the mother-daughter relationship can improve over time, we frequently heard that "distance makes it better." This can be true in terms of the daily, ongoing friction that might crop up if an overabundance of face-to-face time was spent together. As mothers slip into dementia, a loss affects daughters at a heart-wrenchingly deep, gut level. Although there is not definitive data on whether women or men are more likely to suffer from Alzheimer's disease or other forms of dementia, women definitely outlive men and will therefore be more likely to suffer the loss of their cognitive faculties and need care. It has been noted that women use stories to create their identities within families,[7, 8] and when the story includes dementia, it can shape our own view of our personal future. Women are the traditional caregivers of the elderly around the globe,[9] and as they see their mothers slip into cognitive decline, it can raise fear for their own older adulthood years.

One woman, in her seventies, shared that she had cared for her mother-in-law, her husband's aunt, and now her own mother as dementia took hold and stole these women's connections to the present. Her fear is that she will be left alone in a care facility as she had given birth to sons, not daughters, and felt that their wives may be less giving due to the geographical and affective distance between her daughters-in-law and herself. A woman in her early fifties that we interviewed shared that she had gladly opened her home to her elderly mother when she was no longer able to see to her own needs. They had "bumped along nicely together," she said, until her mother's tendency to wander into the kitchen and absentmindedly begin cooking in the middle of the night became a threat to their physical safety when gas burners were left on with food being burnt away in pans. She had to move her mother into a nursing home just a couple of months previously, and her mother still refused to speak with her when she visited.

Another woman, fifty-nine years old, shared a story both poignant and amusing regarding her mother's cognitive decline:

> When I got married, my mother and I seemed to have more in common and more to talk about. And when I became a mother, it was interesting, and sometimes difficult, to watch my mother's interaction with my daughters. She was much more affectionate with them than I remembered her ever being with me. Later, when my father died, my mother needed care as she was in the early stages of dementia. She continued to decline for close to ten years. . . . During that time, she actually became more affectionate toward me and my sister, as she had been as a grandmother to my daughters when they were young. My sister and I would joke that she was much more fun than she had been before she got dementia. And by that point, we had become the adult caregivers for her as she had been for us in our youth.

In addition to the cognitive and emotional distance that accompany dementia, when a mother is arcing toward her final exit from the physical world, geographical distance becomes an obstacle that affects the lives of children in many different ways.

> I lived most of my adult life within a reasonable driving distance of my mother, two to four hours. While I was in graduate school, we lived about two-and-a-half hours apart, and that was ideal. She was in her eighties by then. She always wanted her children to spend the night when they came, so I could drive down, spend a nice twenty-four hours with her, and then go home. I enjoyed visiting her, but there were always moments of stress. I was not always the daughter she wanted me to be, and she wasn't always the mother I wanted her to be. She and I did not handle conflict well, so any little disagreement would

often take on much larger importance that it should have. If it began to escalate, she would say I was acting like my dad. Therefore, we would both pout for a while, then one of us would find a neutral topic and we would carry on.

The last four years of her life, we lived too far apart for frequent visits. The plan had been for her to come live near me when I graduated and found a job, but after spending a couple of weeks with me in the Midwest in the winter, she said that she could not move there. She was not able to get out for her daily walks, and she felt too confined. She eventually moved to live near my older brother and his wife. I would fly down about three times a year and would stay with her for a week to ten days.

Then, during the final seven months of my mother's life, she suffered from dementia, and it was not always easy to figure out what and whom she knew. She lived in a fantasy world in which real life sometimes got mixed up. The most difficult part of seeing my mother like this was that she sometimes knew she was confused and would get a hurt, childlike look on her face. At those times, I felt helpless and sad, because I wanted her always to be the adult.

Losing the adult who took care of the child can clearly be as painful before the eventual decline into death as it is at the end. Another woman shared her contrasting experiences regarding her mother's bout with dementia.

A MOTHERLESS CHILD

Poetry, essays, myths, and stories abound with images of orphans or motherless children finding their ways through adventures and journeys. Books on this topic abound, as well.[10] It has been suggested that this loss is the most significant loss a woman will have to face.[11] When it arrives, we may turn rapidly into spoiled children, demanding that our mothers stay with us and deny their mortality even in the face of sure evidence of just that. Carole, a fifty-seven-year-old woman, only recently lost her mother to the ravages of Alzheimer's, and the memory of her final moments with her mother is still very raw. In her case, while she desperately vocalized her refusal to accept her mother's passing, she was able to find an emotion-charged space in which she was both the caretaker and the cared for:

> The strongest testament to my mother's love and devotion and the unbreakable bond we share happened when she was dying. She suffered from the latter stages of Alzheimer's, but remarkably remembered family, friends, birthdays, and much more than most Alzheimer's patients. She fell and ruptured her eye. For two weeks after the surgery, we were blessed because it was like she was no longer suffering from Alzheimer's. Almost fourteen days after the surgery her dis-

ease suddenly progressed to the most aggressive final stage. I was having a hard time accepting that she was dying.

One day I was in her bedroom with her. She was curled up in the fetal position and had stopped eating and drinking several days prior. My heart broke looking at my mommy lying there so thin and helpless waiting to die. All I could remember was how when I was little, around seven or nine, I would crawl in bed with mama and we would lay on our sides in a half-fetal position and she would hold me tight. Sometimes, as a child, I thought she held me too tight. At that moment, however, all I wanted was to be little again, but I knew my mother needed me. I crawled in the hospital bed behind her, curled up with her in the fetal position, and held her in my arms as she had held me. All my emotions of love, fear, loss, gratitude, and anger flooded my entire being, and I could not control my feelings. I started crying softly at first and then louder and louder until I was wailing at the top of my lungs "DON'T DIE MAMA! DON'T DIE MAMA! What will I do without you? Who will love me? Don't you die, Mama!"

My mother had not spoken in over five days, she was on high doses of morphine, and her Alzheimer's had ravaged her brain and body. As far as most people believed, my mother had already left this life. But while I was having an emotional breakdown and needed my mama the most I had ever needed her, I heard a voice. At first, it was a very soft whisper, "Carole." Then louder, "Carole," then even louder "Carole." It was my mother saying my name over and over to calm me. The only thing missing was how she would hold me while saying it, but I was holding her so it was okay.

Once I heard mama calling my name I immediately began to calm and come to my senses. Realizing how selfish I was being, I stopped crying and kissed mama, telling her how much I adored her and how fortunate I was that she was my mama. I would be okay. It was okay for her to go to heaven. I realize that even when my mother was dying, she was still fighting to love, comfort, and protect me. That is a testament to a mother's love.

Being deeply and emotionally connected through the mother-daughter bond allowed Carole to let go of the physical presence of her mother. Holding onto the emotional legacy can provide an enduring bond.

THE ENDURING BOND

Losing the one who cradled you from the very moment your life began can be a devastating loss for women regardless of their age, and this loss has the power to shape the remaining days of a daughter's own life. Catherine, now sixty-four, shared her reflections on her relationship with her mother who had passed away before they had even had two decades together. Although the loss is still felt today, she is able to celebrate the gift of relationship that they shared during their time together:

My mother, Judith, was an amazing, courageous woman—one who waited until she was thirty-two to marry, which was a fairly old age to be still single back in 1946. She worked in a factory with mostly men, made her own money, and was living independently before marriage to my father. Her beautiful dance to her own music shaped me into the woman I am today and the one I hope to be able to be later in life.

As an only child, I was very close to my mother. The closeness was sprinkled with opportunities and encouragement to go out on my own, go away to college, and generally "do my own thing," which I have done all of my life. I doubt that would have been the case without her as a role model who pushed me toward both rigor and fun, all at the same time. She was completely trusting of my actions and decisions growing up; and in junior high school, I almost preferred to stay around home and do things with her.

Her support of me as a child and then as an adolescent was amazing, and I am grateful that I actually was aware of this at the time. My mother passed away the first semester of my freshman year in college, and I have always suspected that she knew that I would not have her but for what seemed like an instant. I feel her every day of my life, in all my decisions, every bout of sadness and loss, and in my achievements. Her love, my love, and our love together have gloriously lived on, and if there is anything to which I can contribute to my mentorship of others, dedication to education and counseling, and basic lifelong quest as a helper, it is that shared respect and love.

To lose one's mother is to lose a part of oneself—whether one is in childhood or older adulthood, it can shape the surviving daughter's remaining days. And as any daughter grows older, chances are she will one day catch a glimpse of herself in the mirror and see her mother looking back from the reflection. It can be powerful to acknowledge how very much like one's mother a woman has become, and it is hoped that this recognition brings a sense of connection and awareness to the enduring bond we share with the mothers that, at times for most of us, we have longed to deny in our youth but have come to cherish in adulthood.

NOTES

1. Federal Interagency Forum on Aging-Related Statistics, *Older Americans 2012: Key Indicators of Well-Being*. Washington, DC: U.S. Government Printing Office, June 2012.

2. C. Racine, "My Darling Darling: Étude on Muriel's Body," *Journal of the Association for Research on Mothering*, 10, no. 2 (2008): 51–58. *Zenith* is the term used in the author's abstract and connotes the power of the shift in the awareness of a woman's daughter at the point in which she recognizes her mother's finiteness.

3. Ibid., 58.

4. C.-A. Cait, "Parental Death, Shifting Family Dynamics, and Female Identity Development," *Omega: Journal of Death & Dying*, 51, no. 2 (2005): 87–105.

5. T. H. M. Ratti, *I Have to Go On: The Effect of a Mother's Death on Her Daughter's Education*, ProQuest, LLC, EdD dissertation, Arizona State University, 2011.

6. L. L. Bernard and C. A. Guarnaccia, "Husband and Adult-Daughter Caregivers' Bereavement," *Omega: Journal of Death and Dying, 45,* no. 2 (2002): 153–66.

7. M. W. Aleman and K. W. Helfrich, (2010). "Inheriting the Narratives of Dementia: A Collaborative Tale of a Daughter and Mother," *Journal of Family Communication, 10* (2010): 7–23.

8. E. Stone, *Black Sheep and Kissing Cousins: How Our Family Stories Shape Us* (New Brunswick, NJ: Transaction Press, 1988/2008).

9. J. Guerrero-Martin, A. Chaudri, F. Munoz, N. Duran, A. Ezquerro, and P. Suero, "The Relations between Psychosocial Factors, Care Burden, and Depression on the Dementia Family Caregivers," *European Psychiatry, 25* (2010): 567–67.

10. Including Hope Edelman's *Motherless Daughters, Letters from Motherless Daughters,* and *Motherless Mothers.* Diane Hambrook also developed *A Mother Loss Workbook: Healing Exercises for Daughters.*

11. L. E. Schultz, "The Influence of Maternal Loss on Young Women's Experience of Identity Development in Emerging Adulthood," *Death Studies, 31* (2007): 17–43.

III

A Mother's Influence

TEN

Sex and Sexuality

What Do Mothers Teach?

Although we explored earlier the ways that long-term romantic relation-ships can shift the relationship between mother and daughter, we would like to share what we learned about the messages mothers communicate to their daughters regarding sex and sexuality—whether through words of wisdom, warning, or by example.

One researcher, J. Koenig Kellas, looked at the messages that young adult daughters recalled hearing from their mothers concerning adult romantic relationship schemas.[1] She found that memorable messages clustered along four major themes: valuing self, the characteristics of a good relationship, warnings about relationships/men, and valuing of the sanctity of a love relationship. Our own interviews brought forth remem-bered lessons about similar themes, as well, with many women noting that they learned a lot through observing their own parents' interactions. The following are examples of the variety of messages we receive from our mothers as we move from childhood into sexual maturity.

"S...E...X"

Although the media persistently assaults us with sexually charged im-ages and messages, mothers are persistently waging battles to keep their daughters from early entrée into sexual relationships. Whether we were hearing from daughters in their early twenties or those who had passed their sixtieth birthday, the message about sex is that it is best left for marriage. As might be expected, women who are comfortable with the topic are more likely to discuss sexual issues with their children, and mothers tend to be more likely to have these discussions with their daughters than their sons.[2] Unfortunately, many mothers are clearly not particularly comfortable with these discussions, as many young women are coming of age without having heard any explicit discussion of sexual intimacy or romantic relationships. One forty-six-year-old woman shared that her mother "still can't say the word 'sex' in front of me!" Another woman was able to trace back the family's avoidance of the topic a couple of generations. When she had asked her mother about reproduction, her mother's response was simply, "*my* mother never discussed those things with me, so I'm not going to discuss them with you." Some of us may remember a basic "birds and bees" talk or "feminine hygiene briefing" but may have received little guidance beyond that. Other women, however, receive explicit directives about the place of sexual activities in their relationships.

WAIT FOR MARRIAGE

As in generations past, the goal of many a mother is the preservation of her daughter's purity until the wedding bells chime. Some of our mothers are encouraging chastity by passing down folksy bits of advice; one piece of wisdom left a woman chuckling as she recalled her mother warning her not to *ever* sit on a boy's lap. A mid-forties woman recalled her mother's warning, "Keep your panties up and your dress down!" Mothers often send the message that sex is a commodity that should not be traded for anything less than lifelong commitment and a pledge of faithfulness from a man. One woman noted that she was taught that "sexuality is a very powerful force, and it can be used for good or bad, so choose wisely."

Many mothers rely on religious teachings and biblical commandments as they remind their daughters of the sacredness of their bodies and their committed relationships. One woman remembered her mother telling her that her body was her temple and that no man had the right to desecrate it. Another woman noted that her mother's advice about romance was to "follow God's plan." According to one mother, sexual intimacy with partners outside of the marriage would lead to "ghosts in the relationship." While a daughter's decision to maintain virginity until marriage is still many mothers' hope, a realistic view of the world and their daughters encourages some to move beyond sexual abstinence campaigning to "proceed with caution" warnings.

PROCEED WITH CAUTION

Most of us continue to pass along the message that it will be our daughter's romantic partners, not our daughters themselves, who feel the urge to pursue sexual intimacy prior to marriage. As we noted in a prior chapter, refusing to acknowledge or educate our daughters about their own sexuality may create its own problems in our daughters' development. However, one twenty-two-year-old shared a guideline she had been taught regarding sexuality. She called it, "The three-month rule—get to know a man for three months before we engage in sex, it will save a lot of heartbreak." She went on to elaborate that after three months, you would be able to see a man's "true colors." She also shared that she had learned that she should be leery of the man who offers her "the shirt off his back when he is not wearing one." It was a warning to be careful of the man who offers her everything he has but actually has nothing. She believed her mother was protecting her from giving away her most precious gift, sexual intimacy, in return for empty promises.

The fear of an untimely pregnancy for our daughters is a primary motivator for conversations about sexuality. Probably only a very few of us made it past our teenaged years without receiving the implicit, if not explicit, message that early pregnancy would be a very poor choice. In an article from a mid-1960s social work journal, the author described the crisis of unwed motherhood as an "ageless, poignant drama,"[3] and it has grown into an economic crisis, as well. Fortunately, the rate of unwed, teenaged pregnancies has been on the decline over the past few decades.[4] Although it is probably due to greater access to relevant information and services rather than greater effectiveness of mothers' warnings, mothers are still doing their best. An eighteen-year-old shared that her mother used an age-appropriate and definitely effective tactic for encouraging her to avoid pregnancy by warning her that "having children before marriage can put an end to going out and having a good time with my friends." This provided a very clear admonition, as adolescents tend to value their freedom over looking after children.

Not all mothers are able to sit down with their daughters and broach this sort of sensitive subject, which may leave a lot to the imagination. This may be especially unfortunate as research shows that two factors that shape an adolescent's attitudes toward early pregnancy are her mother's message and the quality of the mother-daughter relationship. Perhaps equally as unsatisfying as no conversation is what one thirty-nine-year-old recalled when asked what her mother had said on the topic: "Not a thing! That was taboo. No discussions. I received a booklet and was told nothing!" Hitting the middle ground, perhaps, are those mothers who use euphemisms to warn their daughters about "using protection" and "being careful." Other mothers may use a little more colorful and nuanced language in their directives to their daughters. "Don't be bringing no babies to this house" was the only information that one twenty-nine-year-old received from her mother as she was growing up and beginning to go out with boys. Although she had not received the standard "birds and bees" talk, she affirmed that she and her sisters knew exactly what their mother meant. A similar message that was reiterated by the mother of another young woman was that she "wasn't going to be rocking a baby" for her daughter.

For some of us, telling our daughters to be safe and avoid pregnancy and disease is easier than talking about their romantic lives. As one young woman noted, "When it came to actual relationships, I think she was embarrassed to talk to me about them; but I think she also knew that I was responsible when it came to the romantic part of the relationship." Hypothetical situations can be a lot easier for us to deal with than flesh-and-blood relationships!

THUGS AND GOOD GUYS

As young women begin to date, their mothers may offer warnings about the type of young men they should see. Tied up into our conversations about sexual intimacy are messages about the dangers of some potential romantic partners. A frequently recalled message among interviewees is that some men will try to convince women that they love them with the only goal to bed them. Some of us are warned that we should be careful of the man who only wants to make a fool of us. One young woman related that her mother told her that she knew she would soon be finding boyfriends, but she was not to encourage "thugs and player types."

The qualities of a good mate also popped up in these discussions, and regardless of our cultural background, the message was clear—our daughters deserve a lot from their partners! An African American woman was encouraged by her mother to find a man "who loves you more than you love him" so that she could be sure that he would "do right" by her. In choosing a partner, a European American's mother reminded her that "it didn't matter what the person looked like or what they did for work, as long as they had health insurance, a desire to work hard, and treated me like a human then he was worth it." An Asian American shared that she had been instructed to find a man who would "treat her like a princess." Some mothers warned their daughters to assess how a boyfriend treated his mother as a guide to how she would be treated once the relationship had matured. One young woman was told to date only men who were willing to be seen with her in public, suggesting cheaters should be ruled out early. We want our daughters to find partners that are worthy of them, and it is important that we clearly articulate our respect and positive esteem for our daughters from their birth to build their own sense of self-worth. Yet discussing the qualities of a good partner for our daughters can be an especially difficult task when they are looking for the right *woman*, not man.

ADDRESSING SEXUAL IDENTITY

Approximately 7 to 8 percent of individuals identify as gay, lesbian, or bisexual,[5] yet the overwhelming majority of mothers would prefer that their daughters be 100 percent straight. As one young woman shared in response to the question about what her mother had taught her about sexuality, she stated a line that many of us probably have heard before, "GOD created Adam and Eve, Steve was NO where in the beginning." Another twenty-something related that the only lesson she had been explicitly taught about sexuality was that "romantic relations are for a man and a woman. Period." This need to protect daughters from sexual deviance may spring from a deep and unconscious evolutionary need to ensure our genes stay in the gene pool; from deeply entrenched religious beliefs; or the fear that our daughters may face discrimination and physical harm because of a lesbian identity. For many mothers, it is probably a combination of all of these concerns. It must be borne in mind that when a daughter—or mother—comes out, an eventual "coming out" of the entire family must eventually follow,[6] which can be a frightening task for many mothers.

MY DAUGHTER IS A LESBIAN?

When asked to describe the most difficult conversation between herself and her daughter, one woman responded that it had occurred when her daughter was sixteen years old and had just acknowledged that she was a lesbian. She went on to share, "It was very hard for me. Spiritually I was concerned for her, but I was more concerned with her mental stability and how or if she would be able to handle being a teenager in the South and being gay." She also worried about the hate that others in the community felt toward gay individuals as well as the potential rejection by peers and teachers. "[This] scared me about how hard my daughter's life would be." Luckily for her daughter, this concerned mother affirmed that she "totally accepts her sexual identity and supports her." Another mother, a decade younger, still felt the same fears when her daughter came to her at fourteen and shared that she "liked girls and boys." Two years later, her daughter shared that she had "decided she was 100 percent a lesbian." This was a difficult fact to accept for the mom, but she realized that if she were to try to "change" her daughter, it might cause permanent damage to their relationship.

However, for many young lesbians, the result of their innate sexual identity development is the loss of their mothers' approval. This can be a temporary condition, but it can also be the ultimate end to their relationship. One woman in her thirties related that she had been fully rejected by her own mother when she came out as a lesbian in her twenties. She acknowledged that her mother had struggled with emotional and mental disorders, as well, but that once she had come out, her mother refused to have any further contact with this young woman. Her mother passed away a couple of years ago and, before her death, her daughter had been unwelcome at the hospital, though she did appear at the funeral in an effort to reconnect with her siblings. The loss of connection due to a nonheterosexual identity is not as unusual as lesbian daughters would like it to be. Moreover, for lesbian mothers who do not come out until after having children of their own, the potential for severed mother-daughter relationships due to discrimination is all too real.

MY GRANDCHILDREN'S MOTHER IS A LESBIAN?

A mother of two young daughters (then nine and seven), Sherri came out after having been married for a decade and was quickly confronted with a legal battle waged by her very bitter husband. Sherri faced not only the venomous anger of her husband, but also a wall of rejection by her mother. Her daughters were the object of an ugly custody fight in which Sherri was berated and condemned by her ex-husband, former friends, and members of her own family. Although she was eventually awarded joint custody of the daughters she prized so highly and was raising so well, she has yet to build a bridge back to her family-of-origin.

Another woman, in her late forties, clearly recalls the day that she admitted to her mother the "secret" she had been keeping for decades, even throughout a storybook marriage and the birth of three children. She shared, "When I sat down at my mother's kitchen table that day, and although I was thirty-three, I felt like I was still just a kid. I looked at my mother and mustered up only enough courage to tell her, 'Mom, I like girls, not boys.' And then I waited for her to verbally strike me." Her mother had avowed that it was "just a phase," that she would stop feeling this way if she left the women's tennis league she played in, that she was being ridiculously selfish regarding her children's future, and that they could talk about it later—it was time for her daughter to get her grandchildren home and to bed. "I didn't hear from my mom for a while, and so I called her a couple of weeks later—the longest we'd ever not spoken. She told me that she had gone to bed that night and woke the next morning with the worst case of the flu she'd ever had. Even though she was sick for two weeks, she didn't reach out to me for anything, and I had been too scared to contact her. I was so hurt. . . . I realized then what a blow my coming out had been for her."

Luckily, they were able to patch up the relationship, although it never again felt as comfortable as it had when she had kept her sexual orientation hidden deep inside. Some aspects of a daughter's life cannot bare the scrutiny of the mother who expects perfection or fairy-tale innocence and goodness from her daughter.

ONE BIG HAPPY FAMILY FOR THE NEW MILLENNIUM?

Sexual orientation is perhaps the final culturally accepted target for discrimination, but many mothers are doing their best to embrace their lesbian daughters and their female partners. One interviewee, Mary, related that her own mother had tacitly accepted that she was a lesbian thirty years ago, but that they had never openly talked about the subject and Mary doubted her mother even had a vocabulary with which to address it. Mary went on to share that her mother had always welcomed her current partner with open arms, and since the first Christmas her partner and her partners' children had spent together, her mother had been hanging stockings on the mantel for each of them. Tammy, a fifty-two-year-old lesbian, related a little bit about her coming out story: "I didn't come out to my mom in high school because that was taboo. I know she had known for a long time, and she was very supportive. She did not interfere with my life or in my life, but if I needed her she was always there to provide the help I needed." When she was asked if her mother had accepted her girlfriends over the years, she affirmed, "Yes, she loved a couple of my girlfriends, and as long as I am happy she is happy. As long as my girlfriend is good to me and especially for me, then she is OK with that, too. I have had a few girlfriends I know she did not approve of, but she let me find out for myself they weren't good for me."

As a seventy-one-year-old mother of a happily out and proud daughter shared, it is important to accept your children as they are. She reminds us all to listen to our daughters—even when they are sharing things that you might wish would go unsaid. The mother-daughter relationship is precious—especially as mothers and daughters mature and move into new phases of development. She reminds us that rejecting a daughter is to reject a part of yourself, and that this is a choice that can leave a mother alone and a daughter an orphan. Unconditional love is what motherhood is all about, according to this wise woman. She summed it up, "All I want for my daughter is to be as happy as possible."

WORTHY OF LOVE

Most of us want to raise daughters who have strongly positive self-regard, view themselves as worthy of true love, and are willing to be patient until they find a suitable partner. To that end, we are sending messages that many of our daughters are hearing. Being confident and being smart were seen as positive ways to be attractive to the right kind of partner. Putting education, career, and one's future ahead of a search for love was also a prevalent and valued message. Mothers are encouraging their daughters to respect themselves, love themselves first, take their time in love, and to recognize that being single is an absolutely okay state of affairs.

One young woman shared a lesson that she valued regarding romantic relationships: "My body is precious, and so am I." Daughters are also being explicitly reminded that they do not have to settle for less than they deserve. With the average age of marriage steadily increasing, the overall percentage of women who marry decreasing, and the opportunities to pursue dreams as wide as a young daughter can reach, encouraging independence is likely to pay off big! Some of our daughters, however, may be hesitant in love more so due to the examples that we, as mothers, have provided than our intended teachings.

EXAMPLES NOT WORTH FOLLOWING

Daughters are often witnesses to relationships that should not have begun, much less endured. The need to have a man in their lives will allow some women to place the safety and well-being of their daughters at a priority level much too low. Although research suggests that resilience may develop in daughters who grow up in homes where abuse is present,[7] it is not the kindest way to instill this quality. A thirty-one-year-old mother of a daughter, herself, recalled that her mother modeled "nothing" for her regarding healthy relationships: "She was married to a man for thirteen years who was on drugs and alcohol and who she loved dearly . . . she really didn't want to leave." She went on to share that once her mother finally had the strength to leave this dysfunctional relationship, she chose yet another unsuitable partner, which her daughter believed simply reemphasized how little her mother could teach her about intimate love. She did say that she hopes she can teach her own daughter to be different; she would like to see her daughter become "tenacious and see failures as steps to reach for and achieve higher goals."

One woman, Delia, shared that her mother did not see any value in the open discussions of topics related to sex or intimacy. Delia went on to reveal that her mother had used secrecy about this topic to protect, or perhaps more accurately, to deceive her on many different levels. Not only was Delia spared explicit conversations with her mother about sex, her mother engaged in a secret extramarital affair, left Delia's father for the other man, and then lied about the new relationship, implying that she was legally married to the new man in her life to avoid being accused of "shacking up." Delia is proud that she has raised her own daughters through her own example by modeling acceptance and being open, nonsecretive, and nonjudgmental.

Our parents' interactions and their relationships are often used as models of how to enact healthy relationships or to avoid unsuccessful relationships. It can be very difficult for a young woman to grow up dreaming of finding a "happily ever after" when she has no role models exhibiting how a healthy relationship functions. A client, just twenty, sought counseling to deal with the hurt and anger created by her mother's decision to stay with what she termed "a worthless man." The young woman felt slighted by her mother's inability to be a healthy role model and leave the drug-addicted, unemployed, and ill-tempered boyfriend. The client desperately needed her mother to show her that she could live independently without a man, but her mother fell short in meeting this need. The client was determined not to settle for such poor behavior from a partner, but she was deeply unsettled by her mother's choices, and she felt unsure about her own ability to create the positive romantic relationship that she desired.

Another young woman, in her early twenties, was explicitly told by her mother to avoid making a mistake similar to her own. Only recently, her mother revealed that she had been married to an abusive husband whom she had divorced prior to finding and marrying the young woman's father. Her mother wanted her to avoid a similar fate of victimization. She encouraged her daughter to be patient in finding a long-term partner because rushing into a marriage can be an extremely unwise decision. Sadly, this young woman also shared a story that somewhat echoed her mother's own experience. Her mother had encouraged her to save her virginity for someone she really cared about and who truly cared about her. She then noted, "To this day, I have only slept with one person and I know he did not care for me and that is something I will always have to deal with." Sometimes, family stories are set to repeat themselves, as we often have to learn from our own mistakes, however hard it may be for a mother to witness or daughter to experience.

IF MY DAUGHTER WOULD LISTEN, HERE'S THE KEY

Just because a daughter does not *always* listen to her mother does not mean she does not hear. Some of the words of wisdom regarding healthy relationships that daughters do recall from their mothers include the following suggestions:

- Healthy relationships are a team effort—both partners must contribute equally.
- Always push yourself to be a better partner.
- Be faithful and true—to yourself and your partner.
- Always be willing to compromise, but don't compromise yourself!
- Relationships sometimes require more giving than receiving, but always try to give 100 percent.

- Love your partner fully and only your partner.
- To keep a partner happy, you must meet physical needs as well as other needs.
- Relationships can endure children, teenagers, struggles, and challenges for decades as long as you keep the "spark" alive.
- Be honest, but also keep a little mystery about yourself.
- Support your partner in the decisions that are made.
- It takes two to make a relationship work, so always do your part.

NOTES

1. J. K. Kellas, "Transmitting Relational Worldviews: The Relationship between Mother-Daughter Memorable Messages and Adult Daughters' Romantic Relational Schemata," *Communication Quarterly, 58*, no. 4 (2010): 458–79.

2. E. I. Pluhar, C. K. Dilorio, and F. McCarty, "Correlates of Sexuality Communication among Mothers and 6-12-Year-Old Children," *Child Care, Health and Development, 34*, no. 3 (2008): 283–90.

3. H. L. Friedman, "The Mother-Daughter Relationship: Its Potential in Treatment of Young Unwed Mothers," *Social Casework, 47*, no. 8 (1966): 502–6.

4. K. Kost and S. Henshaw, *U.S. Teenage Pregnancies, Births and Abortions, 2008: State Trends by Age, Race and Ethnicity*, Washington, DC: Guttmacher Institute, March 2013.

5. D. Herbenick, M. Reece, V. Schick, S. A. Sanders, B. Dodge, and J. D. Fortenberry, "Sexual Behavior in the United States: Results from a National Probability Sample of Men and Women Ages 14–94," Journal of Sexual Medicine, 7 (Suppl. 5) (2010): 255–65.

6. J. Beeler and V. DiProva, "Family Adjustment Following Disclosure of Homosexuality by a Member: Themes Discerned in Narrative Account," *Journal of Marital and Family Therapy, 25*, no. 4 (1999): 443–59.

7. K. M. Anderson and F. S. Danis, "Adult Daughters of Battered Women," *Affilia: Journal of Women & Social Work, 21*, no. 4 (2006): 419–32.

ELEVEN

Lessons on Parental Separation and Divorce

What comes to mind when you reflect on the lessons you learned from your mother about intimacy and romance? What are the values and attitudes you hope that your own daughter might carry into her relationships? These questions brought a range of responses from the women with whom we spoke, and their responses were pretty much divided between two poles—what they believed their mothers taught by doing poorly in this area and what they believed their mothers taught by doing well. As indicated in social learning theory,[1] we learn a great deal from our role models.

BROKEN RELATIONSHIPS

Coming from a home in which parents shared a strong and committed relationship can provide a "best of times" perspective for daughters and tacitly encourage a search for a similar relationship. Conversely, daughters growing up in less-than-fairy-tale circumstances, in the best of cases during the worst of times, may be able to use an inadequate role model as the motivation to succeed in ways in which mothers had failed. With about four or five out of ten marriages ending in divorce, depending on the parameters of the population sample (first marriage? second marriage? age at marriage? gender? The variations are endless!), mothers might wonder what they are modeling for their daughters and what effect these impermanent relationships might have on their daughters' expectations of a romantic happily-ever-after.

A mother's romantic misadventures can wreak havoc and create lasting dissension between herself and her children, as described by one woman: "My mother has been married several times, at last count five. The man who was my dad in every way except biologically was number three. She hurt him deeply, and he never seemed to have gotten over it, or he never married again. He [is] the one I spent the most time with, and he is the one I tried to keep happy."

Another woman, the mother of a young daughter, worries about the ways in which poor examples of romantic relationships may show up in each subsequent generation. As she shared:

> My grandmother was incredibly beautiful, and she constantly entered relationships with men—particularly because she could not manage financially on her own. Their home life was unstable; my mother would be filled with dread concerning who my grandmother would date next. Would he be nice to them or would he be hurtful? Regardless of gifts given and pleasantries offered by my grandmother's suitors, my mother was embarrassed that her home did not look like those of the more upstanding neighbors. My grandmother's second husband was abusive to my grandmother as well as her children (including my mother). It took years and suffering much emotional damage to the family before my grandmother left her second husband for the next man, who was a better one. Oddly enough, my grandmother had a fairly strong and highly charismatic personality and seemed to suffer little from these events. My mother, however, has struggled with these events her entire life. She also tolerated a loveless marriage to provide herself and her children with the stability she deeply craved.
>
> I see my grandmother as a reasonably good role model because she was a powerful matriarch in our family and outspoken and demanding (to a degree) with her final husband, the one I remember best. But when it comes to the meat of a committed relationship, I do not have much to go on. My own marriage is not desirable, though no longer toxic. I am afraid the theme that I see when I look at three generations of marriage is mothers who tolerate "crap" from husbands in order to have financial and other forms of security. I would really like to see my daughter enjoy a richer romantic life. Yet I am not sure how she can create something she has yet to see modeled for her.

However, for another family, serial monogamy may bring a different lesson, as shared by a forty-four-year-old woman with two adult daughters of her own: "My mother went through more husbands and boyfriends than Elizabeth Taylor, and was very open and honest about her sexuality." She believed that her mother's openness had allowed her to feel comfortable with her own sexuality that she felt was an unexpected benefit. The climate of a family's home, however, may be the most important factor in how divorce influences the children in the family.

BEFORE THE DIVORCE

It may be that the long-lasting effects of divorce is not always as painful for daughters to handle as are the rocky times between her parents prior to a divorce. One young woman in her early twenties described the most difficult period of her relationship with her mother as involving "the continual arguments and fights between my mother and father prior to their divorce. Everybody in the house was on the edge. It was the worst time of our lives, but we got through it." Living in a battlefield may take a heavier toll than learning to function in a single-parent family. Children who live in homes in which hostility describes the climate between parents are as much at-risk for negative outcomes, such as behavior problems, academic performance concerns, and compromised well-being, as are children whose parents choose to separate and divorce.[2] When a mother and father are subjecting their children to sustained animosity, the psychological health of their children is already at stake.[3]

The difficulties and stressors faced during the period surrounding the disintegration of a marriage can leave a lifelong scar on daughters, as shared by this now twenty-five-year-old woman:

> The time our relationship was strained the most was probably when she and my dad were going through their separation and divorce. My mom completely changed during those five years, and I felt like she was not there for me when I needed her to be and the focus was always on her. I felt like she was not interested in me or my accomplishments or my day-to-day activities, and it made it more difficult because I did not live at home during those years and so there was physical distance between us as well. More and more separation occurred, and walls were put up as protective barriers.

As noted in another chapter, a mother's response to her daughter's accomplishments can be essential in building self-esteem and a sense of self-worth. Yet a mother's self-involvement when a relationship fails speaks volumes about women's tendency to measure their personal success through their relationships to men. The emotional tuning out of a daughter's needs can be as devastating as verbal chastising or abuse.

Another risk, beyond verbal disagreements or emotional cutoff, can be an even more disturbing environmental hazard—substance abuse and physical abuse. Although we expect daughters to be more likely put at risk by their father than their mothers, one young woman described the following background story as to how she came to be raised by her father: "I have never been really close to my mother; she left me at six months old on my dad's door step. She chose the life of men and drugs. I am thankful she gave me to him instead of dragging me into that mess." Asked to describe the lessons she had learned more explicitly from her mother regarding relationships, this young woman had little to share.

Sadly, she described the ways in which her mother's relationships with men provided only lessons on how *not* to form relationships: "When my mother had visitation rights she allowed us to be abused by her boyfriends and she had multiple."

DIVORCE AND INFORMATION OVERLOAD FOR OUR DAUGHTERS

Whether she is seven, seventeen, or thirty-seven, the divorce of a daughter's parents can have a significant impact on her life. While younger kids will feel the shift in virtually every aspect of their daily lives, older daughters may also feel seismic shifts in their emotional balance. When asked about the most difficult conversations she remembered having with her mother, a thirty-seven-year-old revealed that it was just a few years ago that her mother told her she was divorcing her father. As she summed up the worst point in her relationship with her mother, "[it was in its] worst shape during her divorce to my father . . . it's hard to fault your father for anything even if he has hurt your mother." When the parental relationship crumbles, daughters often feel that they may be asked to choose sides, something that mothers may potentially be tacitly and unconsciously encouraging.

When families are split apart by parental divorce or separations, fathers are typically the parents that vacate the family home and the day-to-day lives of children. Not only does this potentially disrupt normal routines, family schedules, and family economics, the loss of a partner often shatters a mother's intimate social support system. Wired for emotional relating, when a woman's closest relationship is disrupted, she feels a strong need to fill the gap. She looks for someone who can provide a sounding board for the regular daily hassles and decisions, but also she wants someone to listen to her as she processes issues surrounding the relationship breakup. Divorce often yields tighter schedules and tighter finances and less time and lessened means to connect with friends. This limits options for long conversations and leaning on others. Thus, those in the household—including her daughters—serve as the most immediate outlet for her sharing, which is not always in the best interest of her children.[4]

Some mothers assume that their adolescent daughters are mature enough for adult, one-to-one sharing of feelings about sensitive topics. They may feel that because their daughters are also, in some way, being "left" by a significant male, that they share their mothers' perspective and reactions to the shift. However, as we know, adolescents are not yet neurologically programmed to respond as adults and still need their parents to guide and support them, not befriend them. Daughters, being relationally oriented just as their mothers are, also tend to worry about their family members, so a mother unburdening herself of her concerns is actually burdening her daughter with inappropriate worries.[5]

Other mothers, however, are cautious about the potential damage that can be done to a child by their own expressed attitude and feelings about a marital split and the ex-spouse, as shared by a forty-nine-year-old mother of two daughters, Kelly and Kristi, who has been divorced around seven years: "Unfortunately, Kristi bore the brunt of our divorce. Her older sister, Kelly, was off to college and Kristi was here. At first, she had a schedule of whom she spent her time with, but then she and her father had a huge fight and she came to stay with me all the time. When they finally reconciled, he was ready for her to come back, but she wouldn't. I know that was very difficult because he was still at the house where she had grown up, so she felt like she was leaving her house. This is probably where we became much closer, but I didn't want her to feel a burden of having to be there for me."

TOPICS THAT MOTHERS SHOULD NOT BROACH
WITH THEIR DAUGHTERS

One area of discussion that can be especially difficult for adolescent daughters is the financial fallout the family is experiencing due to the separation. This, perhaps, is one of the primary and most immediate areas affected by the split household, yet one that a daughter has little ability to influence or resolve. One twenty-eight-year-old woman recalled that after her parents' divorce, her mother had to work twelve-hour shifts after divorcing her husband just to provide for her and her siblings when they were young. As she summed up, "We had to grow up faster than most in order to provide for ourselves." Some of our clients are young women who have revealed that they experienced a sense of "owing their mother financial assistance" and had delayed entering college or wrestled with the conflict of staying in college or taking time off to earn money to help their mothers stay financially afloat. While single parenting and women in the workforce do not carry the stigmas they once did, one woman clearly recalls how different she felt growing up in a one-parent family. "My mother has been married several times, at last count five. Where I was raised, I was the first child to have divorced parents, and while I suspect my classmates really did not notice, I always felt inferior for that reason. [My mother] had to work, and remember this was not the norm in the early 1950s. I hid my feelings most of the time, and when I went away to college where everyone was the same I found I was an 'okay' person."

Other areas that are likely to create psychological distress for daughters included negative feelings toward fathers, difficulties with parenting responsibilities, career and job concerns, and personal problems. It is unlikely that an adolescent daughter can effectively manage any of these concerns, yet their mothers often break the boundaries and open discussions about these topics.[6, 7] One woman clearly recalls the difficult times she experienced after her parents' divorce and her mother's own emotional response to the event. Twenty years later, she still recalls her suffering:

> When my parents divorced, my relationship with my mother was not at its best. She was having a difficult time when my dad left her, and she became very depressed. During those months, she tended to drink alcohol a good bit. I was only eight years old, and felt very sorry for my mother. There were times when I had to take care of her, when it should have been the other way around. It got to the point that when I would leave for my dad's house, I would feel guilty and worry about her being alone. This strained our relationship because even though I felt sorry for her, I was angry and felt things were my fault.

Further, research shows that trying to speak with one's daughters about such adult and relationship-dependent feelings actually creates more distance in the relationship between mother and daughter. In addition, what we may be teaching our daughters about relationships is that healthy ones are much too rare and much too challenging to establish and maintain.

When a woman in her mid-twenties was asked to share a little bit about her own past "difficult conversations" with her mother, she didn't hesitate to provide a poignant list of questions that she had bravely asked of her mother over her twenty-plus years. They speak to the hurt and confusion she experienced because of her mother's unstable romantic relationship history.

As a child:

- Why do I not know my biological father?
- Who are these men that you are dating?
- Why do we have to move all the time?
- Why do I not feel smart?

As a teen:

- Why are boys so afraid to talk to me?
- Why don't I feel very pretty?
- Why don't I know how to be myself?
- Why do I not have any real friends?
- Why does daddy lie so much?

As an adult:

- Why do I not know how to treat men in a relationship?
- Will you ever see me as an adult?

Just reading this list of questions may stir up a host of different feelings for you—they clearly articulate the vulnerability of the speaker and poignantly communicate the pain she experienced from missing consistent interaction with a positive father figure throughout critical developmental periods. Also particularly distressing was her description of what her mother had taught her about family relationships: "A mother is the head of the household, and the man just holds the title of being a father/ husband." When we do not learn how valuable another parent can be in our lives, it is difficult to learn how to be a responsible partner. In our counseling practices, we have both worked with young women who were enduringly affected by the divorces of their parents. Some of the lasting messages that are unconsciously conveyed, but that can deeply wound daughters, include, "Younger women are more desirable," "How you look is what matters most in a relationship," "Men are selfish," and "Life isn't worth living without a man," or a mother's persistent belief that she "just isn't good enough for her husband." Often left to fend on their own emotionally as mothers try to pull themselves together, daughters may need to learn how to navigate shifting relationships of another significant kind, with their siblings.

SHIFTS IN FAMILIAL EMOTIONAL CONNECTIONS

Many women experiencing a transition into a single-parent identity may need to rely on their children to be more independent overall, but also more interdependent with one another as she may be spread thin. This new family constellation can intensify the relationships between siblings—they may show a greater sense of warmth and protectiveness toward one another, or they may experience a higher level of negative affect toward one another.[8] Siblings may also take ownership of responsibility for the dissolution of their parents' marriage. One forty-year-old mother of two daughters noted that one of the most difficult conversations she could recall with them was "when their father left; they didn't understand why and, of course, felt it was their faults." Siblings may try to work together to woo back the absent parent, which is an effort that seldom succeeds.

Another young woman expressed appreciation of her mother's recognition of how difficult divorce could be on children. She recounted, "When my parents divorced, mom knew she could not help me adequately on her own, so she sent my sister and me to counseling. She taught us not to feel shameful about things that can be helpful. There is nothing wrong with asking for a little help every now and then." This young woman greatly benefitted from her mother's willingness to acknowledge and heal the pain felt by her daughters because of the divorce.

Daughters are especially ready to assume guilt and to try to protect others whether they are two or ninety-two. Here is how one young woman described her own sense of responsibility as her parents' marriage dissolved: "Another dramatic shift was probably during the early stages of my parents' divorce when I felt like our roles had shifted because my mom was going through a really rough time mentally and emotionally so I needed to step up for myself, my brother, and her." This was an important turning point for her as she later recognized that she also needed to take care of herself and allow her mother to figure things out on her own. Role clarification can be difficult for daughters who model themselves after their mothers, who are traditionally caregivers and nurturers of a family.

A MOTHER'S ROLE CONFUSION

While the focus has been on how divorce can affect siblings, there are also instances when a mother and her daughter may shift into a pseudo-sibling relationship, of a sort, as described by a now sixty-three-year-old mother. "My mother and I had more of an 'older sister' relationship. She divorced my father when I was three-and-a-half and my brother was three months old. My grandmother basically raised us. She was more of a mother figure to me than my mother was." As this daughter moved through life and continued to witness her mother making poor relationship choices that often ended in the marriage-divorce pattern, she stated that "going forward, I helped her through financial troubles, depression, and multiple health issues. I was more the mother in the relationship till her death."

The loss of a mother figure can leave a daughter especially bitter when her mother is still a part of her life. For those of us who have gone through a divorce or are on the precipice of divorce, we must recognize that our daughters will need our presence in their lives even more keenly. Befriending a daughter as she grows into a woman is not devastating in the way such a relationship shift can be for younger girls. If a mother must move her own family back in with her own parents, it is essential that she not forfeit the mothering role of her children to her own mother. As one woman shared, having a grandmother in the home can be a very satisfying family constellation, if done right: "My parents got divorced when I was five years old and my brother was three years old . . . my grandma—my mom's mom—came to live with us during the week to take care of us for my mom . . . she was like my second mom and also meant the world to me. And in no way can I say that my dad deserted us, or that I did not have a father figure, because I did. Actually, my parents were pretty much the poster children for how divorced parents SHOULD act. But because of that divorce, my mom pretty much dedicated her life to my brother and me. Everything she did, she did for us."

POSITIVE LESSONS FROM BROKEN RELATIONSHIPS

There is no guarantee that any relationship will last, whether built on love, economics, or convenience. When a relationship dissolves, parents should do their best to maintain a healthy communication style with one another, continue to coparent their children as a united team, and provide warm support to their children to allow them to better weather the emotional storms that are virtually unavoidable when the parental relationship dissolves. As a mother, you can provide a strong example for your daughter—in either a negative manner or a positive manner, depending on how you respond to the loss of a relationship.

For instance, when a thirty-five-year-old woman was asked what she had learned from her mother about relationships and intimacy, she summed it up quickly, "Nothing! But by watching her relationships, I learned not to settle for less." Many women, however, are able to manage the divorce and its fallout highly effectively. They are able to show their daughters that women can be strong, secure, self-confident, and capable of living a full and satisfying life without a husband. Contrast this perspective with that of another woman, now forty-eight years old and the product of a single parent home: "I was raised by a single mom who took time for me and herself and taught me the importance of doing that for yourself. From a cultural standpoint, there were not many of my friends with divorced parents, so it was important to fit in, and my mom had a lot to do with that in the way we were in our family life." We have a choice in what we teach our daughters and, ideally, we will model strength, self-confidence, and self-respect.

NOTES

1. A. Bandura, *Social Learning Theory* (New York: General Learning Press, 1977).

2. J. Baxter, R. Weston, and L. Qu, "Family Structure, Co-Parental Relationship Quality, Post-Separation Paternal Involvement and Children's Emotional Wellbeing," *Journal of Family Studies*, 17, no. 2 (2011): 86–109.

3. P. R. Amato, "Research on Divorce: Continuing Trends and New Developments," *Journal of Marriage & Family*, 72, no. 3 (2010): 650–66.

4. S. S. Koerner, S. L. Jacobs, and M. Raymond, "When Mothers Turn to Their Adolescent Daughters: Predicting Daughters' Vulnerability to Negative Adjustment Outcomes," *Family Relations*, 49, no. 3 (2000): 301–9.

5. S. S. Koerner, S. Wallace, S. J. Lehman, and M. Raymond, "Mother-to-Daughter Disclosure after Divorce: Are There Costs and Benefits?" *Journal of Child and Family Studies*, 11, no. 4 (2002): 469–83.

6. Koerner, Jacobs, and Raymond, "When Mothers Turn to Their Adolescent Daughters."

7. K. G. Dolgin, "Parents' Disclosure of Their Own Concerns to Their Adolescent Children," *Personal Relationships, 3*, no. 2 (1996): 159–69.

8. G. Sheehan, Y. Darlington, P. Noller, and J. Feeney, "Children's Perceptions of Their Sibling Relationships during Parental Separation and Divorce," *Journal of Divorce & Remarriage, 41* (2004): 69–94.

TWELVE

Social Support

Your Friends and (Extended) Family Network

As we've noted, women learn how to relate to others from very early in life. Even as infants, we are already seeking out eye contact and building relationships with those important people in our lives.[1] So how much influence might our mothers have on our relational behaviors beyond the genetic contribution? We invited women to share the lessons they had learned about friendships and extended family networks from their mothers, and it does appear that definite messages are being sent.

FRIENDSHIPS ARE IMPORTANT

A young woman in her early twenties shared, "My mother has taught me that nothing in life is worth having if you have no one to share it with, whether it is laughter or tears, good times or bad." Her mother encouraged her to forge and maintain friendships. Many women we interviewed, who dearly value their friendship circles, shared this sentiment. Another woman, in her fifties, noted that although her "mother was a true introvert," her parents' home was always "open to family and friends dropping by" and "she had many friends in the community." The value of relationships was worth the investment of personal energy, she believed, as her mother had modeled this for her even though her introversion made social interactions more work.

Mothers as Models

Another woman noted that her own mother had many, many friends and that she had learned early the importance of getting along with others. "My mother taught me that friends are an important part of life," shared a mid-twenties young woman, and she went on to share that "my mother and her friends take trips together and make 'girls' night out' plans" on a regular basis. This was a great role model for her, and this young woman affirmed that she and her friends do the same. Research findings have indicated that our social skills begin developing early and that our families provide the training ground for "rules of engagement" and acceptable interactions.[2] In fact, many aspects of our earliest family relationships influence our adult friendship support systems. These specifically include our parents' satisfaction with their relationship, the closeness we feel toward our mothers, and the level of negative communication interaction with our mothers as adolescents.[3] Thus, parents should temper their negative interactions in front of their daughters, and mothers should foster positive interactions with her teenaged daughters to encourage future, richly supportive adult friendships for them.

One woman noted that her mother taught her to always be loyal to her friends and that her mother told her—and modeled for her—that she should never let a man come between her and her friends. Another woman joked that "Mom taught me that friendships were essential. She often told me that if it hadn't been for the time she spent with her friends that she probably would have divorced my father." The gift of friendship has probably saved more marriages than spouses might believe!

Friends Are Human

Perhaps we all should take a lesson from the words recalled by one young woman regarding friendships. Her mother told her, "Sometimes, friends or other individuals will disappoint you and that is expected; however, do not hold grudges. Forgive, and let go." Accepting the limitations of others can be easier when you are able to accept that you, too, have limitations. Many women shared that they were taught that true friends would be there for them through the good times and bad—especially when they needed support. One woman shared that her mother told her never to be afraid to ask her friends for what she needed—being there when things were rough was one of the reasons that we have friends in our lives.

HOW STRONG IS YOUR FRIENDSHIP NETWORK?

Clearly, friendship is a valuable commodity—and many mothers emphasize just how important it is to work to keep friendships going strong and running smoothly. One young woman shared that her mother modeled having a lot of good relationships growing up and that she was "always around a lot of people" who could provide support. She was also taught to be "caring and nice," which is the message that many of us receive as females. Learning the rules of friendship begins early. In fact, the most frequently shared lesson from mother to daughter regarding friendships is that daughters should strive to be good friends who are loyal to those about whom they care. As one woman shared, "My mother taught me to appreciate the friends I held close. I learned that loyalty is very important if a friendship is to last." Consciously appreciating your friends for all that they bring to your life was another frequently communicated message between mothers and daughters. As one woman stated, "You only have a very few true friends in life," so the work maintaining the relationship is worth it. Yet many mothers warn their daughters that "not everyone will be caring and nice," so to speak.

BEING SMART IN CHOOSING FRIENDS

One young woman shared only one piece of wisdom that she had learned from her own mother regarding friendships: "You are judged by the company you keep." Other mothers also offer advice about whom you choose to befriend, although not exactly with the same message. Being aware of how others might not have your best interests at heart was a common theme for many women. One woman said her mother put it to her daughter this way, "Do not trust everyone that smiles at you." One young woman recalls her mother teaching her that "the friends you choose will have a major impact on your life, so surround yourself with good people."

Mothers are eager to keep their daughters from being taken advantage of by their acquaintances. Some women remembered their mothers suggesting that family, not friends, were better for long-term support. One woman shared that she was taught that friends are important, but that family is more important. The fear of friendships fading over time was shared by many women who believed that "family is family," no matter where you end up in life. Yet for the most part our mothers encourage the development of strong friendships. As one woman shared, "My mother taught me that friends are good to have and oftentimes, friends can be better than family." Other lasting lessons included reminders that while we don't need a huge number of friends, we do need to choose trustworthy friends. In fact, loyalty and trustworthiness were the qualities that were the most frequently mentioned as being important to good friendships.

Unfortunately, many young women may be warned against being *too* close with friends. One woman recalled her mother sharing the singsong warning, "Have your friends and treat them well, but do not them your secret tell. For when your friends become your foes, out in the world your secret goes!" Other women also received similar messages about the dangers of being too open with nonfamily members. One woman noted that her mother continues to remind her that "close friends and close family are those that have the power to hurt you the most." For some, these warnings may be taken to heart and preclude the development of strong support networks. One woman felt that her mother's example of having only "acquaintances" in lieu of friends had unknowingly provided the model that she had followed. As this mid-forties daughter shared, "My mother belonged to clubs and organizations, but I cannot recall a time when she met a friend for lunch or went shopping with 'the girls' or anything like that. Now I am the same way—my 'friends' are really my immediate family . . . my husband and my kids." While this may build strong nuclear family relationships, it may also cost her the joy of friendship.

BUILDING RELATIONSHIPS THAT WORK *AND* PLAY

The thread of friendship runs throughout the life span and, for some women, it is this thread that holds their lives together. Learning how to get along with others can pay off big as the years pass. One sixty-three-year-old shared that while her mother was more reliant on their large family for support, she had built a different social support network. It was with great joy that she shared this:

> I have some wonderful close friends, those that I can go for long periods without seeing, but there is no change in the relationship. I also have three "bucket buddies." We are doing things together on each of our Bucket Lists. I have a large group of tennis friends, and we do "girls only" weekend trips that are so rejuvenating. We behave like twelve-year-olds that know how to cook and clean up.

Building friendships that allow you to play out your dreams and kick back like kids is a worthy goal for any young woman—or older woman—today. What a delightful way to model the joy of friendship for any generation of girls!

WORDS OF FRIENDSHIP WISDOM FOR ALL DAUGHTERS

- Close friends are just as important as family—you need someone to be there for you when you are going through a difficult situation.
- Be kind, loving, and supportive of your friends, and they will offer these qualities to you.
- Always treat people as if they are somebody.
- Look for the best in people, but stay realistic.
- Always stay on good terms with friends; you never know when you might need their help.

- Maintain true friendships for life, it will always be worth the effort in the long run.
- Choose your friends carefully, and use your intuition when allowing others into your life.
- Always remember that your word is your bond with others.
- Sometimes you must let go of friends who only take away but never replenish your heart and energy.

WHO IS IN YOUR FAMILY NETWORK?

As families have become more geographically transient over the past half-century, extended family bonds are increasingly difficult to maintain. One woman shared that her mother "valued extended family, but did not always maintain contact." Her mother left it up to other family members to keep in touch, but her daughter affirmed that she worked hard to "have always stayed in touch with extended family," as she deeply valued these relationships. She had lost her mother when she was just a young adult and felt a strong need to maintain the family connections that she could to stay close to those who shared her mother's memory. Many women believe that the richness of a family is enjoyed through the interactions between generations and extended family. A woman in her mid-thirties recalls, "My mother loves family gatherings and always invites extended family and friends. As a result, she taught me that the more family, the merrier the gathering!"

And as we already know pretty well, mothers are frequently "the glue that holds a family together." One woman stated this firmly, and added that her mother has taught her that "family is family, regardless of the circumstances that arise." The role of the extended family varies, but respect and acceptance are shared values when it comes to far-flung members of the family. Even though we may have an eccentric aunt that shows up at reunions or that crotchety great uncle who wears us out with complaints, many of us are encouraged to "just get along." One woman remembers her mother telling her, "Do your part and be there for them, no matter how crazy or how hard things may get." Family is important, and many of us are taught early to accept their idiosyncrasies and offer support. However, the limits of the influence of extended family members are often clearly noted. As one woman shared, "Extended family has always been important to us, but not important enough to affect the decisions that happened within our household."

In addition to the geographical variations families represent, family constellations have shifted greatly over the past decades. The rise of divorce rates and the blending of families create new variations on step relationships that widen a family tree. For some women, the addition of stepfamily members can be welcomed. There are some women who are able to forge bonds with all categories of new relations—one woman we know is crazy about the mother of her husband's ex-wife. They met during a holiday event in which the stepchildren/grandchildren were in a school concert. However, another woman revealed that her mother "had an issue with her stepchildren at first. But eventually she just accepted the fact that they were now a part of 'us,' our family." The willingness to embrace all of one's extended kin can provide a model of respect for family that words alone will not do.

A DISTANCE JUST TOO FAR

For some families, the geographical distance and the emotional distance can be too wide to cross, and one generation of a family may have little to no contact with other generations. Many times, the members of the extended family are just names of people in photographs or on holiday cards, if the family still sends these. One woman shared that her mother encourages her to try to stay in communication with her grandparents and extended family, but that "life tends to keep all of us busy," which limits the frequency and quality of contact. Even as the range of communication technology continues to expand, finding the time to Skype, text, or telephone family can be difficult, yet it should be firmly encouraged in each generation. As one woman noted, "I have worked in the medical field for over forty years, most recently with the elder population. I worry about the elder folks who do not have competent extended family. There are so many opportunities for neglect and abuse that it is very scary." We should all take these words to heart and model for our children and siblings how essential it is that we take care of our elders. It is important that all members of our families are acknowledged—especially those who may be aging. One young woman in her mid-twenties shared that her grandmother had just moved into her parents' home and that she is working hard to include her grandmother in her life. She shared that she wants her grandmother to feel appreciated, and so she makes time to "do crossword puzzles with her and ask her advice on all aspects of life, because she is the smartest woman I know!" This active involvement enhances both the granddaughter and the grandmother's life.

APPRECIATION FOR FAMILY IS IMPORTANT

"Family is everything, and at the end of the day, all you really have is your family," affirmed one woman. She went on to add, "That is the reason my sisters and I are so close." One woman shared that her mother taught her that "family is something that you don't get to pick," and that her mother believes that they are "put in your life for a reason." This meant that she needed to show love and support to family members—

which her mother has consistently modeled by remaining close to her brothers throughout her life, even though her mom often complained that her brothers' wives have been less than always kind to her. Another woman shared that her mother always reminds her that "nothing can replace family." This has played out in the strong relationships between her and her "third and fourth cousins," who she was taught to value as "big brothers or sisters." Loving and accepting extended family is a way to keep alive a family's identity and a family's history. It takes time, but it can pay off big.

VALUES WORTH PASSING ALONG

- Family is important, and families should offer support to each family member.
- It is good to know who your people are—they represent where you came from.
- Respect your elders.
- Family and togetherness matter for each generation, so visit as often as you can.
- You don't have to like them, but when you are with them, be nice and hold your tongue.

NOTES

1. R. T. Leeb and F. G. Rejskind, "Here's Looking at You, Kid! A Longitudinal Study of Perceived Gender Differences in Mutual Gaze Behavior in Young Infants," *Sex Roles, 50*, no. 1–2 (2004): 1–14.

2. H. Baril, D. Julien, E. Chartrand, and M. Dube, "Females' Quality of Relationships in Adolescence and Friendship Support in Adulthood," *Candadian Journal of Behavioral Sciences, 41*, no. 3 (2009): 161–68.

3. Ibid.

THIRTEEN

Do Mothers Influence What We Want to Be When We Grow Up?

Even as the number of working mothers has grown substantially over the past three decades,[1] we are still getting a bad rap if we try to balance a job and a family,[2] even though "involved fathers" are patted on the back for taking time to spend quality time with the kids that mothers must be raising for them. Approximately 60 percent of mothers are working outside of the home, and 85 percent of them agree that they are "very happy" or "pretty happy," which is actually a higher percentage than of those who are stay-at-home mothers.[3] Conversely, 42 percent of us believe women really should not work outside the house at all.[4] It appears that especially aversive to us are mothers who make the choice to work because they *want* to work, not because they *need* to work, outside the home.[5] Mothers who are taking on traditionally male positions or clearly finding success in the workplace are also especially disliked. It is apparent that our culture still has a long way to go in terms of making the professional world a "woman's world," as well as a "mother's world."

Times may not be changing as quickly as we would like, but many of the mothers with whom we spoke are fully encouraging their daughters to seek fulfillment in their career aspirations. In addition, the daughters interviewed also shared their experiences with maternal encouragement in terms of vocational and educational attainment. It seems that even as the world of work keeps changing, the lessons shared through the generations are still consistent in that they address education, hard work, compensation, and vocational commitment. The recent recession did not just end through the increase of jobs for men, but women made a significant jump in breadwinning status—a double-digit percentage increase in the number of women who are earning as much or even more than their partners are.[6] However, women continue to do the same jobs for less pay

149

than men who hold the same position and levels of responsibility. In fact, women earn only about 77 percent of what a man makes in the same job.[7] Our daughters are part of an increasingly valuable source of energy and strength in the workplace, and it is clear that mothers, for the most part, are encouraging them to make wise decisions as they grow into their professional identities; for many of us, our first directive to our daughters is to seek an education.

EDUCATION

The value of an education is clear to mothers of preschool daughters all the way to mothers of fully grown daughters who are now mothers themselves. An older woman shared with us that "Mother said education is the key to having a great career." In fact, a college education is pretty much a "non-negotiable" step into adulthood for most women. As an early thirties African American woman recalled, "College was not an option—it was a requirement. By the time I was a senior in high school my mother had already applied to several colleges on my behalf, and it was a matter of negotiating which ones she and I agreed upon. There was no discussion, question, or debate on that one."

"[My mother] always stressed the importance of getting an educa-tion . . . I will need an education in order to progress, and once I receive that degree no one can take it away," recalled another woman. Her moth-er's point struck home for many daughters with whom we spoke in that education, unlike possessions, will be theirs forever and is a goal that is worth the energy and financial investment. She went on to note that it is best to get an education before other responsibilities start stacking up in a woman's life: "Get all of the education [you] can before starting a family, because life becomes hard when juggling school, work, and family time." When asked about the most important lesson she hopes to instill in her two daughters, thirteen and six years old, a thirty-seven-year-old re-sponded, "Education is the key. That's my motto around the house. I want them to be leaders and not followers. Independence!"

The perceived linear connection between education, career, and life success is etched into the American worldview. This sentiment was echoed by a twenty-two-year-old who noted that "my mother didn't fin-ish college, so she has always pushed me to go to college and become the best teacher I can be." A daughter's decision to follow an alternate path can leave lasting disappointment for a mother. When a sixty-five-year-old mother of a thirty-five-year-old daughter was invited to share about decisions her daughter had made that had been difficult for her to accept, she responded with only one. It was her daughter's decision "not to go to college." For women who were themselves unable to move into the world of higher education, this loss can influence their perceived sense of accomplishment throughout their lives. From a forty-four-year-old woman who was unable to make that first step on the path, we heard this regret, "I tried very hard to be better than my mother, but I realized too late that not getting my education first influenced everything else in my life. Surviving became the most important thing." The drive for daughters to live lives different from their mothers was a strong theme in terms of professional goals and paths.

NOT LIKE MY MOTHER

As the cultural expectations of a daughter's career success have shifted dramatically in the last few decades, so, too, have the individual ambitions of young girls, which especially may be fashioned by witnessing the struggles of their own mothers. When a woman in her thirties was asked about the career advice or direction she had received from her mother, she adamantly replied, "Nothing!! That's one of our differences. She has worked as a factory worker, and though there is nothing wrong with an honest living, but I've always wanted more for her. She has not had a full time job since 1999, [and she is] settling for these lousy part timers." The daughter of another lifelong factory worker shared that what she learned from watching her mother's employment path was that she wanted to make sure that she, herself, was successful in her own career, as she summed up, "[My mother] worked in a factory, and I knew that I did not want to do that."

In a related vein, mothers who have spent their lives in unfulfilling or unstable jobs often directly ask their daughters to learn from their examples. As a forty-four-year-old shared, "My mom worked up to three jobs at a time, and she stayed on us about getting an education so that we may never struggle as she did." "[My mother] wanted the best for me. She made sure I had every opportunity to be successful. She had less than a sixth-grade education, but she expected great things from me," shared a thirty-nine-year-old. As a counterpoint to this inspirational message, a woman in her fifties revealed, "Neither my mother or father finished high school, so they never pushed [education or career]. They just pushed me to find a good job and be a hard worker." These values of hard work and a strong work ethic are also frequently communicated from mothers to daughters.

HARD WORK PAYS OFF

The one piece of advice that daughters are given most often by their mothers regarding career is that they should work hard to be the best that they can be. Whether it is the simple directive "always do your best" or that "hard work pays off," a strong work ethic is being passed down between generations. Not only are mothers encouraging their daughters to be hard workers, there is also a message that success does not necessarily come easy. As one woman recalled being told, "It takes hard work and dedication to make it." In providing a similar message, another mother also invested in her daughter's self-esteem and self-worth as she passed along the lesson, "Be independent and strive to be the best that YOU can be. Give the best that you have to offer and know that it is enough."

Integrity and honesty are being instilled in daughters through such reminders as we must "give an honest day's work for our pay," or the affirmation that we have to "work hard for every dime we make." A fifty-two-year-old woman shared that even now, as she relates news to her mother about her promotions or increasing responsibilities on the job, her mother always reminds her, "Don't forget where you came from." Her daughter interprets this as her mother's edict that she should be mindful of the individuals she manages in addition to being a reminder that she shouldn't let her professional success influence her connections to her family-of-origin. Mothers can be extremely potent role models for their daughters regarding upward mobility and career achievement. One daughter was proud to share that her mother "climbed the corporate ladder over the years, and I admire that about her." A woman in her late twenties shared, "My mother taught me to work hard for everything that I want in life. She was an entrepreneur at heart; therefore creative in her career goals." An increasing number of women are joining the workforce as entrepreneurs and business owners,[8] and this can provide daughters with a wonderful resource and inspiration as they move into their own careers.

Career versus Job?

When a mother dreams about a daughter's future, it often includes seeing a young woman enjoying a fulfilling career, not toiling away at "just" a job. Moreover, the hopes of a mother might actually be important in shaping a daughter's aspirations and future professional life.[9] Researchers have shown that evolution plays a role in a mother's investment in her daughter—low-status parents (mothers) typically invest more strongly in their low-status offspring (daughters). In relation to this information, a recent longitudinal study found that a mother's hopes for her daughter's future play a stronger role in her daughter's adult outcome than a mother's aspirations for a son.[10] In fact, a mother's expectations of her ten-year-old daughter are related to her daughter's sense of control twenty years down the road at age thirty. In addition, it was found that a girl's level of internal locus of control, meaning a sense that she commands her own fate, has a direct relationship with her income as an adult. Thus, there are good reasons to encourage a young girl to strive for a career, not just a job; however, not every mother will do this.

The messages mothers send their daughters can create a sense of long-term regret in their girls. One woman noted that her mother had "not so much discussed career as much as having a job. I realized the difference later on in life." When asked about her mother's advice regarding a career, a now forty-year-old woman recalled sadly, "My mother wanted me to go to vo-tech in high school so that I could work in an office, she told me I'd never make it in the real world . . . and that I needed a man to take care of me." She elaborated to describe the lack of support her mother offered her when she was young: "My mom taught me that I could not be independent or have the ability to take care of myself . . . she also didn't see any reason for me to pursue an education outside of high school, so I can't really say that she taught me any valuable lessons. I think I learned more from my grandmother and my father." In response to the damage done to her own self-efficacy and self-worth by her mother, she is consciously parenting her own two daughters to believe in themselves and their potential. The lessons that she most wants to convey are that "being true to yourself is important and that following your dreams is also important." She has created a richer, supportive relationship with her girls and feels proud that they are able to discuss their fears and hopes with her. Another mother, though, feels that all of the efforts she has made to encourage her daughter to succeed were fruitless—and she feels that the values she modeled were ignored: "My daughter has not tried to excel as much as she is capable of career wise. I fear she is 'settling,' and I continually strived to be the very best." Mothers, like counselors and teachers, can only plant the seeds—they cannot force growth to occur on their own timetables.

Do What You Love and Love What You Do

Many of us have seen the inspirational poster or coffee mug decorated with the adage that titles this section—two decades ago, my officemates gave me the mug as a going-away gift as I moved to a new job some thousand miles away. This was an important reminder to a young career girl all those years ago—raised by a well-educated, extremely intelligent mother who had "settled," herself, for a job, not a career, I wanted to make good and make my parents, especially my mother, proud. Fortunately, the primary career advice received throughout my life was that I had the power to reach my goals and that I should do something that brought happiness to my life. Although I would follow a few dead-end paths and fall down a rabbit hole or two, my mother's advice always carried me on to the next career opportunity and adventure.

As one woman was told by her mother, "Get it while you can. . . . There is so much opportunity to take advantage of!" Ideally, following the right career opportunity will involve a love story between a girl and her job, as well as bring professional satisfaction. A young woman in her early twenties recalled:

> My mother has told me since I was a little girl that I can be anything I want to be, and with hard work, dedication, and God I can get here. Maybe not always on my time and in my way, but in a way that if I truly work for it, I will succeed.

Believing that our daughters have what it takes to achieve their dreams will make them that more likely to come true.[11] Always verbally reminded by her mother that "if you have a dream, live it out," a young woman recalled that her mother had modeled this adage. Fifteen years ago, her mother opened her first retail clothing store, and that was a dream that her mother had held onto since her own childhood. For another young woman whose mother has not been able to realize her own dreams, she is grateful that her mother has worked hard to allow her daughter to reach for her dreams. She shared her mother's view on a career:

> That was the most important thing to her. My mother isn't very educated and never had a chance to live her dreams. But she always told me that I could be and do anything that I wanted to and that the resources were available. She encouraged and supported me to go to college and achieve the things that she hadn't been able to achieve . . . career was very important in my family.

Many women shared memories of the hopes their mothers had that they would find a job that would allow them to be not just successful, but happy as well. As one woman shared, her mother told her to "choose something that I will be passionate about and love for the rest of my life." Some mothers are able to let their daughters know that it is happiness, not cash, that is the measure of career satisfaction. A thirty-something woman shared that she had been raised to believe that "money isn't everything—if you don't like the job you have, look for something that will make you happy and be dependable." Not only should a job be "dependable," but also many women feel strongly that its compensation should allow them to be *independent*.

Becoming Independent

Although we are reminded that "money isn't everything," many young women are being educated about the value of a dollar and the need to earn a sufficient number of them to allow them to be self-sufficient. The wisdom passed down to one woman was a three-part litany: 1) a career is a necessity; 2) independence is a must; and 3) independence should be attained before sharing her life with anyone. Her mother wanted her to have a better life than she, herself, had lived. Another woman in her thirties shared that her mother had always instilled the importance of work, and she was warned, "Don't look for handouts—you have to get things for yourself." A forty-three-year-old was told to "choose a career that pays a lot of money so that [she] wouldn't have to depend upon a man to take care of [her]." Another young woman recalled her mother's down-to-earth advice: "She taught me how important it is to be able to stand on your own two feet without needing the financial support of someone, because you never know when tragedy will strike or when life will take unexpected turns."

Once upon a time, girls might have been expected to go to college only to earn a *Mrs.* degree, but independence and career success are now the preferred outcomes of a college education. Today, the opportunities that college can offer in terms of career choice and career success are the focus. Although not every mother sees college as the ticket to a good life for her daughter, there is wisdom in encouraging daughters to find a job that brings independence and satisfaction of both the financial and personal kinds. Whether a mother encourages a daughter to "obtain a career that is enjoyable and make enough money to live comfortably" or "get a good job to enjoy the finer things in life," or "choose a career that you love and are passionate about doing, not for the money," the message is clear that daughters are on the receiving end of heartfelt educational and career advice. A young girl reported being encouraged by her mother "to get my degree and aim for a career, NOT a job." This is advice that crossed age barriers as well as cultural barriers.

Cultural Beliefs Shifting?

We wondered if there were any unique cultural differences—beyond generational influence—in career input from mothers to their daughters. Although there are suggestions that Asian women, traditionally, were less likely to envision personal career identities,[12] it appears that a mother's influence may be shifting this pattern. A mother can positively affect a daughter's self-image, and it has been found that a close and connected relationship between mother and daughter may actually inspire a daughter to move toward a professional career path. On the opposite end of the spectrum, it turns out that daughters with conflict-laden relationships with their mothers may also have a stronger sense of self-efficacy about their careers.[13] Although this particular finding was developed based on a sample of Asian daughters, it makes sense that the results translate across cultures. Researchers suggested that the negative emotions (such as guilt, anger, and resentment) that are typically experienced during the years in which emerging adults struggle against parental control may help propel young adult women toward greater self-reliance as they work to gain autonomy from their mothers. As the sense of autonomy increases, the sense of self-efficacy about the ability to manage a new adult identity also grows.

Holding nontraditional sex-role stereotypes can also support the de-velopment of vocational aspirations. In congruence with the research, a young Asian woman we interviewed shared what her mother had ad-vised her in terms of career: "Be career-oriented and financially stable. Don't depend on anyone for financial stability. Even if you have to [rely on others], don't be so vulnerable that if you are left alone, you can't survive and take care of yourself." Another woman shared that her moth-er had always encouraged her to "be independent." These mothers clear-ly recognize the need for self-sufficiency, indicating the rejection of the once traditional assumption than women need men to ensure that their survival resource needs are met.

BALANCING ACTS

Some of us are encouraged by our mothers to prepare for the balancing act that we need to master to manage a career and a family. We have found out that this can be a challenge for all women, regardless of how much money we earn. Some of the biggest challenges are long hours on the job as well as the lack of support from others as we face an oversized workload.[14] These three circumstances are also examples of the type of situation that can quickly throw off the delicate balance achieved by working mothers—too much time away from home, too much work, and too little support—or even empathy—from others on the job or in the home! Moreover, those of us who are unable to keep the balance are more likely to be coping with physical and mental health concerns as well as suffer from lower satisfaction at work and at home.[15]

Researchers have frequently explored the success of women in high-status occupations, those who are able to "break the glass ceiling" or "have it all," which usually means paid help and live-in childcare. The experiences of those mothers who are waiting on these "having it all mothers" in discount stores or fast food restaurants seem to get much less attention, and yet they face the toughest challenge keeping things bal-anced! In one of a few studies on this group, researchers found that low-wage earners had a difficult time handling the frequently unpredictable work demands alongside their family's demands.[16] An interesting find-ing of this research was the way in which a woman's *moral identity* influ-enced her success in achieving and maintaining a balance between di-verse poles of obligation. In essence, our need to be a good mother was often translated into the need to be a responsible employee. Thus, it seems that the greater drive we have to succeed in the role of mother is directly correlated with the need to succeed in the role of employee. Helping our daughters prepare for taking on the dual roles required of working mothers is a priority for some, as we learned through our inter-views.

WHO'S TAKING CARE OF THE KIDS?

In most cases, mothers are directly influencing their daughters' plans to stay home and raise their children or enter the workforce and leave the children's daily care to others.[17] If a mother is able to manage successfully both career and family life, then her daughters will be more likely to follow in those footsteps. It is not surprising, however, that fathers who are able to spend a significant amount of time with their children in addition to keeping their career path on track are called "involved fathers," but the mothers who are able to accomplish both tasks are merely called "working mothers." The double standard of care is likely to be a part of our culture for another generation or so, and this may continue to influence young children's career goals. Researchers have found that young women frequently assume that their professional trajectory will probably include times of full-time, part-time, and no employment as they move through the reproductive trajectory.[18] One interviewee shared that while her mother taught her the importance of having a career, she also emphasized that she should "find the balance between work life and home life."

My Place Is Home

Just as some little girls are encouraged to imagine themselves as businesswomen carrying their laptop bag as they board the corporate jet, there are those who are still encouraged to imagine themselves carrying diaper bags and sippy cups as they load up the stroller for a walk to the park. A few years ago, researchers looked at the generation of women who came of age during the times in which a woman's place was definitely in the home as compared to the generation of daughters that they raised.[19] They found that although about two-thirds of the older generation had been less professionally successful than their daughters had been, there wasn't really any negative fallout regarding their self-esteem or satisfaction with their choices. In fact, the older generation felt quite good about having spent their time caring for their children. Caring for kids and a house was also recalled as being a much easier task than what they believed their daughters were trying to accomplish by balancing work and family responsibilities.

Earning money and helping provide for a family can be a necessity, but some mothers reiterate that their daughter's family responsibilities should take priority over any job. One twenty-four-year-old woman was taught a similar belief: "My mom did not have a career. She took care of the family, so I guess she taught me that having a career is not important." From a twenty-two-year-old, we heard that her mother had taught her that raising a family is more important than a career. Family values, and expectations about women's roles, reflect family experience. One fifty-one-year-old shared that her mother was a product of her times in that she believed "boys should get an education and girls should stay home barefoot and pregnant." Although there may be some exaggeration in her retelling of the lesson, there is enough truth that her professional achievements are still difficult subjects for her to share with her mother. To sum up this section, here are the words of a thirty-four-year-old who is looking forward to having her first child and shaping her career trajectory around her own vision: "[A career] can be good, but being a stay-at-home mom is good, too."

CONCLUSION

To answer the question posed in this chapter title about maternal influence on girls' career goals, we reply with a resounding "yes!" Empirical studies, qualitative studies, and our own interviews clearly indicate how strongly influenced daughters can be by their mothers' career advice. The messages most clearly communicated are that mothers would like to see their daughters achieve a high measure of happiness in their careers and that mothers believe their daughters are capable of achieving whatever their professional goals may be. Higher education is a "given" for most of the young women growing up today, and this is seen as a "first step" on the career trajectory. Young women are also being reminded to work hard for their goals and to work toward financial independence. No longer do mothers dream of their daughters marrying a doctor or lawyer; they are joining in their daughters' dreams of professional accomplishment on whatever career path it takes.

NOTES

1. U.S. Department of Labor, Bureau of Labor Statistics, "Women in the Labor Force: A Databook (2010 Edition)," 2011. Retrieved from http://www.bls.gov/cps/wlf-databook-2011.pdf.

2. T. G. Okimoto and M. E. Heilman, "The 'Bad Parent' Assumption: How Gender Stereotypes Affect Reactions to Working Mothers," *Journal of Social Sciences, 68,* no. 4 (2012): 704–24.

3. Pew Research Center, U.S. Bureau of Labor, Harvard Business Review, September 2012.

4. Ibid.

5. Okimoto and Heilman, "The 'Bad Parent' Assumption."

6. S. J. Glynn, "The New Breadwinners: 2010 Update," Center for American Progress, April 2012. Retrieved from www.americanprogress.org/issues/labor/report/2012/04/16/11377/the-new-breadwinners-2010-update/.

7. A. Hegewisch, C. Williams, & A. Henderson, *The Gender Wage Gap by Occupation,* Institute for Women's Policy Research, April 2011. Retrieved from www.iwpr.org/publications/pubs/the-gender-wage-gap-by-occupation-updated-april-2011 from the website.

8. S. Gelardin, "Narratives: A Key to Uncovering Mother-Daughter Influences on Life and Work," *Career Planning and Adult Development Journal, 17* (2001): 135–47.

9. E. Flouri and D. Hawkes, "Ambitious Mothers—Successful Daughters: Mothers' Early Expectations for Children's Education and Children's Earnings and Sense of Control in Adult Life," *British Journal of Educational Psychology, 78* (2008): 411–33.

10. Ibid.

11. Ibid.

12. H. Song, "The Mother-Daughter Relationship as a Resource for Korean Women's Career Aspirations," *Sex Roles: A Journal of Research, 44* (2001): 79–97.

13. C. Mao, Y. Hsu, and T. Fang, "The Role of the Mother-Daughter Relationship in Taiwanese College Students' Career Self-Efficacy," *Social Behavior and Personality, 40,* no. 9 (2012): 1511–22.

14. I. Losoncz and N. Bortolotto, "Work-Life Balance: The Experiences of Australian Working Mothers," *Journal of Family Studies, 15* (2009): 122–38.

15. Ibid.

16. K. Backett-Milburn, L. Airey, L. McKie, and G. Hogg, "Family Comes First or Open All Hours?: How Low Paid Women Working in Food Retailing Manage Webs of Obligation at Home and Work," *Sociological Review, 56,* no. 3 (2008): 474–96.

17. M. Fulcher and E. F. Coyle, "Breadwinner and Caregiver: A Cross-Sectional Analysis of Children's and Emerging Adults' Visions of Their Future Family Roles," *British Journal of Developmental Psychology, 29* (2011): 330–46.

18. E. D. Looker and P. A. Magee, "Gender and Work: The Occupational Expectations of Young Women and Men in the 1990s," *Gender Issues, 18* (2000): 74–88.

19. D. Carr, "'My Daughter Has a Career; I Just Raised Babies': The Psychological Consequences of Women's Intergenerational Social Comparisons," *Social Psychology Quarterly, 67,* no. 2 (2004): 132–54.

FOURTEEN

Lessons in Economics and Finance

What lessons do you most want to convey to your daughter about money? What do you wish that you had been taught by your own mother about finance? For many families, discussions about financial affairs are still one of the basic taboos—growing up, many of us were taught that money, age, and politics were subjects never to be broached or questioned in our homes. Of course, sex was another generally verboten topic, but it was a sensitive enough subject that many families did not even talk about *not talking* about it. In this chapter, we will share what we discovered about the sharing of information about finances and family economics between mothers and daughters. While one young woman we interviewed noted that the only lesson she had learned from her mother about financial issues was that you should "[n]ever discuss them with your children," it is important to bear in mind that a mother's openness to discussing finances with her daughter may play a significant role in her financial, psychological, and personal well-being.[1]

MUM'S THE WORD?

As the economy has been riding the waves of a tsunami for the past decade, many families are being forced to acknowledge—some overtly and some covertly—the influence cash flow has on a family's lifestyle, although many parents still consider money to be a taboo topic.[2] Separation, divorce, single parenthood, and organizational downsizing are just a few of the environmental/cultural factors that may substantially affect the financial freedom of a family. For the generation of women coming of age in the 1950s and 1960s, education about money matters may have been as minimal as the sharing of the adages "save for a rainy day" and "two can live as cheaply as one." Mothers might also have suggested that their daughters keep a little "mad money" at hand, in case of emergencies or irresistible impulse purchases. Although a large number of women are still being encouraged to save for that "rainy day," in just those words, the areas that are least likely to receive explicit discussion include family income, family savings, and family debt.[3]

Researchers have shared that mothers are still hesitant to discuss family finances with their daughters, although 87 percent of graduating high school seniors consider their parents the primary information source for their financial education.[4] As a topic of family conversation, money has similarity to the topics of drug/alcohol use and education—parents' perspectives and opinions are the ones that close these topics in a conversation.[5] Examples of the final authority a mother would convey to her daughter in these areas might include the conversation stoppers, "just say no," "finish your homework," or "we can't afford it."

Other researchers have found that a fair number of parents are more comfortable talking about sex and dating or drug and alcohol use than about money.[6] Mothers may find it a lot easier to tell their daughters to "just say no" than "start a 401K savings plan as soon as you can." Mothers are models for their daughters in virtually all aspects of adult womanhood, so it can be especially important that they recognize the messages that are transmitted about financial matters through their behavior, not just their words. Cynthia, a yoga teacher in her early fifties, still worries about the messages she sent to her young daughter whom she delivered when she was just a teenager:

> Our relationship has been anything but conventional or normal; it was dysfunctional, at best. I had her when I was a baby myself at seventeen years of age. No time to be having a child . . . Of course, at seventeen and a dropout from school, my resources were meager and so was my support system. Soon she would be swept away from me to be cared for by my mother until I could get my so-called act together. That would be years and mournful tears away. Had I known then what I know now, things would be very different for us . . . But as a satellite mother, at best, and working a million different jobs, sometimes all at once, trying to make a living for us would prove to be hopeless. Working so much left little time for me to be with her, let alone care for her. I was on the wheel of no end.

Over two decades later, she still worries that her daughter may have a skewed view of the financial hardships and sacrifices experienced as an integral aspect of how their mother-daughter relationship evolved. It is also a testament to the research finding that mothers who are separated, divorced, or raising their daughters on their own are likely to be motivated to address family financial issues with their daughters.[7, 8]

"GENERALLY SPEAKING" VERSUS "BEING SPECIFIC"

In a recent qualitative research study, Lynsey Romo interviewed parents to explore their experiences in discussing financial issues with their children.[9] She found that while parents were willing to provide more general education about finances to their children, they typically did not discuss a family's financial specifics such as income, budget, assets, and others. The reasons behind the reticence included *protecting* children from a concern not their own as well as an acknowledgement of the pervasive general taboo about discussing money matters. In our own conversations with mothers of daughters, we asked what lessons they most wanted to convey to their daughters as they grew into adulthood. Only about a quarter of the mothers queried responded with lessons related to financial matters.

Gender also may play a role, as many women we interviewed noted that it was traditionally a male's responsibility to handle a family's financial affairs. However, for those mothers who did touch on this area, their aspirations centered on hoping their daughters would be able to be self-sufficient in life, work hard, and be financially secure. One mother stated simply that she wants her daughter to be able to "balance a checkbook!" Of those who strived to teach their daughters about independence, a sixty-three-year-old mother of two daughters shared that she and her husband sought to instill in their daughters the acknowledgment that "you need to be with a man by choice, not necessity." The need for young women to be financially self-sufficient is well supported by the statistics showing the shrinking number of women who marry and the increasing age at which they do. So what are the lessons that are being taught by our mothers about money?

LEARNING WHAT NOT TO DO

Although we may not consciously consider financial lessons as those we most want to impart to our daughters, it is clear from our interviewees that both spoken and tacit lessons are being passed along by their mothers. Some lessons may be less overt than others may, as noted by a young woman who revealed, "We didn't talk much about financial matters. I just knew that I wanted to make a life for myself where I didn't have to struggle or live paycheck to paycheck." Having witnessed her mother's struggles, she wanted to live an easier life, as she knew the hardships associated with financial stress. This young woman also admitted that she and her mother never really discussed sex, either; communication was through more modeling and informal interactions than verbal disclosures.

Not only was one twenty-five-year-old interviewee's mother not in a position to care for her when she was born, neither her mother nor grandmother were in a good place to educate her on financial matters. When asked what she had been taught about money growing up, she responded, "Not much at all. I was raised by my grandmother who also was not able really to support me with this [education]. I had to learn the hard way about financial matters." Another woman sadly responded that she, too, had received no explicit information about finances as she shared that she was taught "nothing. I [saw my mother] struggle and choose cigarettes and men and such. She would spend her last [dime] and we hardly had food to eat." These women are not alone, as many women believed that their mothers offered little worthwhile education regarding finances, as one woman summed up, "[My mother] is poor with finances; if anything, she taught us how *not* to be financially stable!" Hoping to change the tide of financial illiteracy being passed down to another generation, one woman shared that "financial matters [weren't] discussed . . . hard lessons were learned as I got older, which is one reason why I started discussing [the topic] with my son from the age of six."

EXPLICIT EDUCATION ABOUT M . . . O . . . N . . . E . . . Y

In talking with women of different ethnicities about the financial education they received, it was interesting to discover that our racial identity may influence the most frequently shared lessons between mothers and daughters. Findings from a recent study indicated that adolescents from higher-income African American families had greater financial knowledge than those from lower-income homes, yet Caucasian students from lower-income families had greater financial knowledge than those from higher-income homes.[10] The young women in this study had more overall knowledge than young men, perhaps because mothers were more likely to discuss financial topics than fathers were. We, too, found many themes were shared across cultures in our own interviews, but the messages and the emphases were frequently quite distinct based on culture.

Save, Save, Save

We found that African American mothers appeared much more likely to stress the importance of saving money above all other lessons. Whether the goal was preparing "for a rainy day" (a phrase that clearly has withstood the test of time as it was recalled by daughters from their late teen to their sixties) or planning for retirement, saving money is considered a priority by many women. A thirty-year-old African American woman shared the following story about her mother's efforts to instill good financial habits in her from a young age:

> Well, she was not too savvy financially, but she made me deposit all my money for summer jobs into a checking account, and I had to budget and plan for what I would spend that money on. Fast food purchases were not an option—LOL. . . . [And] I loved french fries! She taught me to pay bills on time, as well.

African American mothers were also were more likely to explicitly address the necessity of paying bills on time and building and maintaining credit. One woman recalls her mother's admonition to her: "Always handle your business. Your credit and character define a large part of who you are." A thirty-seven-year-old woman recalled her mother telling her, "Make your own money, child. And keep your credit. . . . If you don't have good credit, you don't have nothing."

Religious Values

For those of us who grow up in strongly religious homes, we generally learn early about the importance of tithing to our churches. Although this message was shared by women of different cultures, it was more prevalently a financial lesson explicitly shared between African American mothers and daughters. A twenty-two-year-old was taught early "that my Father God supplies all my needs according to His riches . . . and to be led by the Holy Ghost with my finances and to always pay my tithes first!" The need to be a good steward of both one's faith and one's finances was a well-instilled message. Another woman recalled that her mother told her that she should tithe first, save a little next, and then budget the amount that was left for daily needs.

Living within Your Means

The Caucasian women we interviewed were more likely to recall messages about "living within your means" as the primary explicit financial admonition of their mothers. One woman shared that her mother used the example, "even if something only costs a dollar, if you don't have a dollar, then you can't afford it." Yet this message was definitely reiterated by women from all cultural identities in our interviews. One young Asian respondent shared her mother's wisdom about money by noting that in her family culture, they had the saying, "spread your legs only so far as your blanket can cover them," indicating that she should not try to live beyond her means. Whether directed to "live within your means" or "don't spend more than you have," the message of spending wisely is a correlate of this message that was often directly addressed.

Spend Wisely

When you reflect on the messages you received from your own mother about *spending* money, what stands out for you? We received a wide variety of lessons taught regarding this topic. Frugality is an explicit lesson many of us may learn from our mothers. One forty-eight-year-old Caucasian recalled that her mother advised her, "do not over extend" and that her mother would tease her as an adolescent that she had "champagne taste on a beer budget, even though she didn't drink!" Some of us are reminded that it is foolish to waste money on items that are not on sale, and many of us have learned the importance of "bargain shopping" by watching our mothers in action. Other daughters, however, may learn a different lesson from their mothers, as one thirty-four-year-old woman recalled, "She did not teach me very much because she did enjoy shopping and the best things in life."

For many of us, explicit lessons are often shared regarding the decision-making process of which items are worth an investment—one woman mentioned that her mother warned her to buy a house, not a new car, as houses always increased in value whereas new cars depreciated the moment they "left the lot." Of course, the housing crises we have witnessed in the recent past may make this suggestion less of a truism, but mothers try to do their best to encourage their daughters to make smart purchases.

One young woman recalled that her mother warned her that she would have to work to buy the things she wanted. A thirty-year-old African American woman was amused to share the following bit of wisdom shared by her mother: "This is funny, but my mom's thing is that if you want things, you will have bills. Just get things little by little and don't put yourself in a financial crisis." Another thirty-year-old shared a somewhat similar piece of advice from her mother: "Always try to save a 'nest egg,' but don't deprive yourself . . . you deserve to buy the things that you want."

A similar message was recalled by a twenty-nine-year-old as she described her mother's advice: "Well, she was not the best steward over money. She liked nice things and she was willing to work hard to survive and enjoy the things she desired." Many women are victims of "self-esteem sabotage," as they feel they must put others' needs first and only do for themselves if there is something left over. Therefore, these explicit beliefs passed along that women and their daughters deserve the best may indicate a needed positive shift in culturally gendered expectations. Self-worth is often tied up into the acquisition of possessions for many women, and the ability to treat ourselves well and do so independently is a strong theme in some mother-daughter communications.

Love or Money?

A young woman who is in the midst of the "emerging adult" stage, which also indicates that she is focused on the Eriksonian conflict of intimacy versus isolation, was given lessons on finance in terms of long-term relationship partnering. This twenty-two-year-old's mother had stressed the importance of financial matters to her and impressed upon her that financial well-being affects every aspect of daily life, and most especially, a marriage. The young woman related, "My mom taught me that money cannot buy happiness, but it sure does help. She taught me that in looking for a spouse, love does matter, but so does [a spouse's potential for] providing for me and my future family; stability is not always certain in any field, but being financially able is the best way to be." The lessons her mother taught her regarding finance also carry meta-messages about the roles women and men are expected to play in committed relationships. While this young woman is being prepped to find a mate on whom she can depend for economic stability, many women are hoping to instill a strong sense of financial autonomy in their daughters.

Financial Independence Is Valued

Regardless of cultural identity, women are committed to teaching their daughters to avoid being economically dependent on anyone else. As one twenty-four-year-old shared, "My mother taught me that I should always be independent and to always have my own money. She taught me to never ask for money from men because men would use that as a way to take advantage of a woman." Mothers who were not financially independent themselves may often be the most vocal on this issue. Many women who were unable to get on their feet financially, much less stay on their feet, would like to see a better economic outcome for their daughters. One woman recalled her mother telling her, "Sometimes it will get hard, but don't stop going, and never give up!" Even the woman cited earlier, whose mother enjoyed "nice things," was told by her mother that she needed to always have a job and her own money, because "even when I get married, it is still possible to be an individual." Another important lesson that we may want to teach our daughters is that having a strong work ethic is directly tied to less financial stress. We will further address lessons on work and career in a subsequent chapter, but many women are encouraged early to build strong professional and work ethics as an aspect of financial education.

Some women are forced to learn financial lessons the hard way rather than through early training. As one woman recalled, "My mother never discussed finances with me or showed me how to take care of things. I had no idea how to do things when I left her home. I had to rely 100 percent on my ex-husband to take care of me." When she divorced her husband, she was forced to learn how to manage bills and a household independently for the first time. Somewhat similar to divorce, death is another integral life transition through which financial education can be passed along.

When a mother has the financial smarts to keep her affairs in order, it can be an unexpected gift and learning opportunity for a daughter. A thirty-four-year-old daughter shared a poignant, yet motivating, story about her mother's final affairs:

> She was great about saving money, and she had all her affairs in order when she died! Everything was taken care of; we didn't have to struggle to try to afford to bury my mom. She had more than one insurance policy and had a retirement plan, as well.

While her mother's choices during her life bespoke a strong understanding of financial concerns regarding end-of-life issues and provided a valuable example of how to manage one's business affairs, hopefully we can provide this same information to our daughters while we are still around to discuss these topics! Encouraging our daughters to see the big picture financially—not just the present moment—can help them make decisions that will allow them to be confident, financially independent women.

IS IT ABOUT THE "MONEY, MONEY, MONEY"?

Even in light of the sobering statistics on divorce, our culture still sends young girls the message that happiness is found in finding a successful husband who earns lots of money, owning expensive designer clothing, and living in a beautifully decorated McMansion in the "right" neighborhood. Luckily, many mothers are doing their best to encourage their daughters to view happiness as an experience, not a commodity that could be tied to a scale of dollars and cents. Many of our interviewees were told that while money might "make the world go round," it certainly would not buy happiness. A woman in her late twenties was taught to value money but to refrain from making money the most important goal in her life. Another mother communicated a similar message to her twenty-something daughter: "Money and possessions are not important to be happy, but money is necessary in order to obtain necessities." Encouraging our daughters to view financial health as just one aspect of overall well-being can prepare them to recognize that joy is not found in the acquisition of material goods but in the everyday experiences in life. In addition, being able to independently manage their finances can provide a sense of security that will contribute even more so to their overall feelings of satisfaction and accomplishment in life.

GIVING CREDIT WHERE CREDIT IS DUE

As we have shared, there is a range of lessons that are transmitted from mothers to daughters from generation to generation about money. While we receive both overt and covert messages about financial health, spending, saving, and managing credit, there are some of us who receive explicit financial management training from their mothers. As one young woman responded to the question of what she had been taught by her mother, "Everything! My mother does all the home finances, and she is very practical. She taught me to live within my means and that financial peace is a must!" Another woman shared about her own mother that "she taught me that I should always have good to great credit. She also taught me how to manage and budget my money. She helped me open up my first banking account . . . which I still have." Whether we are learning from our mothers' examples or learning from their mistakes, money matters are an essential area about which we must educate our daughters.

SHE NEEDS TO KNOW . . .

The economy is an unpredictable force, and we should be consciously providing as broad an education as we can for our daughters regarding sound financial decision making and money management techniques. To help our daughters avoid financial disasters or short-term shortfalls, we should provide them with 1) knowledge about the value of money and the work involved in earning it; 2) the need to understand the basic economics of income and expenses on a short-term and long-term basis; 3) the importance of saving for future purchases rather than being overwhelmed by debt; 4) planning for retirement; 5) balancing their bank statements; and 6) developing a strategy for financial independence, regardless of their marital status. By providing an economic education to our daughters, we are giving them the tools to appreciate their net worth as well as their self-worth.

THE BOTTOM LINE

In closing, we would like to share a final bit of our interview with Cynthia, the yoga teacher we mentioned earlier, who clearly is still trying to find balance in her relationship with her daughter. In reflecting on the financial lessons she was inadvertently teaching her preschool daughter about the value of paid income as she struggled to make ends meet as a single mother, she shared this story:

> My favorite story was when my daughter was about three or four years of age, and I was getting ready for work in my mother's bathroom, as

she sometimes allowed me to stay there. I heard "Mommy, Mommy" from the hallway [and the sound of little footsteps] running toward the bathroom. I opened the door to see my daughter, Amber, holding a paper bag of loose change saying, "Mommy, Mommy . . . look you don't have to work anymore, we are rich!" . . . Needless to say, all of the makeup I had just put on my go-to-work face had to be redone from my crying over such beautiful innocence.

I still cry when I think of it, and now that my daughter is a mother, I watch her picking up the pieces from where I left off. She learned from me what not to do as she discovers now on her own what to do. When she was expecting her firstborn and was struggling with work decisions, I told her that being a mother is the most important job she will ever have. Even though we are now older and I am still her mother, I realize how much I missed out. I am a grandmother now, and this is the second most important job I have and one that I love.

NOTES

1. J. Serido, S. Shim, A. Mishra, and C. Tang, "Financial Parenting, Financial Coping Behaviors, and Well-Being of Emerging Adults," *Family Relations, 59*, no. 4 (2010): 453–64.

2. L. K. Romo, "Money Talks: Revealing and Concealing Financial Information in Families," *Journal of Family Communication, 11*, no. 4 (2011): 264–81.

3. M. W. Allen, "Consumer Finance and Parent-Child Communication," in J. J. Xiao (ed.), *The Handbook of Consumer Finance Research*, 351–61 (New York: Springer, 2008).

4. Capital One, As High School Graduates Open their Gifts, Parents Have Key Opportunity to Talk Money Management, June 14, 2011, retrieved from http://phx.corporate-ir.net/phoenix.zhtml?c=70667&p=irol-newsArticle&ID=1573673&highlight.

5. L. A. Baxter and C. Akkoor, "Topic Expansiveness and Family Communication Patterns," *Journal of Family Communication, 11* (2011): 1–20.

6. ING Direct Harris Interactive Poll.

7. S. S. Koerner, S. L. Jacobs, and M. Raymond, "When Mothers Turn to Their Adolescent Daughters: Predicting Daughters' Vulnerability to Negative Adjustment Outcomes," *Family Relations, 49*, no. 3 (2000): 301–9.

8. S. J. Lehman and S. S. Koerner, "Family Financial Hardship and Adolescent Girls' Adjustment: The Role of Maternal Disclosure of Financial Concerns," *Merrill-Palmer Quarterly, 48* (2002): 1–24.

9. Romo, "Money Talks."

10. P. O. Mullins, "Financial Knowledge and Communication of Teenagers and Their Parent or Guardian," [Abstract]. *Dissertation Abstracts International Section A: Humanities and Social Sciences, 68*, no. 12-A (2008): 5220.

IV

The Maternal Legacy

FIFTEEN

Shaping a Daughter's Identity

MOTHERING A DAUGHTER AND DAUGHTERING A MOTHER

I doubt that many of us made it through our girlhood and adolescence without vowing at least once, "I'll *never* be like my mother when I grow up!" Then, at some point in our lives as we move into young womanhood, we may catch a glimpse of ourselves in the mirror or listen to something we have said aloud, and we are startled to realize just how much *like* our mothers we actually are! This can be a shocking revelation for some of us, as we saw so clearly—from our own perspectives and limited vision—the faults and failings of our mothers. Fundamentally shaped by our mother's presence in our lives, she is both a model and a responder to our own behaviors, even our frustrations and ruminations.[1] We gauge the acceptable realm of responses to life's events, in a large part, based on our mother's interactions with the world and with us. This truth invites an exploration of how we, as mothers, might consciously mother our daughters in such a way that we allow them to blossom as daughters and into women.

ALLOWING DAUGHTERS "TO DAUGHTER" THEIR MOTHERS

How do you, as a woman, *daughter* your mother? In 1993, J. van Mens-Verhulst, J. Schreurs, and I. Woertman authored a book in which they repurposed the noun, *daughter*, into a verb, *to daughter*.[2] We all understand that children are mothered, but it may seem like a totally new concept to ponder as we recognize that female offspring actually "daughter their mothers." Van Mens-Verhulst and colleagues used this term to describe the state of a girl/woman *being in relation to* her mother. A few years later, van Mens-Verhulst[3] went on to assert that by *daughtering*,

173

girls/women are present to receive the love of their mothers as well as to elicit the love of our mothers. From our early years, we are refining our ability to solicit actively the love and validation we need, such as being sweet, obedient, or loving, in order to receive a mother's approval. Our subjectivity, as daughters, develops as we work to differentiate, or become independent and separate beings, from our mothers, such as when an adolescent daughter begins to resent and rebel against her mother's rules. In effect, according to van Mens-Verhulst, daughters must reorganize their perspectives in a fourfold manner as they grow into adult daughters. These address the following areas: 1) differentiation from mothers; 2) awareness and knowing the physical self; 3) adolescent turbulence and development; and 4) acceptance of the inevitable aging and decline of parents. The following sections will expand on her ideas as we present related findings from our own qualitative research.

DAUGHTERLY DIFFERENTIATION

The first task faced by a daughter involves differentiation from her mother and acceptance of her mother as a woman with both strengths and flaws. As daughters, we must seek to give shape to our own identities and separate from our mothers, at the personal level, sociostructural level, and the symbolic level.[4] Not only are we shaping our own identities as daughters and women, we are also, by default, redefining our ideas of who our mothers[5] are and what they represent. As we move from childhood into adolescence and then into adulthood, our perspectives related to the power and authority held by our mothers will shift. As children, we clearly need our mothers to be sovereign rulers and omnipotent caretakers. Attachment theory suggests that an infant believes that she and her mother are a single entity. As the child increases in perceptual skills, however, she realizes that they are separate beings, and this new recognition gives rise to separation anxiety. We depend on the caretaking and the emotional embrace of our mothers, and, as children, we often believe our mothers to be "all powerful." A popular humorist some years ago, Erma Bombeck, noted that as her children grew older, she missed those days when her children believed she could blow on the stoplights to make them turn green.[6] Yet for our daughters to develop into self-confident adults, we must allow them to revision motherhood and mothers in a way that allows for imperfections and humanness in their embodiment. Only by encouraging our daughters to see our fallibility and our acceptance of our own shortcomings will we be able to give them the freedom to accept themselves as they are.

Many mothers may be reluctant to give up the image of omniscient, omnipotent authority in the family. Seldom do working mothers enjoy the full amount of respect that should be theirs—either in the home or at the workplace. For many mothers in traditional two-parent households, their male counterparts may hold the place at the head of the table. Thus, mothers may enjoy the opportunity to be seen by their daughters as powerful and flawless. A generation of mothers of emerging adult daughters today were raised on the "Aviance night" philosophy that we may drudge through the daily housekeeping chores or nine-to-five work-day but by evening we are expected to be ready to be the objects of our partners' sexual desire. While this myth of having it all surrounded the upbringing of many young women in the 1970s and 1980s, the fear of not being able to have—and keep—it all still keeps many of us from allowing our daughters to "see us sweat." Being a mother is a difficult job, and yet we are often doubly taxed to maintain a sense of calm competence even when facing plumbing emergencies, children's calamities, muddy paw prints from pets, and dinner guests on the way.

A sense of satisfaction can be found in being seen as capable of magic by our daughters—whether it is the ability to blow on the stoplight to make it turn green, banish the monsters in the closet, kiss away the pain of a skinned knee, or heal hurt feelings with gentle words. A now twenty-four-year-old daughter remembers a time when she and her younger brother were occasionally whisked up the stairs at bedtime in a race to the top, she in their mother's arms and he in their father's. Although the first parent on the stairs would always win the "race," Gigi was still young enough to believe that there was a mystery in who would be the victor. One evening, she recalled, she and her mother were two stairs behind her father and brother, yet she and her mother ended up in the children's shared bedroom first. The story behind the surprise finish was that her father had stopped for a moment on the stairs, and Gigi and her mother had kept moving past them. Two decades later, Gigi still enjoys sharing the story of the "magic" outcome of that bedtime race and contin-ues to keep the magic alive by wondering aloud just how it happened. The magic her mother created for her as a little girl is treasured, she shared, and she laughs when she described the terminology her mother used to describe it—Mommy Magic. As is often the case, however, as Gigi grew up, her parents divorced and she was let down by both her parents in different ways. She also realized that "Mommy Magic" was not infallible, mothers were not perfect, but that the relationship can remain sacred and strong regardless of imperfections found in either member of the mother-daughter duo. It was in accepting the limitations of her mother that allowed Gigi to take risks in her own life and to feel confident that even as she strikes out in ways quite different from her mother's path, she will always be able to count on loving support and complete acceptance from her mother.

ALLOWING DAUGHTERS TO ACKNOWLEDGE
THEIR SEXUAL SELVES

The second of the four areas of focus is the female body and female sexuality.[7] As van Mens-Verhulst noted, seldom do mothers openly discuss sexuality, especially female sexual desire, with their daughters. The messages most frequently broadcast from mother to daughter revolve around the importance of chastity and the expectation that daughters are expected to keep boys from taking advantage of them sexually. With public school education in sexual health limited to little more than basic anatomy and abstinence preaching, our daughters are given little opportunity to learn about the multiple facets of sexual health or sexual relationships within a health-promoting or self-respecting manner.[8] In the interviews we conducted with adult women, from their early twenties into their late sixties, the most difficult mother-daughter conversations they recalled having as adolescents addressed menstruation and managing their virginity. One woman, now twenty-eight, recounted that when she started menstruating, she was terrified to tell her mother—and that when she did, her mother told "everyone," male and female, of her daughter's developmental milestone. This created multiple moments of horrendous embarrassment for her. Another woman, about the same age, described how uncomfortable any talks about sex and menstruation made her feel, and that she grew up dreading car rides, as that was when her mother would hold her captive and broach those topics. She also noted that the conversation was always about the importance of being smart and not letting boys get *their* way with her. Mention is seldom made of the fact that even adolescent females experience sexual desire.

However, this latent sexual desire, which daughters are taught neither to acknowledge nor to handle, may be transformed into aggressive feelings toward mothers during late adolescence.[9] Confusion over her own sexual longings can force a daughter to face the fact that her mother, too, is a sexual being. This knowledge can create inner conflict for daughters, especially when they are not prepared to manage their own sexuality. Moreover, in the current climate, young women are exposed to overly sexualized media images, yet mothers still lean toward overly depersonalized and sterile reproductive health discussions. Many young women move from childhood into adulthood never having engaged in a healthy discussion of what it means to be a woman *and* a sexual being. We do not have the conversations that we should have with our daughters, and our own hesitation and silence likely communicate much more than what little content we actually do provide regarding even basic topics such as menarche and puberty.

Menstruation in Historical Times

As a topic of discussion, menstruation has traditionally brought shame for many of us females. In fact, there is quite an historical precedence for this when we reflect on the etymological origin of the word that describes topics that *should* be avoided—*taboo*. *Tupua* is a Polynesian word that means menstruation, and the word *taboo* is a derivative of this word. It is well known that the ancient treatment of menstruating women was to have them isolated in separate dwellings during their monthly cycle. McKeever[10] and Ernster,[11] as cited by Costos, Ackerman, and Paradis,[12] generated lists of slang terms for menstruation, and there were 128 of them! It came as no real surprise that the ones most frequently used were the most derogatory. They ranged from "the red plague," "the curse," to a more recently coined term, "shark bait," due to the loss of blood. Costos et al. also noted that among the messages (perhaps the word *propaganda* might be applicable?) communicated to young women by the feminine hygiene product manufacturers is that our periods are "hygiene crises"[13] in need of expert assistance in finding the product that is appropriate for "mopping up the mess."[14]

A further obstacle to opening the discourse between mothers and daughters regarding menstruation has been the "menstrual divide." Traditionally, research has shown that women who are open to talking about menstruation are distrusted by those who are not.[15] Thus, being open about this aspect of a daughter's development may require that a woman risk crossing that divide and breaking generational patterns of silence on the subject. Therefore, open conversations with daughters about this specific fact of life are not as common as some of us might expect.

Findings from the Costos et al. study described above indicated that over half of the women had never discussed menstruation with their mothers. One of our interviewees, a woman of forty-six, noted that her first period started during a school day, and she had asked a teacher what to do. When we asked how she approached her mother about the topic or if her mother approached the topic with her, she related that she and her mother had never discussed the topic at any point in their relationship. Her mother had not asked for details or additional information that afternoon when her daughter informed her that she now needed pads and tampons. Her mother had avoided a difficult conversation, which probably made things easier for this mother but left her daughter convinced that no sexuality- or body-related topics were open for discussion in her home.

Menstruation in Contemporary Times

As we fast forward to current times, we are beginning to see a new attitude toward the menstrual cycle. It appears that women are growing in their openness *to prepare* their daughters for menarche and *to support* them once they enter that gate. In one study,[16] the reactions of mothers, as remembered by their now nineteen- to twenty-two-year-old daughters, were categorized by qualities that ranged from celebratory, emotionally connected, helpful, and unsupportive. Presenting a vast attitudinal shift, almost a third of the recalled responses were classified as "celebratory" at the advent of their daughter's first period. Almost half of the mothers were emotionally connected, and a third of the others provided responses that their daughters described as being helpful. Distressingly, the mothers whose reactions were less than helpful or positive represented the lower socioeconomic standings of the group, and women of color were overrepresented in this group, as well. In consonance with this particular study, our interviewee who had no communication—helpful or otherwise—with her mother about her period grew up in a rural, almost below subsistence-level income family. Yet when her own daughter revealed that she had started her first period, she was in a much better economic situation, and she and her nuclear family had been exposed to a world far different from the narrow one of her small hometown. At the news of her daughter's menarche, she responded with both a celebratory gesture of allowing her daughter to pick out the menu and dessert for that evening as well as a supportive effort by picking up feminine hygiene products "just for her daughter" and a heating pad to have on hand if cramps accompanied her daughter's periods.

Demographic factors play a substantial role in shaping the ways in which mothers are able to respond to their daughter's developing sexual self. In family cultures in which each generation is playing out the past struggles (financial, ethnic, educational, and so on) of the prior generation, there is seldom opportunity to develop more inclusive and expansive worldviews. Mothers typically continue to behave as their own maternal relatives did, and regardless of how they may believe that they want things to be different for their daughters, they tacitly encourage their daughters to follow their example through unconscious modeling. Women in the Lee study who had received less than enthusiastic responses by their mothers at their menarche, but who now recognized the potential to have a more positive and supportive response to their future female offspring's menarche, may be more likely to shift the family messages related to menstruation and "becoming a woman." Regardless of the positive support we can offer our daughters, we must not lose sight of the challenges inherent in being a fertile, young female in our culture. Beyond the monthly hassles of dealing with such things as tampons, pads, cramps, PMS, and shame, young women are being bombarded with messages regarding their sexuality and their bodies. Once the hurdle of menstruation has been cleared, the subsequent conversations that *should* happen between mother and daughter may present an even more difficult challenge for the pair.

Sexually Charged Topics and Failing Conversations

Speaking to a daughter about female sexual desire is still likely to be verboten in most families, which is in stark contrast to the promotion of flaunting and fulfilling female adolescent sexual needs in today's media. One woman, twenty-nine, shared a story that illustrates clearly the wall between sexual covertness in the home and sexual explicitness in the external world. As one of many sheltered female middle schoolers, she knew little about sexual matters or the slang terms that referred to sexual acts. One afternoon a boy on the bus asked her for oral sex, using the slang term *blow job*. She was confused and did not have a clue what this boy was asking her to do. She went home and naively asked her mother what the term meant; her mother refused to answer and referred her to her father. Her father refused to answer and referred her to the dictionary. Unfortunately, she said, the dictionary in her house did not include that particular term. She returned to her father, who directed her to her mother. Her mother relented and provided an explanation of the term. She still blushes as she recalls the extreme awkwardness of the moment and her embarrassment as her mother's words sank in.

With the widespread hesitation of parents, especially mothers, to discuss sexual matters with their daughter in an educational manner, it is no surprise that young women are reluctant to ask questions about desire or birth control and are heartbreakingly reluctant to reveal sexual victimization to their mothers. When mothers tacitly affirm that healthy sexual development and budding desire are topics that "nice girls" do not discuss, it only follows that some young women will believe that incidents in which others take sexual advantage of them are to be kept hidden, as well. In fact, several women interviewed noted that when they broached the subject of sexual molestation with their mothers, they were not only silenced, but also disbelieved. One thirty-five-year-old African American woman shared that the most difficult conversation she had ever had with her mother occurred during her early teen years when she worked up the courage to reveal that her mother's boyfriend had attempted to rape the young teen. Her mother refused to believe her and refused to discuss the issue further. Not only do some mothers allow their daughters to be victimized, their own discomfort in discussing sexual issues may keep them from even acknowledging this victimization.

Afraid to Talk the Talk or Unable to Walk the Walk?

A mother's comfort level in discussing sexual behavior is an important factor in determining the nature of the communication with her daughter.[17] It is clear from our current sample of mothers and daughters that comfort is hard to come by. Talking to daughters about the anatomical aspects of sex may be easier than addressing the emotions and attitudes surrounding sexuality. A growing number of schools are now offering much richer and more textured lessons on sexual health, but it might be another generation before the mother-daughter sex talk loses its power to make even the most loquacious mother clam up. However, it is a talk that definitely needs to happen—and mothers must be cognizant of the walk they are walking and not simply the talk they are talking. Again, there seem to be obstacles based in demographics that hinder the sexual education and emotional maturation of a wide swath of daughters. In a paper exploring race and class in messages sent to daughters by African American mothers, Townsend emphasized that the messages verbally transmitted may be at cross-purposes with the messages that mothers are communicating as models of sexual beings. [18] The author noted that at the same time a mother asks a daughter to "protect her jewel," [19] the mother may be openly sexually promiscuous or openly allowing herself to be victimized in others ways by men. The conflict in this message may be a symptom of the conflict inherent in the ways in which African American mothers express their concern and protectiveness of their daughters. [20]

It has been noted that African American mothers exert a good amount of energy into the protection of their daughter from sexual harassment, physical abuse, and sexual abuse. [21] However, in transferring these survival skills, these mothers may be unable to communicate the emotional support and affection they feel for their daughters into the messages transmitted; thus, the mother-daughter relationship can be negatively charged with intense emotions that lack a sense of tenderness and mutual appreciation. Several African American interviewees acknowledged that hostility was a palpable aspect of their relationships with their mothers, and that the enmity seemed to grow stronger as they reached puberty and sexual maturity. Several of these women also noted that they looked to grandmothers, aunts, or other maternal figures for unconditional positive regard and tenderness. This underscores the role of the *othermother*[22] in African American culture, or the "village mothers" who are necessary to raise a child. Collins hypothesized that the othermothers can provide an encompassing love that is free from the burden of responsibility to protect the survival of the daughter. Yet as our cultural norms shift, the informal kin networks that once were available to oversee the raising of each new generation are no longer present in the form they once had been. Whether we lose our family support systems through geographical relocation or employment's claim upon our schedules, our daughters are often growing up in a culture created and bounded by both the entertainment media and the social media.

Drug and substance abuse, once primarily the vice and disease of the males in a community, are no longer gender-selective as methamphetamine, cocaine, and alcohol are taking away increasing numbers of mothers. In communities where drug abuse seizes both the fathers and the mothers, young girls are left on their own regarding their sexual and social development. In a society that labels women as either victim or temptress, and in minority cultures in which women are already subjugated by the men of the minority and the dominant group, young female adolescents are likely to wield their sexuality as a tool of power or, conversely, as a vehicle of victimization.

Also complicating the sexual socialization of young African American females is that their mothers are likely to be the sole economic and emotional resource of their families. Thus, daughters may grow up assuming more masculine roles and holding more masculine expectations of how their lives will unfold, whether for good or for bad. Unfortunately, daughters who exhibit masculine attitudes toward sexual experimentation and behavior are prone toward engaging in more sexually risky behaviors. Daughters who exhibit the more feminine traits and view motherhood as a passage rite into adulthood are also more likely to engage in risky sexual behaviors.[23] Townsend suggested that the original mother-daughter relationship should be the focus of educational efforts regarding the healthy sexual socialization process of young minority women. And in an encouraging postscript, our interviewee who shared how difficult her own adolescence had been with her mother noted that she is working hard at letting her own daughter know how much she loves and treasures her — as she works to help her daughter know how to make smart decisions regarding priorities including education and sexual relationships. She wants her daughter to be able to trust her and know that she is there for her, whether her daughter is making good choices or having "learning experiences" along the way.

ADOLESCENCE IS A BATTLEFIELD

The third level of self-conceptualization occurs in our daughter's travels into and through their adolescent years.[24] Mothering a daughter moving through adolescence is almost as difficult as daughtering a mother while being in the midst of adolescence! These years are essentially devoted to a daughter's efforts toward individuation from her mother, and this requires having a mother who will allow a daughter to develop an identity outside of the family. A mother must provide her daughter with permission to separate from the family in terms of thinking for herself and seeing herself as her own person, not through the biased perspective of her parents' eyes. Lastly, an adolescent daughter must receive the opportunity to develop autonomy and respectfully to begin to express her own ideas and beliefs that might diverge from traditional family values.

In our chapter on adolescent daughters, we provide additional examples and suggestions for successfully mothering adolescents. In brief, it is important to recognize that adolescent daughters are following paths that are hardwired into their neurological makeup. A young woman's genetically encoded goals include finding a mate/potential father for her children; leaving her family-of-origin to create a new family; and building alliances and relationships with others of similar beliefs, values, and interests. All of these tasks are age appropriate, but it can be hard for many mothers to allow their teenaged daughters to develop autonomy and create independent identities. The need for mothers to submerge their own sense-of-self into their daughters can limit the mutuality of the mother-daughter relationship. Daughters can feel pressure to own the unrealized dreams of their mothers, and mothers can fear the threat of competition from the daughter as she grows into a woman. Allowing our daughters to become strong, independent, and self-confident women can be the greatest gift we can offer them. However, it requires that mothers allow themselves to become strong, independent, and self-confident women so that they may teach by modeling versus trying to teach by preaching.

EVEN MOTHERS GROW WEARY

The last transition our daughters must experience on their way to personhood and self-subjectivity is to grow to accept and handle the aging of their mothers and fathers.[25] It is during this period in which we may see our daughters yet again engulfed in their role of daughter at a time when they are also likely to be in the midst of rearing their own children or comfortably ensconced in a life they have worked hard to achieve. Developmentally, daughters first must identify with their mothers, as the same gender parent, then separate from the woman with whom they will always share the secret awareness and similarities that only females will share. Next, they must watch as their mothers begin to face the ravages of time, illness, frailty, and inevitable decline; a woman may move from witness to guardian as she assumes the role of caregiver, authority, and mother. For many women, this role is the culmination of a lifetime of training; *woman as nurturer* is a prototypical role in our culture. We have addressed these late challenges to the mother-daughter relationship in a separate chapter, as well. While a daughter may bear a burden of caretaking for a mother who is no longer able to manage independently, there are rich narratives describing the joys and satisfaction felt in giving back, in some small part, to mothers they believed had given them so much. Ultimately, this can be the most poignant and meaningful period in a woman's life as she uncovers a new layer of the gift of being invited to daughter her mother.

CONCLUSION

In this chapter, we have highlighted aspects of the template developed by van Mens-Verhulst to outline the development of self-subjectivity of daughters. No event takes place in a vacuum, and the act of "daughtering" only occurs within a familial or social constellation peopled by those for whom a woman may take on the role of daughter. To grow into a fully functioning adult female, we must travel from self-in-relation-to-mother, to sexually aware and mature adult, through an adolescence in which we are given the freedom and trust to create our own self-identities, and then to return to the role of intimate family member as we daughter an aging mother. This path, this circle of life, is one that speaks of the interplay between interdependence and independence. We cannot raise daughters without being mothers, and we cannot be daughters without sacrifice given by mothers.

NOTES

1. S. J. Cox, A. H. Mezulis, and J. S. Hyde, "The Influence of Child Gender Role and Maternal Feedback to Child Stress on the Emergence of the Gender Difference in Depressive Rumination in Adolescence," *Developmental Psychology*, 46, no. 4 (2010): 842–52.

2. J. van Mens-Verhulst, K. Schreurs, and I. Woertman, *Daughtering and Mothering: Female Subjectivity Reanalyzed* (London/New York: Routledge, 1993).

3. J. van Mens-Verhulst, "Reinventing the Mother-Daughter Relationship," *American Journal of Psychotherapy*, 49, no. 4 (1995): 526–38.

4. Ibid.

5. Ibid.

6. E. Bombeck, *At Wit's End* (New York: Ballantine Books, 1967).

7. J. van Mens-Verhust, "Reinventing the Mother-Daughter Relationship."

8. M. Fine and S. I. McClelland, "Sexuality Education and Desire: Still Missing After All These Years," *Harvard Educational Review*, 76 (2006): 297–338.

9. E. K. Dahl, "'Last night I dreamed I went to Manderly again': Vicissitudes of Maternal Identifications in Late Female Adolescence," *Psychoanalytic Inquiry: A Topical Journal for Mental Health*, 24 (2004): 657–79.

10. P. McKeever, "The Perpetuation of Menstrual Shame: Implications and Directions," *Women and Health*, 9, no. 4 (1984): 33–45.

11. V. Ernster, "American Menstrual Expressions," *Sex Roles*, 1 (1975): 3–13.

12. D. Costos, R. Ackerman, and L. Paradis, "Recollections of Menarche: Communication between Mothers and Daughters Regarding Menstruation," *Sex Roles, 46*, nos. 1 & 2 (2002): 49–59.

13. Ibid., 50.

14. These are our words, not the words of the original source, but they seem most appropriate given the negative, messy connotation of a woman's menstrual cycle in popular media, still today.

15. Costos et al., "Recollections of Menarche."

16. J. Lee, "'A Kotex and a Smile': Mothers and Daughters at Menarche," *Journal of Family Issues*, 29, no. 10 (2008): 1325–47.

17. E. I. Pluhar, C. K. Dilorio, and F. McCarty, "Correlates of Sexuality Communication among Mothers and 6-12-Year-Old Children," *Child: Care, Health, and Development*, 34, no. 3 (2008): 283–90.

18. T. G. Townsend, "Protecting Our Daughters: Intersection of Race, Class and Gender in African American Mothers' Socialization of Their Daughters' Heterosexuality," *Sex Roles, 59* (2008): 429–42.

19. Ibid., 429.

20. Ibid., 437.

21. P. H. Collins, *Black Feminist Thought: Knowledge, Consciousness, and the Politics of Empowerment* (New York: Routledge, 2000).

22. Townsend, "Protecting Our Daughters," 437.

23. Ibid.

24. J. van Mens-Verhust, "Reinventing the Mother-Daughter Relationship."

25. Ibid.

SIXTEEN

Learning the Maternal Role within Cultural Perspectives

When you think of your cultural identity, what aspects of identity come to mind? For many women, their religious faith, their ethnicity, or their geographical locations are clear descriptors of how they locate themselves within their cultures. Our mothers are essential to the development of our positive self-concept and self-identity.[1] The socialization we receive via our mother's cultural identity and our developmental milieu greatly affect how we define who we are and where we fit in the universe. In the words of an African American woman invited to share about the role cultural identity played in her relationship with her mother, "It influenced it greatly because the culture you grow up in will always be a part of you."

GROWING UP AFRICAN AMERICAN

Much has been written about the influence of skin color on how a person is perceived by others in this world. In fact, African American mothers are encouraged to begin instilling racial pride early in a young infant's life.[2] Mothers must prepare their children for life as an outsider in a predominantly white-powered world. Described as "racial socialization," nonwhite mothers prepare their daughters to know what to expect from their world, how she should conduct herself in the world, and ways in which she can best handle a bicultural identity.[3] Factors that have been found to be important in the successful socialization of an African American child include how the mother feels about her own heritage as well as her ability to establish a relationship with her child.[4] In addition, judging from empirical studies[5] and our own interviews, it appears that

185

African American mothers do a much better job instilling a strong sense of self-identity and self-esteem in their daughters than their dominant culture counterparts!

Self-Esteem and Self-Respect through Adversity

Although many of us would like to believe that equal opportunity exists for everyone, regardless of ethnicity, this is clearly not the case, according to many of the women with whom we spoke. One nineteen-year-old woman shared that "where I'm from, your name is all you have. My mother raised me and my sister to always respect ourselves," and it was implied that they were to expect respect from those with whom they developed friendships and romantic relationships. Building a strong sense of self-esteem can be necessary to handle the prejudice and bias still found in many areas today, as attested to by one of our interviewees: "I was taught that African Americans will always have a strike against them, and it is because of the color of our skin. I was also taught that some people still live today as if we were still in segregation, but you have to overlook them and do the best you can in life."

Dealing daily with the hurtfulness and hatefulness of others quickly might wear away at the self-esteem of some, but it clear that there is a confidence that can be planted into the belief systems of young girls, if needed. As a twenty-something shared, "As an African American female, I was taught that we are underestimated and oppressed. I was taught that it is not just okay to be average or as good as the rest, but I must be better than the rest. I must be able to walk, talk, and think with the power to move the mountains that will be placed before me."

It also is interesting in the way that self-esteem can be encouraged from one generation to another, as we see one woman expressing strength of commitment to her own belief system while inspiring her daughter to share that strength of will, although her daughter's beliefs may be in complete opposition to those of her mother. One woman shared that her mother believed her word was law and was adamant about having the final word on family affairs. Her daughter admired her mother's strength but just as firmly believed that all voices deserve to be heard in a dispute. The belief that your words carry weight and that you have value in this world are messages that African American mothers take pains to communicate to their female children.

A mother of a four-year-old daughter is doing her best to instill a strong sense of positive self-concept in her young daughter, while clearly acknowledging cultural identity and the existence of racist attitudes:

> I want her to know that "her blackness is beautiful" . . . she attended a predominantly white preschool and she wanted "long, flowing hair." I need her to know that she is different, but that she is also beautiful . . . a beautiful, lil' "brown" girl.

Strength of Relationship

Whether a woman was describing her current relationship to her mother or extended family relationships, many African American women expressly described the value of strong connections to family. One interviewee, now a mother to two daughters of her own, noted that she believed that this family-oriented background built a strong foundation for developing the women she, her mother, and her daughters are to-day—strong, self-confident women. Women described the close-knit relationships between generations, siblings, and extended family. "Family is an important part of my culture. I was raised to support my family and to help others," shared one thirty-year-old. Another woman affirmed, "I think our family-oriented background built the foundation for who we are today. My daughters are being raised as an extension of how my own parents raised me."

The connection between strength of relationship through the generations seems to parallel the strength mothers want to instill in their daughters. One thirty-three-year-old reiterated how important the mother-daughter bond should be: "I was taught that, regardless of what happens, you have to be good to your mother. To honor her. I think that has a lot to do with our culture." As a woman in her early thirties summed up, "My mother comes from a family of very strong women that believe in being highly involved in children's lives as well as being very nurturing."

Independence and Drive

Cultural images of African American women often focus on the "strong, black woman" who must stand firm as the matriarch and solo parent while the father of her children stays hidden in the back alley up to no good. Whether this image is merely a deeply ingrained stereotype across lines of ethnicity or is a true description of many African American women, many of the women we interviewed used this prototype to describe their mothers and the self-perceived cultural expectations of who they should become. This ideal woman, who is described as "strong and independent," may also present a sense of aloofness and distance from others as she steels herself for daily life, which many women suggested could resemble a battleground. While there may be definite advantages to being this untouchably tough individual, the need for genuine and authentic connection and vulnerability may be lost in the identity development of these women. However, the women with whom we spoke are adamant about the value that strength plays in becoming a woman.

One woman, as clearly a voice for many, affirmed, "In the black community, the mothers are very strong and independent. This had a great effect on *my* life." Another mother shared that she is raising her daughter with awareness of the struggles that she will face due to the color of her skin, "Being black in America makes me teach my daughter how to work for things she wants. Nothing will be given to her easily. But she is smart enough to make things happen in her life and become successful." Speaking about independence and control, one young woman shared that a cultural message that was passed down from her mother was that the mother, not the father, is the head of a household. This woman was also raised to be self-sufficient and not to wait on others to do what needs to be done. In her family, women are seen as the backbone of the family and the community. In addition, being African American women, they must not only lead the family as matriarchs, they must also stand united and strong against the external prejudice that they may face. One woman recalls her mother making statements that might begin, "Black people don't do that or that's a white thing." She does not attribute these statements to her mother carrying a prejudice against other ethnicities, but she does acknowledge, "There was no trust for white people" in her family.

The explicit lessons shared between generations of African American women often address ethnicity in ways that other cultures might not and that provide valuable lessons for those of the majority ethnicity. One barely twenty-two-year-old woman shared that cultural identity played a significant role in her upbringing: "Because we were black, I was taught we had to work twice as hard to get what we need and wanted. I was also taught that not everyone will accept me because of my skin color. I think this helped me to become independent, strong, and driven." Another woman noted that she and her sister had been raised by their mother "to be strong African American women." And this self-confidence was echoed by the young woman, noted above, who was brought up believing that she can move mountains: "I was raised to get the most from my education, and to become independent from all those who may hold me back." Moreover, many mothers are able to inculcate this self-confidence without the presence of a father in the home.

Single-Parent Households

As we described in an earlier chapter, there is a greater likelihood of single parenthood or children being raised by extended family rather than birth parents for African Americans. Both of these situations strongly influence the dynamics within the mother-daughter dyad. On one end of the spectrum, this can give rise to a painful childhood. As one young woman recalled, her mother became pregnant with her before she was in a place to be a caring mother, and this young woman "was taught how to love by my grandmother and aunt. My mother taught me how not to treat a child." On the other end of the spectrum, being raised in a single-parent household positively influenced other women's relationships with their mother. As one noted, "I think being African American influenced my relationship with my mom—it is what made us extremely close because all we had was each other. We were most definitely not rich, but we were happy."

Another woman summed up, "As is common to African American culture, a lot of older children were raised by grandparents due to unwed parents. I felt [strongly] attached to my grandmother since birth." Although there seems to be a loosening of the "old ways" of childrearing, the effects of stern, unyielding parents are still being felt: "My Momma was raised strictly by her uncle and aunt. No one discussed family issues. Love wasn't displayed. That upbringing was normal among older black people. Being that Momma was forty when she had me, the old ways transferred to her children." This sternness can be interpreted as strength by some and encourages the new generation of daughters to value the ability to hold fast to their dreams for a better life, as one young woman shared: "[As a result of my cultural upbringing,] I didn't have to make those same mistakes that I witnessed as a child, teenager. I became very stern and knew exactly what I didn't want in life."

The value of the mother-daughter relationship may be especially high in a single-parent home, as a daughter shared: "Personally, I feel that my cultural identity made our relationship stronger just because of some of the things we faced on a daily basis. It also helped me to admire my mother for being the strong, single mother that she was throughout my whole childhood and teenage years. [Having daughters of my own,] I feel that our cultural identity has made us stronger as women, and I can only hope that it has enhanced the way that I am raising them." Now twenty-four, the former teenaged mother of a five-year-old daughter still feels the pressure that was placed on her when she gave birth: "I feel I have to work more to prove myself since I was a black teen mother." The lesson she most hopes to pass down to her daughter? "Don't let anyone or anything discourage you. Believe in yourself and you can accomplish anything!"

Family Faith

The need to find solace from a culture that can be oppressive is often filled through active involvement in the church. As one woman described her own experiences, she noted that African American families spend a lot of time in church: "Church becomes a place of support and healing." Another noted that African Americans identify strongly with their religious beliefs and worship sites and shared that "this is the source of our strength and empowerment." The connection between family and faith was clearly drawn by many women and neatly summarized as this: "Christian faith is ingrained in the African American community. Because my mother represented the face of our Christian faith, I feel like this bonded us together and resulted in a closer relationship. It certainly played a key role in how we were raised."

The role of faith and religion provide a strong sense of structure to life as well as pave the way for an opening up to those whose cultures differ, in the best of cases. As a thirty-seven-year-old woman shared about the influence of religious teachings in how her mother raised her, she related, "I am glad my mother instilled in me that no matter how much money you have, your skin color, or your beliefs, we are all God's children, and no one is better or worse than you. And you are no better than anyone else." She went to share that she is working to ensure that she teaches her own daughter to "love herself, because God made us all."

GROWING UP WHITE

Inviting women who represent the predominant, power-wielding ethnicity to discuss the role of cultural influence on their relationships to their mothers yielded a variety of different perspectives on how culture may be defined. Although few women were able to discuss openly race and ethnicity as their cultural marker, one forty-year-old woman was very vehement in describing how her mother had inculcated her regarding the issue of diversity and race:

> As a child, I was constantly given the message that certain cultures were "not as good" as others. More specifically, I was told (and continue to be told) outright that certain ethnic groups were not as smart, were not as capable as others were. This is something that I feel passionate about and adamantly disagree with. It is unfathomable to me that simply because I was born a certain color that I should receive more or be viewed as more important. WHAT is that about? It seems our world is becoming more and more violent. Given this new environment of violence, I believe it is even more vital to come together and encourage one another. My mother continues to view different cultures as "less than."

Regarding other women who shared the role of culture in their upbringing, many women looked to their religious belief system as the location of the identifier of family culture. Others looked to their geographical region as the pinpoint on their personal cultural map, and still others looked to the ethnic heritage of their families in terms of countries from which their forebears migrated. Socioeconomic status and family constellation were also chosen as distinct cultural descriptors. Clearly, there is not a similar sense of "Caucasian identity" in the same manner that others use ethnicity as a cultural designation.

Family Faith

As might be expected, the religious traditions that are handed down from generation to generation strongly flavor the mother-daughter relationship for many women. One woman shared that being raised in a Christian home brought "many blessings" that have allowed her to "have an advantage over many others." Another woman shared that "I was raised in a Christian home where respect was asked of us and we worked together as a group." She hopes that she is able to teach her own daughters the same Christian values that were communicated by her mother.

While many women mention the strong values from their faiths that their mothers emphasized in their upbringing, they also note that these basic values influence their own childrearing practices. Other women, however, go through a spiritual/religious transformation as they move into adulthood that can create problems in previously close mother-daughter relationships. One woman still regretted the difficult time she has caused her mother who "has a hard time understanding my reasoning for choosing more of a spiritual path rather than a religious one."

Who I Am Is Where I Am

"I was raised in what I considered to be a fairly typical, southern household," one woman began, and went on to discuss the intergenerational households common to her community and her strong appreciation for communication between the generations. Another proud southerner described her mother's inculcation of culture as "all about manners and hospitality, and I believe she instilled both equally and I'm so glad she did. When I travel or when I have lived in other parts of the country, I feel like people appreciate this and recognize it as one of our strongest traits." Although this woman enjoys bringing her ingrained southern hospitality to new places, spending your childhood in many different places can leave a young girl looking for hospitality.

A young woman who was raised as a "military brat" spent her younger years watching her family try to make a home in many places. The experience of moving around a lot and being home alone with her mother while her father was gone so much has left her feeling that her lack of roots and sense of home during those years has left her with a residual sense of insecurity in all of her relationships. Without a place to call home and having a mother who is handling the shifting roles required of a "sometimes two-parent, sometimes one-parent" household, the mother-daughter relationship might be dramatically influenced by these factors. Another self-labeled "military brat," however, shared that she was able to develop friendships with a widely diverse group of individuals, whereas her own mother still wrestled with the challenges that took her beyond her small-town, impoverished upbringing.

A woman born into a Scandinavian-Lutheran community found that it greatly affected her relationship with her mother in ways that she believed may sound "negative" to others but that she appreciated. She went on to describe the extremely conservative, stoic, and guilt-driven community as supportive of her mother's efforts to raise her to be hardworking and caring; however, she noted that she felt that the lack of praise and affection between family members was a sad loss. She is raising her own daughters to feel free to think for themselves, not feel the need to rely on a man to take care of them, and to feel that it is okay to feel positive about themselves.

Friends and Family Values

Our friends and our family provide our most integral sense of cultural community, as many of us look to these communities as our place of center. One woman was grateful that her mother had not only raised her well but also had encouraged her to develop a solid group of friends throughout her youth. She went on to describe this group as sharing "similar morals and beliefs, had decent relationships with their parents, and whose parents were also engaged and involved" in their children's lives.

"Because my mom treated me with respect, I have a lot of respect for her," shared one twenty-two-year-old interviewee. She felt that her mother's ability to value her as a female has positively influenced her in many aspects of self-worth and self-esteem. Another woman felt that her mother's valuing of the mother-daughter relationship built a strong, close bond that others might not be able to develop due to family culture differences of strict mother/daughter role expectations. Close mother-daughter relationships are clearly a treasured aspect of family connection, as many women acknowledged this belief, but the relationship may not be as close from its early stages as it has been for many of our interviewees.

Born approximately forty years prior, one mother we interviewed shared that her mother strongly personified the saying that "children should be seen and not heard." As she wrote:

> In my home growing up, I did not argue with my parents. This was seen as disrespectful and the height of arrogance. Although I do not believe in disagreeing for disagreement's sake, I do believe that opinions and beliefs held by children should be acknowledged. I believe that by not allowing children to explore and have varied experiences, that the parents are doing their children an incredible disservice. I want my two daughters to know that I love them unconditionally. We may have disagreements, but I always want them to know that they have a voice and that their voice matters. By not allowing me to have a voice, I ended up not thinking my voice mattered, my opinion was worthless. After all, I was simply a child. Not having a voice or an opinion that matters is something I continue to struggle with, and now I am forty. It is difficult for me to think that anything I say has value or merit. I hope to never hinder my children in this way.

Another woman, born two decades prior, provided an interesting "point-counterpoint" experience. She asserted her belief that her own mother had been raised in a family culture in which distance and formality were modeled, as she felt that once she, herself, became a young adult, her mother has been "telling me everything she has been holding in for all of my own life, no matter what comes to mind!" In an extremely similar revelation, another woman shared how she was now breaking the traditional silence on women in her own family culture: "Culturally, I was taught to be guarded and not 'spill' too much information. So I have been like that with my own mother until very recently." She is grateful that she has begun to enrich her relationship with her own mother through the introduction of authentic and honest deep communication about significant topics.

Socioeconomics and Mothering?

A family's financial status may also be viewed as an important aspect of cultural identity for women. Whether a family is rich or poor, it can strongly determine the experiences and opportunities for relationship development in a home. When we are raised in a home free of concerns related to daily survival, the mother-daughter relationship can provide a sense of emotional, as well as material, security. As one twenty-five-year-old woman noted, "As one of the only white families in a small, low socioeconomic status (SES) town, we were more privileged than other families. I was able to have . . . home cooked meals every night." For her, the pleasure she took in sitting down to meals prepared by her mother has developed into a great enjoyment in entertaining—she felt that her family's relative wealth allowed her mother to pass down cultural experiences and traditions that others might have missed. However, she went on to note that her own mother had grown up in relative poverty, thus her mother strongly instilled an appreciation for the good fortune that a good education might bring.

There can be a downside to living the high life, as our work with the daughters of wealthy parents has revealed. Although many parents engage in their childrearing practices as do parents in other tax brackets, some parents seem to engage in a privileged kind of "distance parenting." This might include the introduction of nannies, boarding schools, and elite summer camps to the mother-daughter relationship. This may occur in order to allow mom either to work in the boardroom or perfect her swing. In these families, a daughter's sense of herself is still intertwined in the mother-daughter relationship, although the relationship may be layered with extra levels of caregiving persons or institutions. Though the relationship may be prone to some of the same perils of other mother-daughter relations, it seems less likely to hold as much intimacy as those found in other SES family systems.

Although the current economic times seem to be squeezing the middle class out of existence, many of our interviewees were raised in self-described middle-class families, and the experience seems to have been a very positive one for mother-daughter relationships, for the most part. Through our experience with college students, it appears that most students will self-define their family incomes as "middle class," but many young women are unaware of just how far they underestimate their family's income. Many young women are oblivious to the additional opportunities and choices they may actually have as compared to their truly "middle class" peers. One young woman did share her awareness of just how spoiled she felt due to financial and family circumstances. She noted that she had grown up an only child to older parents in a middle-class home, and she experienced a very protective mother who babied her throughout her youth. She recalled how her family's relative financial ease and her only-child status provided her the opportunity to throw tantrums when she didn't get her way and that her mother frequently gave in to these fits. She felt that she was allowed to rely on her mother more than what might have been best and that she now encourages her own daughter to be a leader and to be more independent from her than she had been from her own mother.

Down a rung on the SES ladder, a woman revealed that when she had been in first grade, socioeconomic factors had driven her mother to return to work. While this changed the dynamics of the family, to some degree, her mother had found a job as a schoolteacher, which allowed her daughter to continue to spend "massive amounts of time with my mother." She was raised to believe that a mother's first responsibility was to attend to the needs of the family and keep career a second priority. As she continued to reflect on her early education on the mother-daughter relationship, she noted that she also thought that her "mother was raised to think that your children were your greatest accomplishment, and so she did whatever she could to make life easier for us."

One woman shared that her single mother had raised her for many years, although her grandmother was her guardian for a time before her father eventually got custody when she was in her teens. She shared that while she and her mother were "always poor, except through one of Mom's brief marriages," she had a great deal of responsibility growing up that she had resented. It was only as she entered adulthood that she began to understand and appreciate her mother's plight, and then her relationship with her mother was able to grow much stronger. Now a mother of two young adult daughters herself, she admits that while she "tried very hard to be better than my mother," she realized too late that by not getting her education earlier, that influenced so much in her own life that "surviving became the most important thing."

Family Constellation

Trying to figure out if her culture had influenced her relationship with her mother, one woman shared that she did not think it really had, as "it's acceptable for a woman to be a single mother in the United States, and that's about it." Although the shame once associated with single-parent households has dissipated, growing up in a family that doesn't "look like" the neighbor's family can have a significant influence on how some daughters experience their relationships with their mothers. Another woman reported that her mother had been married multiple times and that she had always felt different from other girls her age—"Where I was raised, I was the first child to have divorced parents and . . . I felt inferior for that reason." This woman shared that she had a difficult time establishing a healthy relationship with her mother and that she worked hard to get attention in a "good way," such as academic achievement.

A woman who describes herself as "part Irish, part German, but both parts being generations removed," noted that it was probably the fact that her mother was divorced that was the aspect of cultural identity that most shaped their relationship. She went on to share that it had not been until she entered school that she realized her family was any different from any other family. Reflecting on the unique family constellation, she wondered, "Perhaps, if my Mom had been a typical stay-at-home mother, our relationship may have been different." She is raising her own daughters to embrace her husband's Italian cultural heritage, and she shared: "From the food, passion, and the funny stereotypes. Family is the priority. Unconditionally. I love it!" The strong commitment to family among Italians was described by one woman succinctly as "family is a religion." In a recent qualitative study of individuals of Italian descent—female caregivers of older relatives with dementia—the cultural values related to family, similar to the Hispanic populations' *familismo*, was an integral component of these women's decisions to care for suffering older family members.[6] The Italian heritage of commitment to family identity and well-being is clearly self-regenerating in subsequent generations as daughters observe their mothers' caregiving across the age spectrum from infants to the oldest person.

Another woman recognized that even having a two-parent home does not guarantee two-parent access for daughters. Recounting the need for her father to work a night-shift job, she felt that her mother had to take on more responsibility in the raising of her daughters, and that changed the traditional mother-daughter relationship that might have developed without the added burden of solo parenting the majority of the time.

GROWING UP DIFFERENT

Although we only heard from a very few women of Asian or Hispanic descent, those within each group described shared experiences within their respective cultures. For Asian women, the clearly shared theme was that they must often give up a strong sense of personal identity and individuality as they move into adulthood. A title of a qualitative research study by Helene K. Lee[7] fully captures the sublimation of individual identity described by our own interviewees—"I'm My Mother's Daughter, I'm My Husband's Wife, I'm My Child's Mother, I'm Nothing Else." To be a young Asian daughter in North America, according to an interviewee, means that you may have to accept feelings of guilt for choosing to follow the ways of one's dominant-culture friends. When asked about the mother-daughter relationship, specifically, she replied, "I feel guilty if I don't please my mother," and she implied that this was a culturally embedded belief that went beyond what she believed was the "ordinary guilting" that mothers liked to do to their offspring.

While respect for older family members is a virtue shared across most cultures, an Asian daughter also noted that within her culture, not only must youth compromise and obey their elders, but also females must compromise in their relationships with males. While she has been encouraged to succeed in her education and career, she still carries with her the knowledge that her will is not going to win out against the men in her life. And with the domestic violence rates comparatively high among Asians—some studies suggest that as many as 60 percent of Asian females will experience physical or sexual violence during their lifetime[8] — it is clear that mothers are at a disadvantage to attempt to instill a strong sense of independence or self-determination in their daughters.

A young Pacific Islander noted that she felt less close to her mother because they had been born into different countries and different cultures. She wondered if their relationship and understanding of one another might have been different if they shared a birth country. Another young woman shared a similar perspective: "I don't believe my cultural identity has influenced my relationship with my mother much. Being adopted had more of an influence than traditional cultural identity things."

Education as an Hispanic Family Value

Traditionally, *familismo* is considered a strong component of the cultural heritage among Hispanic cultures. As one young woman shared,

> Most women in the Mexican culture are expected to get married and have children right away. Some do not even make it out of high school before they find themselves doing both, married and with one or two kids. . . . I remember being about thirteen years old, hearing my grand-

ma tell one of our neighbors that before you know it, I was going to make her a great grandma, and how she couldn't wait.

However, she felt that her own family's expectations targeted her educational achievement rather than motherhood status. She shared that she had known from an early age that she did not want to have children and that she had shared this decision with her mother. Although her mother accepts this decision, this daughter noted that

even now as an adult, the expectations keep coming; my mother expects me to find a job that is related to my field. My mother is very active in the Hispanic community and at church, she expects me to go to church every Sunday, but I don't. She expects me to be listening to her at all times and complete all her requests, and I fail to do so all the time. She expects me to be more relaxed and not so quick tempered in regards to other family members including my husband, but that does not always happen. The ultimate expectation I have from my mother is to be an individual who helps other less-fortunate members of the community. I am glad to have her as one of my most influential critics as well as the person who expects the most from me.

Another woman of Hispanic descent, roughly twenty-five years older than the young woman described above, also recalls the value of education being impressed upon her by her mother:

Mom pushed education hard because we had so much more opportunity than the women of her time did. She sometimes felt my sister and I were not aggressive or assertive enough in our careers. I really did not see what she saw. . . . I do not think my sister did either. Maybe we liked being in our "comfort zone" and played it safe and conservative. Neither one of us had mates, but family responsibilities were very important in our culture. My mother would probably have expected us to try and balance out career and family obligations, but honestly something would have to "give" . . . maybe it wouldn't be family or career but personal mental/emotional health? I can honestly say I don't know for sure. I wonder if raising a family was more important to my mother because she never went back to college after she married my dad.

CONCLUSION

While we have gone into detail sharing the reflections of women on their cultural identity as well as its influence on their mother-daughter relationships, it is clear that we determine the power of culture to influence our relationships. Many women felt that they were creating a relationship with their daughters that would be governed by their sense of what is most beneficial to their daughters, consciously choosing to develop new qualities in the relationship that they may not have experienced as daughters themselves. Moreover, the construct of "cultural identity" can shift as new patterns and new connections to community are developed. We are not as "culture bound" as we may believe we are; as mothers, we can follow the wisdom of the woman who shared her secret to breaking the ineffective cultural imprint: "I try to live so that my daughter will know how to live."

NOTES

1. D. J. Thomas and C. T. King, "Gendered Racial Socialization of African American Mothers and Daughters," *The Family Journal: Counseling and Therapy for Couples and Families, 15*, no. 2 (2007): 137–42.

2. R. L. White-Johnson, K. R. Ford, and R. M. Sellers, "Parental Racial Socialization Profiles: Association with Demographic Factors, Racial Discrimination, Childhood Socialization, and Racial Identity," *Cultural Diversity and Ethnic Minority Psychology, 16,* no. 2 (2010): 237–47. doi: 10.1037/a0016111

3. Ibid.

4. B. F. Turnage and C. L. Dotson, "Parenting of Female African American Infants," *International Journal of Childbirth Education, 27* (2012): 54–57.

5. H. Ridolfo, V. Chepp, and M. Milkie, "Race and Girls' Self-Evaluations: How Mothering Matters," *Sex Roles, 68* (2013): 496–509.

6. R. Benedetti, L. Cohen, and M. Taylor, "'There's Really No Other Option': Italian Australians' Experiences of Caring for a Family Member with Dementia," *Journal of Women & Aging, 25*, no. 2 (2013): 138–64.

7. H. K. Lee, "'I'm My Mother's Daughter, I'm My Husband's Wife, I'm My Child's Mother, I'm Nothing Else': Resisting Traditional Korean Roles as Korean American Working Women in Seoul, South Korea," *Women's Studies International Forum, 36* (2013): 37–43.

8. M. Yoshihama, "Domestic Violence against Women of Japanese Descent in Los Angeles: Two Methods of Estimating Prevalence," *Violence against Women, 5*, no. 8 (1999): 869–97. San Francisco: Author, 2005 (Revised).

SEVENTEEN

Attitude and Gratitude

In this chapter, we are celebrating joys found in the mother-daughter relationship through the sharing of "high moment," or, alternately, "critical incident" stories that were shared with us. We invited women to speak about the qualities in their mothers that they were proud that they saw in themselves as well as about the aspects they treasured most in their relationships with their mothers or daughters. Heartwarming stories abounded—and, true to form, even those who had what might be described as "strained" relationships were frequently able to note something hopeful in their mother-daughter connections.

CELEBRATING DAUGHTERS

Inviting mothers of daughters to share a favorite story about their daughters brings mothers a lot of joy. Of course, many of the stories described times when their daughters were still somewhat young—before the angst of the teenage years or the potential for disappointment in their adult choices had begun. Mother to a now twenty-four-year-old daughter, Suzy remembered the pride she felt when a Sunday school teacher complimented her then seven-year-old daughter on the uninhibited creativity she showed in class each week—whether it was art, singing, or acting out Bible stories. The Sunday school teacher pushed Suzy to explain how she had raised her daughter to be so enthusiastically creative. The mother's response? "I try to say, 'Yes' to my daughter more often than I say, 'No.'" Suzy said she reveled in her daughter's unbridled curiosity and creativity: "If no one is getting hurt and the mess isn't permanent, why not encourage kids to be creative?" Moreover, now that her daughter is grown and is a high school teacher, she loves hearing of the creative ideas her daughter used to teach reluctant teenaged students geometry and algebra.

BUFFALO GALS

Kate is the mother of a beautifully creative and joyful daughter herself. She had no trouble providing a story of a special moment in their relationship together. The recollection was as clear as a bright, full moon and yields anecdotal evidence of the deep, some say lunar-based, connection shared by all women:

> Some years ago, when my daughter was about eight years old, "the gals" got together and went camping. My daughter and I, along with my friend and her daughter, pitched a tent in the wilderness (okay, it was a campground with bathrooms, and a swimming pool). One night there was an enormous full moon that shone so brightly we did not even need lights inside our tents. At midnight, my daughter and I decided to take a walk around the campgrounds. The moon was so big and bright that our figures cast moon shadows along the trail. We walked up a hill at the edge of the campground and began singing that old song "Buffalo Gals, Won't You Come Out Tonight." When we got to the line about dancing by the light of the moon, we had reached the top of the hill, and we started dancing. Two silly silhouettes at the top of a hill, spotlighted by a golden moon, dancing a dance of blissful lunatics. Crazy gesticulations. Off-key singing. Cheek-to-cheek cheesy rumbas, with big dips. Laughing. Dancing. Happy. Free.
> When we had worn ourselves out and were headed back to our tent, arm in arm, I said to my daughter, "Sarah, when you are older, and have kids of your own, will you tell them about all the crazy things we did together when you were young?"
> To my surprise, she said, abruptly, "No."
> "You won't?" I asked.
> "No," she said, "I'll show them."

There is joy and abandon in Kate and her daughter's connection that celebrates the freedom that lucky moms and daughters find in their relationship.

LEARNING ALONG THE WAY

Renee, a mother of two beautiful daughters approximately twelve years apart, emphasized that her daughters were extremely different in temperament and interests, but that made it so easy to love each of them in just the unique way each needed. As Renee shared:

> Sara has always been a very headstrong, independent person . . . from the minute she was born. So it was no big surprise that when her sister,

Megan, was born that Sara stepped in to be my assistant. Megan, on the other hand, is a very quiet go-with-the-flow kind of person who won't speak up. So I find myself caught in the middle sometimes and having to switch gears. . . . Expecting one reaction from one and one reaction from the other, and there are times when I so wish Sara would just go with the flow like Megan does and times that I wish Megan would just speak up like Sara does. But regardless . . . I wouldn't change a thing about either one of them.

Though her older daughter became quite independent, she was a crier as a baby, and a tantrum thrower as a child. By the time Megan was born, Renee had realized that she could avert drama if she were to give her younger daughter the attention she needed before the crying and the tantrums started. She believes the best way to raise children who are so different is simple—"All you have to do is listen to them . . . children tell you what they want . . . it's just not always as plain as day as we would like it to be."

Today, Renee shared that her older daughter is still the "responsible one" and "the one who no matter what will always be there." She also related that she and her husband had just returned from a trip out of the country, and before they left, Renee realized just how much she now relied on her older daughter:

She was the one we gave power of attorney to along with my mom, in case something happened to her sister while we were gone and she was the contact person—and without her, I could not have enjoyed the vacation as much—I knew that if I needed anything taken care of, that she was on top of it! That was the moment I realized that I could trust her—and she did not let me down.

She summed up her feelings about raising two very different daughters with the following wisdom that is clearly worth sharing:

The difference between the first and last child? The first one is like training for a new job . . . you think you know everything already—which is why you applied in the first place! Then you find out you do NOT know everything, after all. But you forge on, hoping to one day get it right. And then, by the last child, you are finally pretty confident. You walk away, smiling, saying, "I've got this all figured out!"

Moreover, for Renee and other mothers, her words ring true—you do have motherhood pretty well figured out once you have raised a couple of kids!

CELEBRATING MOTHERS

Daughters appreciate and can articulate the connection and presence of their mothers in their lives. Even the traits and qualities that some daughters are less than happy to have inherited from their mothers bring a sense of connection. As one young woman shared, "We are both stubborn, and we both love hard!" Stubbornness, persistence, and being headstrong are traits that many women are glad that were passed down, but they also recognize them as stumbling blocks to their relationships with their mothers, among others. Another woman loves that her mother is loving and kind to everyone, traits she likes in herself, but she does sometimes wish "we didn't care so much about others' feelings." "Being outright nosy" is how one young woman described a shared trait—she smiled about this and said that she might rather call it "being involved in the lives of those we care about."

Regardless of what we like or do not like about our mothers, research shows that their influence on our identities as children is magnified in shaping who we are as adults. In fact, it is our ability to reshape our relationships to our mothers into a reciprocal configuration that actually gives evidence of our maturity and adult status.[1] By being able to perceive the reciprocity of the relationship in that both mothers and daughters receive and give something of worth, we become the women that mothers have been hoping they could raise. The following are stories that attest to the success that mothers can achieve.

SHARING HONESTY

A twenty-five-year-old woman is very grateful to her mother for always bringing honest communication to their relationship. As she described her mother's frankness, she said:

> One thing I can say about my mother is she has always been very honest. She has never "sugarcoated" anything. I felt that she told me the necessary things that would make me a better person or make the right decision. I think the conversation about the finality of death is the most difficult conversation that we had. My mother simply explained that it was inevitable and you have to appreciate every day you are given.

This young woman's awareness of the finiteness of life has allowed her to develop an authentic appreciation for every moment she shares with those she values in her life. Another mid-twenties daughter shared a similar appreciation for the honesty in the communications between her mother and herself. As she shared with a smile, "We both always make sure to tell each other the truth about things even if it's something about the outfit we have on or the need for a breath mint."

MOTHER AND DAUGHTER ON FOREIGN SOIL

A woman in her thirties described a foreign adventure that happened when she and her mother traveled to her mother's homeland in Asia. Although she has three sisters, it was only this woman and her mother who went on this trip. She valued this chance to have her mother's "undivided attention," as that was something that she felt was always in short supply with so many siblings vying for her mother's ears and eyes growing up. She went on to share that she "learned tons about their family history." In addition, she was able to enjoy a very different side of her mother that she treasured:

> [My mother] would ask me advice about outfits, gossip about family, and we shared unique experiences like the time we had to run off squatters from our family's land! To thank my mom for letting them stay for as long as they did, they gave us a chicken, and we drove home with a bound-up chicken in the backseat of our car—and I, the American-born city girl—was terrified! Good times!

It is clear how much this young woman treasured the one-on-one time and individual attention she received from her mother during this adventure. However, other women feel that their mothers were much less available to them and left them expressing gratitude for what little of both of these commodities that they did receive.

AN ARID CLIMATE

Although the following story does not provide such a heartwarming conclusion as the one on foreign soil offered, it, too, is planted in a foreign landscape, of sorts. In creating an analogy of her and her mother's relationship, a thirty-year-old woman used the following story:

> My mother and I have a relationship like a gardener who grows cacti. I would be the cactus and my mother the gardener. The gardener can do very little, but the cacti can survive. The gardener does not have to water the plant much because in spite of its appearance, the cactus has very strong roots and durable skin.

Although her mother was unable to offer her much as she grew and matured, her daughter was able to take what she needed and grow into a strong, self-confident woman who is trying to right the remembered wrongs of her mother through the attentive nurturing of her own three-year-old daughter.

A MOTHER KNOWS WHAT A DAUGHTER NEEDS

Most mothers know that there exists a powerful communication tool known as a "mother's intuition." Mothers know when things are going poorly for their daughters, and they can sometimes feel it thousands of miles away. We ache when our daughters suffer, and we often have to blink back the tears in our own eyes when we see them cry. An early-twenties woman shared that she and her mother share a deep respect as well as "really get each other at a deep level." She went on to share the following story, illustrating just how deeply her mother's intuitions about her really are:

> One afternoon, I came home from work and I was exhausted mentally, physically, and emotionally. I did not talk to anyone about the way I was feeling, but I was feeling just so down and that I had nothing left to offer anyone. My mother called me later that night and encouraged me and talked to me about her experiences in a similar job. I had not told her anything about what I was feeling, but she just knew what I was going through. She prayed for me and encouraged me. That is the type of mother that she is—she knows even when I don't tell her what I am feeling. She cares. I know she ALWAYS will be there for me!

Another woman described a "daughter's intuition." She shared that she can "sense when my mother needs to talk. I have called her on many occasions and asked if everything is okay. She will respond by admitting that she was just considering giving me a call!"

Although not so much a matter of a woman's intuition, another mother was able to give a daughter exactly what she needed at the right time. A young woman remembers being a young adolescent and was just hanging out shooting hoops in her driveway. She was delighted when her mom stepped outside and joined her on the driveway. As she summed up, "I just enjoyed it so much! I loved that she wanted to do something that I wanted to do!" And these memory-making moments can be created by even the busiest of mothers and the powerful impression that they leave can last a daughter's lifetime.

A DAUGHTER KNOWS WHAT A MOTHER WANTS

From speaking to so many women about the frequently complicated relationships they have with their mothers, we have learned to "expect the unexpected" story from time to time. Although most of us who have raised children recognize just how entertaining television can be—especially for our children, we did not expect so many women to use television shows as "anchor points" in their relationships with their mothers—perhaps because it was our own "little secret" with our mothers or daughters. A couple of stories stood out regarding the role that shared television viewing can play in cementing relationships. Perhaps the comment made by the young woman who traveled to Asia with her mother regarding their relationship is a helpful barometer of mother-daughter relationship closeness. In response to the question about how she would describe her relationship with her mother today, she answered, "I'd describe it as close, but not 'American TV sitcom' close. We have a mutual respect for one another." This suggested that television shows possibly portray examples of the way that some women believe relationships *should* be or, at least, might be. We use the media as barometers of how we might live our lives, and television viewing is often a part of the bonding time between mothers and daughters.

Suzy, the mother of the twenty-four-year-old daughter mentioned at the beginning of this chapter, shared that during her daughter's turbulent adolescent, Goth-obsessed years Thursdays were the only day they knew they would be in agreement for any length of time. The weekly saga of Lorelai and Rory Gilmore, aka *The Gilmore Girls*, invited them to snuggle up on the couch with popcorn, Diet Cokes, and harmony for an hour each week. Later, they added a weekly yoga class to their *Gilmore Girls*–inspired truce, and they kept these two traditions going strong until Suzy's daughter moved out and into her own place just a couple of years ago.

We learned about another *Gilmore Girls* fan duo from a daughter's perspective, as well. Relating that her father started working the evening shift during her senior year in high school, a young woman shared that "it was just me and mom at home for dinner. We started the tradition of eating ramen noodles and watching *Gilmore Girls* together at 4 o'clock every day!" The American sitcom focused on the drama and love between a mother and daughter clearly captured the hearts of women everywhere—those who had actually experienced such a warm and loving relationship with their mothers or daughters as well as those of us who still hoped we could establish such a close relationship.

We want to share one other story that presents shared television viewing as an anchor for connection. This story, however, has a funny twist to it that probably is appreciated best by fans of the particular show. A woman who lost her mother several years ago recalled a gift that she had given her mother that represented her efforts at pleasing her mother while also highlighting the sense of humor she and her mother shared: "[We] loved the show *NCIS*, and my mother loved Abby's farting hippo. The last Christmas that she was alive, I made her a pooting hippo, and she absolutely loved it. She would cuddle with it when she was feeling bad." Knowing that she had given her a gift that would bring a smile to her mother's face, as well as a belly laugh, brought her great satisfaction. As an interesting counterpoint, this daughter revealed the ways in which she was like her mother: "I am very thoughtful, like my mother. I am also pretty old fashioned and traditional. I have older values that are like her, and I like that." Perhaps the "pooting hippo" was an "old fashioned in a sentimental way" gift to let her mother know how much she loved her — and she certainly knew what would make her mother smile.

HANGING OUT IN THE KITCHEN

When we grow up and move into our own new lives as women, what do we miss most from the days we lived at home with our mothers? For one daughter, it is spending time in her family kitchen. She and her mother are able to recreate the closeness they felt there when she is able to get home to visit. As she recollected:

> When I go home for a holiday . . . my mother and I pretty much have a ritual. When I get to her house, we will cook dinner together and visit. Once we have eaten dinner, we always go to the living room and play all of our favorite songs. We tend to sing and dance with each other. We have done this since I was a little girl, and it has always been so much fun. Sometimes after that, we will sit up and talk for hours about life, relationships, or whatever is on our minds that night. We love to spend fun, communicative time together. We both enjoy each other's company very much.

Another woman shared that her favorite time spent with her mother was "just cooking in the kitchen together — priceless!" The sharing of time in the kitchen preparing a meal together is a wonderful, prototypical feminine ritual. The kitchen is clearly the "heart of the home" for many of us. In the following story, however, a woman recalls hanging out *under* the kitchen table while secretly enjoying her mother's company.

ENCOURAGING OUR DAUGHTERS TO DREAM

What do we remember most fondly about our childhood experiences with our mothers? For some women, it is not just the good meals, the shared laughter, or the warm hugs. One woman, Stephanie, recalled that her mother was a guitarist, a singer, and a songwriter. Some of her earliest childhood memories are of her mother playing and singing while sitting at the kitchen table while she was hanging out under the table. She went on to say,

> I certainly did not get her musical talent, but she always asked me to join in singing her songs. She encouraged me and made me feel like a star. She wrote a song about me called, "Dreamer." It's about a little girl with dreams of becoming so many things when she "grows up"! It always brought a smile to my face to hear her sing that, as I got older.

Although she is still coping with grief at the loss of her mother, Stephanie shared that she felt good knowing that her own young daughter had brought great joy to Stephanie's mother during the last few years of her life.

ALWAYS TAKING CARE OF HER NOT-SO-LITTLE GIRL

A number of women shared similar stories about the moments with their mothers that they cherished most. These often involved the caregiving they received from their mothers well into adulthood. One young woman shared how much she valued the times that her mother would bring her into her bed to sleep when she was ill with a stomachache or fever as a child. What she likes best, though, is that her mother has allowed this to be "continued into adult years. This truly captures what I see is her best trait and what brings our relationship together. [She has] a pure, trusting heart." Another woman shared that she and her mother had "just begun to get close again . . . we were more affectionate and shared really funny moments" shortly before her mother passed away. When asked to share a story that epitomized their relationship, she shared:

> I was sick one weekend that I came home from college and she was able to tell by my voice on the phone that I was sick. By the time I got home, she had cooked soup, changed the bed linens on her own bed, and made me tea. She told me to shower and go get in her bed, not mine. We laid there all day watching movies.

Clearly, when we are sick there is no one we need more and no one more eager to care for us than our mothers. However, when an illness is powerful enough to threaten a daughter's life, a mother faces more challenges than just putting together a bowl of chicken soup.

One mother we spoke to had very recently witnessed her twenty-three-year-old daughter experience an unexpected and critical health crisis. Her daughter had to be hospitalized twice and she then returned to her parents' home afterward for recuperation and recovery both times. Although she is now back in her own apartment, her mother is still reeling emotionally from the ordeal: "No matter how independent our daughters are, there are going to be life obstacles that make their needs even greater. As the mother, you have to swallow your pride and be the mom when they need it. But you will know they are beginning to get better when they began to talk back and argue again. Of course, then you, as the mother, have to relearn how to let go again without going through the whole 'empty nest depression' all over again." She feels she is still learning.

Another mother we interviewed had to experience the terrifying discovery that her adolescent daughter, a front seat passenger, had been in a serious automobile accident and rushed by ambulance to the hospital where she had to remain several days as she healed. The driver suffered even more severe injuries, and the backseat passenger died at the scene. All three girls were just seventeen years old. When we asked this woman how she had handled what is so many mothers' nightmare, she responded:

> I would like to make just a couple of comments that helped me cope with my daughter's accident back in 2009. Anyway, who really knows how we will handle such events in our lives until we have to? As the mother of a daughter and because of our relationship in the family, it was I who ended up giving her all the bad news about what had happened to the other girls—worst of all that her friend did not make it. This was a truth my husband and I had decided to wait to tell her until our youth minister had arrived. But I was with her alone and she was so worried and because of the depth of our bond, I knew the time was right. It is not easy being the bearer of that kind of news, and it was very painful to see her reaction. I guess all of us are given the tools to deal with the worst news, but to see my daughter suffer both physically and emotionally took a lot. It may sound cheesy but I turn all my troubles over to God and I believe He gives me the wisdom and strength to deal and He gave me the wisdom of how to help my daughter, who still is dealing with the effects of the accident.

Being a mother can be a surprisingly difficult role, and it often requires that we take on tasks that we wish were never required of anyone. Fortunately, this young woman is now happily moving through her college years, and she and her mother are extremely close and bonded in a way that reflects a shared resiliency and strength.

THE BEST FRIEND A DAUGHTER COULD HAVE

In an earlier chapter, we shared the ways that the mother-daughter relationship grows into a friendship as a daughter grows into a woman. One daughter—already well past fifty—shared with us how much she values her friendship with her mother, who is approaching eighty:

> My mother and I spend a lot of time in our flower gardens together and share new ideas about gardening and crafts. We also try to go out to eat and window-shop about once a month. I cherish every minute that I can spend with her. I will be so lost when she passes away.

Another daughter, however, recognized the close kinship that she felt with her mother early on as just a little girl. As she recollected, "I'm the knee baby out of a family of four boys and me the only girl. My mom and I always shared this strong bond being the only women in the family— until the grandchildren arrived." For those unfamiliar with the term, a *knee baby* it refers to the second youngest child in a family of four or more. The closeness developed into their ability to see themselves as "best friends who share almost everything." She went on to summarize, "My mom is my sister, best friend, and my dear mom at all times!" Susan, the mother of an adolescent daughter, shared the events that inspired her to give her best to her daughter:

> Losing my dad at fifteen has given me a different perspective on raising [my] daughter. It hit home that we, as parents, are not guaranteed tomorrow. So, I have spent the last eighteen years investing all my time into nurturing her . . . and to being her best friend. If I die today, I will have given Claire more amazing experiences than most people get in a lifetime.

In closing this topic, we would like to share a recollection of a woman who has lived long enough to know just how valuable a mother can be through the ups and downs of life:

> I can honestly say my mother is a mother when I need my mother and a friend when I need one the most! We have been through a lot together, but . . . there is no one else with whom I would rather have experienced my life's journey so far. I am everything I am today because of my mother, and I am blessed to have the kind of relationship we share.

CONCLUSION

As we hope is visible throughout this book, there are as many ways for the mother-daughter relationship to evolve as there are mothers and daughters to relate! In fact, there are many more stories and nuances than we could possibly convey in a single book. However, we have attempted to touch on the major themes and concerns that were revealed by the mothers and daughters with whom we spoke. Not surprisingly, this relationship may be the most seminal and influential relationship in which a female will participate. We hope that the stories we have presented illustrate how powerful and challenging it can be to mother a daughter or daughter a mother. The unique identity of each mother and daughter dyad influences the path the relationship follows, but as the book's subtitle indicates, each pair will spend a lifetime "living, loving, and learning" within the relationship.

Struggling to create separate identities from our mothers can lead us to intentionally follow paths much different from those of our mothers. However, a mother's influence goes much deeper than we might recognize until we come to a space in which we can safely explore that most primary relationship and allow ourselves to acknowledge the positive *and* the negative ways in which we were shaped by our mothers' interactions with us. Our experiencing of the relationship changes as we mature and it is over the course of our lifetimes that we are able to fully appreciate the depth, breadth, and strength of the relationship's power to mold us into adult women.

In summation, we would like to remind readers that even the women who had regrets about their early interactions with their mothers were often able to recognize the positive personal outcomes that had been borne from these less than ideal relational circumstances. It is over the course of time and maturity that women can begin to perceive this relationship with a clarity that is less clouded with the early disappointments or disillusionment. When we began to recognize our mothers as women as human as we, ourselves, are, we begin to see more clearly the ways in which we can be better women as a function of the mother-daughter relationship.

For mothers of daughters, we encourage you to revel in the joy that your daughters bring to you at every age and stage. Mothers have a magic about them that can be lost as a daughter grows into adolescence, but hold fast to the promise that as a daughter grows into a woman, the bond can again blossom into a new form in which both women equally share the joy of a familial relationship that becomes a relationship of deep friendship and mutuality. No matter where we come from, or how long we are allowed to share the earth with our mothers or daughters, we are all given a full lifetime of opportunities to live, love, and learn from this relationship.

NOTE

1. E. Hancock, *Reckoning the Relationship between Daughters and Mothers: Transforming a Critical Tie*. Paper presented at the Annual Convention of the American Psychological Association, Anaheim, California, August 1983.

Bibliography

Aleman, M. W., and Helfrich, K. W. (2010). Inheriting the narratives of dementia: A collaborative tale of a daughter and mother. *Journal of Family Communication, 10,* 7–23.

Allen, M. W. (2008). Consumer finance and parent-child communication. In J. J. Xiao (Ed.), *Handbook of consumer finance research* (pp. 351–61). New York: Springer.

Amato, P. R. (2010). Research on divorce: Continuing trends and new developments. *Journal of Marriage and Family, 72,* no. 3, 650–66.

American College of Obstetricians and Gynecologists. (2011). Frequently asked questions: Labor, delivery, and postpartum care. www.acog.org/~/media/For%20Patients/faq091.pdf?dmc=1&ts=20130616T0852124419.

Anderson, K. M., and Danis, F. S. (2006). Adult daughters of battered women. *Affilia: Journal of Women & Social Work, 21,* no. 4, 419–32.

Armstrong, M. J. (2003). Is being a grandmother being old? Cross-ethnic perspectives from New Zealand. *Journal of Cross-Cultural Gerontology, 18,* no. 3, 185–202.

Askling, J., Erlandsson, G., Kaijser, M., Akre, O., and Ekbom, A. (1999). Sickness in pregnancy and sex of child. *The Lancet, 354,* 2053.

Assor, A., and Tal, K. (2012). When parents' affection depends on child's achievement: Parental conditional positive regard, self-aggrandizement, shame and coping in adolescents. *Journal of Adolescence, 35,* no. 2, 249–60.

Backett-Milburn, K., Airey, L., McKie, L., and Hogg, G. (2008). Family comes first or open all hours?: How low paid women working in food retailing manage webs of obligation at home and work. *Sociological Review, 56,* no. 3, 474–96.

Bakalar, N. (2010, April 19). Despite advice, many fail to breast-feed. *New York Times,* 7.

Bandura, A. (1977). *Social learning theory.* New York: General Learning Press.

Baril, H., Julien, D., Chartrand, E., and Dube, M. (2009). Females' quality of relationships in adolescence and friendship support in adulthood. *Canadian Journal of Behavioural Science, 41,* no. 3, 161–68.

Baruch, G., and Barnett, R. C. (1983). Adult daughters' relationships with their mothers. *Journal of Marriage and Family, 45,* no. 3, 601–6.

Baxter, J., Weston, R., and Qu, L. (2011). Family structure, co-parental relationship quality, post-separation paternal involvement and children's emotional wellbeing. *Journal of Family Studies, 17,* no. 2, 86–109.

Baxter, L. A., and Akkoor, C. (2011). Topic expansiveness and family communication patterns. *Journal of Family Communication, 11,* 1–20.

Beck, C. T. (2002). Postpartum depression: A metasynthesis. *Qualitative Health Research, 12,* no. 4, 453–72.

Beeler, J. and DiProva, V. (1999). Family adjustment following disclosure of homosexuality by a member: Themes discerned in narrative account. *Journal of Marital and Family Therapy, 25,* no. 4, 443–59.

Benedetti, R., Cohen, L, and Taylor, M. (2013). "There's really no other option": Italian Australians' experiences of caring for a family member with dementia. *Journal of Women & Aging, 25,* no. 2, 138–64.

Berenson, K. R., Crawford, T. N., Cohen, P., and Brook, J. (2005). Implications of identification with parents and parents' acceptance for adolescent and young adult self-esteem. *Self and Identity, 4,* no. 3, 289–301.

211

Berger, P. L., and Luckmann, T. (1966). *The social construction of reality: A treatise in the sociology of knowledge*. Garden City, NY: Doubleday.

Bernard, L. L., and Guarnaccia, C. A. (2002). Husband and adult-daughter caregivers' bereavement. *Omega: Journal of Death and Dying, 45*, no. 2, 153–66.

Bombeck, E. (1967). *At wit's end*. New York: Ballantine Books.

Bos, H. M. W., van Balen, F., and van den Boom, D. C. (2004). Experience of parenthood, couple relationship, social support, and child-rearing goals in planned lesbian mother families. *Journal of Child Psychology and Psychiatry, 45*, no. 4, 755–64.

Bowlby, J. (1977). The making and breaking of affectional bonds. *British Journal of Psychiatry, 130*, 201–10.

Boyce, P. and Hickey, A. (2005). Psychosocial risk factors to major depression after childbirth. *Social Psychiatry Psychiatric Epidemiology, 40*, no. 8, 605–12.

Britton, J. R., and Britton, H. L. (2008). Maternal self-concept and breastfeeding. *Journal of Human Lactation, 24*, no. 4, 431–38.

Bystrova, K., Ivanova, V., Edhborg, M., Matthiesen, A. S., Ransjo-Arvidson, A. B., Mukhamedrakhimov, R. et al. (2009). Early contact versus separation: Effects on mother-infant interaction one year later. *Birth, 36*, no. 2, 97–109.

Cait, C.-A. (2005). Parental death, shifting family dynamics, and female identity development. *Omega: Journal of Death & Dying, 51*, no. 2, 87–105.

Callister, L. C. (2006). Doing the month: Chinese postpartum practices. *MCN, The American Journal of Maternal and Child Nursing, 31*, no. 6, 309.

Carr, D. (2004). "My daughter has a career; I just raised babies": The psychological consequences of women's intergenerational social comparisons. *Social Psychology Quarterly, 67*, no. 2, 132–54.

Carter, J. D., Mulder, R. T., Frampton, C. M. A., and Darlow, B. A. (2007). Infants admitted to a neonatal intensive care unit: Parental psychological status at 9 months. *Acta Paediatrica, 96*, no. 9, 1286–89.

Chapman, D. J. (2012). Longer cumulative breastfeeding duration associated with improved bone strength. *Journal of Human Lactation, 28*, no. 18, 18–19.

Cherlin, A., Cross-Barnet, C., Burton, L. M., and Garrett-Peters, R. (2008). Promises they can keep: Low-income women's attitudes toward motherhood, marriage, and divorce. *Journal of Marriage and Family, 70*, no. 4, 919–33.

Chien, L., Tai, C., Ko, Y., Huang, C., and Sheu, S. (2006). Adherence to "doing-the-month" practices is associated with fewer physical and depressive symptoms among postpartum women in Taiwan. *Research in Nursing and Health, 29*, no. 5, 374–83.

Chisholm, J. S., Quinlivan, J. A., Petersen, R. W., and Coall, D. A. (2005). Early stress predicts age at menarche and first birth, adult attachment, and expected lifespan. *Human Nature, 16*, no. 3, 233–65.

Chodorow, N. (1991). *Feminism and psychoanalytic theory*. New Haven, CT: Yale University Press.

Cohen Engler, A., Hadash, A., Shehadeh, N., and Pillar, G. (2012). Breastfeeding may improve nocturnal sleep and reduce infantile colic: Potential role of breast milk melatonin. *European Journal of Pediatrics, 171*, no. 4, 729–32.

Collins, P. H. (2000). *Black feminist thought: Knowledge, consciousness, and the politics of empowerment*. New York: Routledge.

Condon, M. C. (2004). *Women's health: Body, mind, spirit: An integrated approach to wellness and illness*. Upper Saddle River, NJ: Prentice Hall, 472.

Corter, C., and Fleming, A. S. (1995). Psychobiology of maternal behavior in human beings. In M. Bornstein (Ed.), *Handbook of parenting* (pp. 87–116). Hillsdale, NJ: Erlbaum.

Costos, D., Ackerman, R., and Paradis, L. (2002). Recollections of menarche: Communication between mothers and daughters regarding menstruation. *Sex Roles, 46*, nos. 1 & 2, 49–59.

Courtwright, D. T. (2008). Gender imbalances in history: Causes, consequences and social adjustment. *Ethics, Bioscience and Life, 3*, 32–40.

Cox, S. J., Mezulis, A. H., and Hyde, J. S. (2010). The influence of child gender role and maternal feedback to child stress on the emergence of the gender difference in depressive rumination in adolescence. *Developmental Psychology, 46*, no. 4, 842–52.

Dahl, E. K. (2004). "Last night I dreamed I went to Manderly again": Vicissitudes of maternal identifications in late female adolescence. *Psychoanalytic Inquiry: A Topical Journal for Mental Health, 24*, 657–79.

De Magistris, A., Coni, E., Puddu, M., Zonza, M., and Fanos, V. (2010). Screening of postpartum depression: Comparison between mothers in the neonatal intensive care unit and in the neonatal section. *The Journal of Maternal-Fetal and Neonatal Medicine, 23*(S3), 101–3.

de Tychey, C., Briancon, S., Lighezzolo, J., Spitz, E., Kabuth, B., de Luigi, V., Messembourg, C., Girvan, F., Rosati, A., Thockler, A., and Vincent, S. (2008). Quality of life, postnatal depression and baby gender. *Journal of Clinical Nursing, 17*, no. 3, 312–22.

Degges-White, S., and Marszalek, J. (2006/2007). An exploration of long-term, same-sex relationships: Benchmarks, perceptions, and challenges. *Journal of LGBT Issues in Counseling, 1*, no. 4, 90–120.

Dolgin, K. G. (1996). Parents' disclosure of their own concerns to their adolescent children. *Personal Relationships, 3*, no. 2, 159–69.

East, P. L., and Jacobson, L. J. (2003). Mothers' differential treatment of their adolescent childbearing and nonchildbearing children: Contrasts between and within families. *Journal of Family Psychology, 17*, no. 3, 384–96.

Edwards, B., Galletly, C., Semmier-Booth, T., and Dekker, G. (2008). Antenatal psychosocial risk factors and depression among women living in socioeconomically disadvantaged suburbs in Adelaide, South Australia. *Australia and New Zealand Journal of Psychiatry, 42*, no. 1, 45–50.

Erikson, E. (1968). *Identity: Youth and crisis.* New York: W. W. Norton.

Ernster, V. (1975). American menstrual expressions. *Sex Roles, 1*, 3–13.

Federal Interagency Forum on Aging-Related Statistics. (June 2012). *Older Americans 2012: Key indicators of well-being.* Washington, DC: U.S. Government Printing Office.

Fine, M., and McClelland, S. I. (2006). Sexuality education and desire: Still missing after all these years. *Harvard Educational Review, 76*, 297–338.

Finer, L. B., and Zolna, M. R. (2011). Unintended pregnancy in the United States: Incidence and disparities. *Contraception, 84*, no. 5, 478–85.

Flouri, E., and Hawkes, D. (2008). Ambitious mothers—successful daughters: Mothers' early expectations for children's education and children's earnings and sense of control in adult life. *British Journal of Educational Psychology, 78*, 411–33.

Fouquier, K. F. (2011). The concept of motherhood among three generations of African American women. *The Journal of Nursing Scholarship, 43*, no. 2, 145–53.

Fowler, L. A. and Moore, A. R. (2012). Breast implants for graduation: A sociological examination of daughter and mother narratives. *Sociology Mind, 2*, 109–15.

Fowler, L. K. (1999). *Family life month packet, Ohio State University, 1999.* Retrieved from http://www.hec.ohio.state.edul/famlife/.

Fox, G. L. and Inazu, J. K. (1982). The influence of mother's marital history on the mother-daughter relationship in black and white households. *Journal of Marriage and the Family, 44*, 143–53.

Friedman, H. L. (1966). The mother-daughter relationship: Its potential in treatment of young unwed mothers. *Social Casework, 47*, no. 8, 502–6; 502.

Fulcher, M. and Coyle, E. F. (2011). Breadwinner and caregiver: A cross-sectional analysis of children's and emerging adults' visions of their future family roles. *British Journal of Developmental Psychology, 29*, 330–46.

Gardner, D. K., Wale, P. L., Collins, R., and Lane, M. (2011). Glucose consumption of single post-compaction human embryos is predictive of embryo sex and live birth outcome. *Human Reproduction, 26*, no. 8, 1981–86.

Gelardin, S. (2001). Narratives: A key to uncovering mother-daughter influences on life and work. *Career Planning and Adult Development Journal, 17*, 135–47.

Girl power: Single mothers are more likely to have daughters. (2004). *Economist, 373,* no. 8398, 79–80.

Glynn, S. J. (April 2012). The new breadwinners: 2010 update. Center for American Progress. Retrieved from www.americanprogress.org/issues/labor/report/2012/04/16/11377/the-new-breadwinners-2010-update/.

Grant, V. J. (1994). Maternal dominance and the conception of sons. *British Journal of Medical Psychology, 67,* no. 4, 343–51.

Gremigni, P., Mariani, L., Marracino, V., Tranquilli, A., and Turi, A. (2011). Partner support and postpartum depressive symptoms. *Journal of Psychosomatic Obstetrics & Gynecology, 32,* no. 3, 135–40.

Guerrero-Martin, J., Chaudri, A., Munoz, F., Duran, N., Ezquerro, A., and Suero, P. (2010). The relations between psychosocial factors, care burden, and depression on the dementia family caregivers. *European Psychiatry, 25,* 567.

Gunlicks, M. L., and Weissman, M. M. (2008). Change in child psychopathology with improvement in parental depression: A systematic review. *Journal of the American Academy of Child and Adolescent Psychiatry, 47,* no. 4, 379–89.

Hall, J. C. (2008). The impact of kin and fictive kin relationships on the mental health of black adult children of alcoholics. *Health & Social Work, 33,* no. 4, 259–66.

Hammock, E. A., and Young, L. J. (2006). Oxytocin, vasopressin and pair bonding: Implications for autism. *Philosophical Transcripts Royal Society London B Biological Sciences, 361,* no. 1476, 2187–98.

Hancock, E. (August 1983). *Reckoning the relationship between daughters and mothers: Transforming a critical tie.* Paper presented at the Annual Convention of the American Psychological Association, Anaheim, California.

Harter, S. (1998). The development of self-representations. In W. Damon & N. Eisenberg (Eds.), *Handbook of child psychology: Social, emotional, and personality development* (5th ed., Vol. 3, pp. 553–617). New York: Wiley.

Harvard Mental Health Letter. (September 2011). Beyond the "baby blues." Volume 28, no. 3.

Hatzinikolaou, K., and Murray, L. (2010). Infant sensitivity to negative maternal emotional shifts: Effects of infant sex, maternal postnatal depression, and interactive style. *Infant Mental Health Journal, 31,* no. 5, 591–610.

Havlicek, J., Dvorakova, R., Bartos, L., and Flegr, J. (2006). Non-advertized does not mean concealed: Body odour changes across the human menstrual cycle. *Ethology, 112,* 81–90.

Hayden, J. M., Singer, J. A., & Chrisler, J. C. (2006). The transmission of birth stories from mother to daughter: Self-esteem and mother-daughter attachment. *Sex Roles, 55,* 373–83.

Hays, S. (1996). *The cultural contradictions of motherhood.* New Haven, CT: Yale University Press.

Hegewisch, A., Williams, C., and Henderson, A. (April 2011). *The gender wage gap by occupation.* Institute for Women's Policy Research. Retrieved from www.iwpr.org/publications/pubs/the-gender-wage-gap-by-occupation-updated-april-2011.

Helle, S., and Lummaa, V. (2013). A trade-off between having many sons and shorter maternal post-reproductive survival in pre-industrial Finland. *Biology Letters, 9,* no. 2, 20130034.

Henderson, C. E., Hayslip, B., Sanders, L. M., and Louden, L. (2009). Grandmother-grandchild relationship quality predicts psychological adjustment among youth from divorced families. *Journal of Family Issues, 30,* no. 9, 1254–64.

Herbenick, D., Reece, M., Schick, V., Sanders, S. A., Dodge, B., and Fortenberry, J. D. (2010). Sexual behavior in the United States: Results from a national probability sample of men and women ages 14–94. Journal of Sexual Medicine, 7 (Suppl. 5), 255–65. doi: 10.1111/j.1743-6109.2010.02012.x

Hoffman, L. (2004). When daughter becomes mother: Inferences from multiple dyadic parent-child groups. *Psychoanalytic Inquiry, 24,* no. 5, 629–56.

Holroyd, E., Lopez, V., and Chan, S. W. (2011). Negotiating "doing the month": An ethnographic study examining the postnatal practices of two generations of Chinese women. *Nursing and Health Sciences, 13*, 47–52.

Howard, C. R., Lanphear, N., Lanphear, B. P., Eberly, S., and Lawrence, R. A. (2006). Parental responses to infant crying and colic: The effect on breastfeeding duration. *Breastfeeding Medicine, 1*, no. 3, 146–55.

Ickovics, J. R., Reed, E., Magriples, U., Westdahl, C., Rising, S. S., and Kershaw, T. S. (2011). Effects of group prenatal care on psychosocial risk in pregnancy: Results from a randomized controlled trial. *Psychology and Health, 26*, no. 2, 235–50.

Capital One. (2011). As High School Graduates Open their Gifts, Parents Have Key Opportunity to Talk Money Management, June 14, 2011. (June 2008). Retrieved from http://phx.corporate-ir.net/phoenix.zhtml?c=70667&p=irol-newsArticle& ID=1573673&highlight.

Ivanov, P. C., Ma, Q. D. Y., and Bartsch, R. P. (2009). Maternal-fetal heartbeat phase synchronization. *Proceedings of the National Academy of Sciences, 106*, no. 33, 13641–642.

Jadva, V., Hines, M., and Golombok, S. (2010). Infants' preferences for toys, colors, and shapes: Sex differences and similarities. *Archives of Sexual Behavior, 39*, no. 6, 1261–73.

Jones, B. C., DeBruine, L. M., Perrett, D. I., Little, A. C., Feinberg, D. R., and Law Smith, M. J. (2008). Effects of menstrual cycle phase on face preferences. *Archives of Sexual Behavior, 37*, 78–84.

Kanazawa, S. (2005). Big and tall parents have more sons: Further generalizations of the Trivers Willard hypothesis (hTWH). *Journal of Theoretical Biology, 235*, no. 4, 583–90.

Kanazawa, S. (2007). Beautiful parents have more daughters: A further implication of the generalized Trivers Willard hypothesis (gTWH). *Journal of Theoretical Biology, 244*, 133–40.

Kellas, J. K. (2010). Transmitting relational worldviews: The relationship between mother-daughter memorable messages and adult daughters' romantic relational schemata. *Communication Quarterly, 58*, no. 4, 458–79.

Kiel, E. J., and Buss, K. A. (2006). Maternal accuracy in predicting toddlers' behaviors and associations with toddlers' fearful temperament. *Child Development, 77*, no. 2, 355–70.

Kitamura, K., and Muto, T. (2001). The influence of adult mother-daughter relationships on daughters' psychological well-being: Life events of marriage and childbearing. *Japanese Journal of Developmental Psychology, 12*, 46–57.

Ko, Y., Yang, C., and Chiang, L. C. (2008). Effects of postpartum exercise program on fatigue and depression during "doing the month" period. *Journal of Nursing Research, 16*, no. 3, 177–85.

Kobayashi, Y. (2010). Assistance received from parturients' own mothers during "satogaeri" (their perinatal visit and stay with their parents) and development of the mother-infant relationship and maternal identity. *Journal of Japan Academy of Midwifery, 1*, 28–39.

Koerner, S. S., Jacobs, S. L., and Raymond, M. (2000). When mothers turn to their adolescent daughters: Predicting daughters' vulnerability to negative adjustment outcomes. *Family Relations, 49*, no. 3, 301–9.

Koerner, S. S., Wallace, S., Lehman, S. J., and Raymond, M. (2002). Mother-to-daughter disclosure after divorce: Are there costs and benefits? *Journal of Child and Family Studies, 11*, no. 4, 469–83.

Kost, K., and Henshaw, S. (March 2013). *U.S. teenage pregnancies, births and abortions, 2008: State trends by age, race and ethnicity*. Washington, DC: Guttmacher Institute.

Kvitvaer, B. G., Miller, J., and Newell, D. (2012). Improving our understanding of the colicky infant: A prospective observational study. *Journal of Clinical Nursing, 21*, 63–69.

Lagerberg, D., and Magnusson, M. (2012). Infant gender and postpartum sadness in the light of region of birth and some other factors: A contribution to the knowledge of postpartum depression. *Archives of Women's Mental Health, 15*, no. 2, 121–30.

Lee, H. K. (2013). "I'm my mother's daughter, I'm my husband's wife, I'm my child's mother, I'm nothing else": Resisting traditional Korean roles as Korean American working women in Seoul, South Korea. *Women's Studies International Forum, 36*, 37–43.

Lee, J. (2008). "A Kotex and a smile": Mothers and daughters at menarche. *Journal of Family Issues, 29*, no. 10, 1325–47.

Leeb, R. T., and Rejskind, F. G. (2004). Here's looking at you, kid! A longitudinal study of perceived gender differences in mutual gaze behavior in young infants. *Sex Roles, 50*, no. 1–2, 1–14.

Lefkowitz, D. S., Baxt, C., and Evans, J. R. (2010). Prevalence and correlates of post-traumatic stress and postpartum depression in parents of infants in the neonatal intensive care unit (NICU). *Journal of Clinical Psychology in Medical Settings, 17*, no. 3, 230–37.

Lehman, S. J., and Koerner, S. S. (2002). Family financial hardship and adolescent girls' adjustment: The role of maternal disclosure of financial concerns. *Merrill-Palmer Quarterly, 48*, 1–24.

Leung, S. S. K., Arthur, D., and Martinson, I. M. (2005). Perceived stress and support of the Chinese postpartum ritual "doing the month." *Health Care for Women International, 26*, no. 3, 212–24.

Lichtenstein, A. (1984). The maternal instinct in Scripture: Toward a literary understanding. *Journal of Evolutionary Psychology, 5*, no. 3–4, 147–48.

Looker, E. D., and Magee, P. A. (2000). Gender and work: The occupational expectations of young women and men in the 1990s. *Gender Issues, 18*, 74–88.

Losoncz, I., and Bortolotto, N. (2009). Work-life balance: The experiences of Australian working mothers. *Journal of Family Studies, 15*, 122–38.

Lynch, B. (July 2004). Postpartum culture: The loss of the lying-in time. Speech given at Doulas of North America (DONA) Annual Conference in New Orleans.

Maestripieri, D. (2001). Biological bases of maternal attachment. *Current Directions in Psychological Science, 10*, no. 3, 79–83.

Mao, C., Hsu, Y., and Fang, T. (2012). The role of the mother-daughter relationship in Taiwanese college students' career self-efficacy. *Social Behavior and Personality, 40*, no. 9, 1511–22.

Marazziti, D., and Dell'osso, M. C. (2008). The role of oxytocin in neuropsychiatric disorders. *Current Medical Chemistry, 15*, no. 7, 698–704.

Mauthner, N. (1998). Re-assessing the importance and role of the marital relationship in postnatal depression: Methodological and theoretical implications. *Journal of Reproductive & Infant Psychology, 16*, no. 2, 157–76.

McKeever, P. (1984). The perpetuation of menstrual shame: Implications and directions. *Women and Health, 9*, no. 4, 33–45.

McVeigh, C. (1997). Motherhood experiences from the perspectives of first time mothers. *Clinical Nursing Research, 6*, no. 4, 335–48.

Mendell, D. (1997). The impact of the mother-daughter relationship on women's relationships with me: The two-man phenomenon. *Issues in Psychoanalytic Psychology, 19*, 213–23.

Mercer, R. T. (2004). Becoming a mother versus maternal role attainment. *Journal of Nursing Scholarship, 36*, no. 3, 226–32.

Mizuno, K., Mizuno, N., Shinohara, T., and Noda, M. (2004). Mother-infant skin-to-skin contact after delivery results in early recognition of own mother's milk odour. *Acta Paediatrica, 93*, no. 12, 1640–45.

Morrongiello, B., and Dawber, T. (1999). Parental influence on toddlers' injury-risk behaviors: Are sons and daughters socialized differently? *Journal of Applied Developmental Psychology, 20*, no. 2, 227–51.

Moses-Kolko, E. L., Perlman, S. B., Wisner, K. L., James, J., Saul, A. T., and Phillips, M. L. (2010). Abnormally reduced dorsomedial prefrontal cortical activity and effective connectivity with amygdala in response to negative emotional faces in postpartum depression. *American Journal of Psychiatry, 167,* 1373–80.

Mottram, S. A., and Hortacsu, N. (2005). Adult daughter aging mother relationship over the life cycle: The Turkish case. *Journal of Aging Studies, 19,* no. 4, 471–88.

Mullins, P. O. (2008). Financial knowledge and communication of teenagers and their parent or guardian. [Abstract]. *Dissertation Abstracts International Section A: Humanities and Social Sciences, 68,* no. (12–A), 5220.

Nicolson, P. (1999a). The myth of the maternal instinct: Feminism, evolution and the case of postnatal depression. *Psychology, Evolution & Gender, 1,* no. 2, 161–81.

Nicolson, P. (1999b). Loss, happiness, and post partum depression: The ultimate paradox. *Canadian Psychology/Psychologie canadienne, 40,* no. 2, 162–78.

Nolan, M. L., Mason, V., Snow, S., Messenger, W., Catling, J., and Upton, P. (2012). Making friends at antenatal classes: A qualitative exploration of friendship across the transition to motherhood. *The Journal of Perinatal Education, 21,* no. 3, 178–85.

Noorlander, A. M., Geraedts, J. P. M., and Melissen, J. B. M. (2010). Female gender preselection by maternal diet in combination with timing of sexual intercourse—a prospective study. *Reproductive BioMedicine Online, 21,* no. 6, 794–802.

Notman, M. T. (2006). Mothers and daughters as adults. *Psychoanalytic Inquiry: A Topical Journal for Mental Health Professionals, 26,* 137–53.

O'Hara, M. W. (2009). Postpartum depression: What we know. *Journal of Clinical Psychology, 65,* no. 12, 1258–69.

Ojanen, T., and Perry, D. G. (2007). Relationship schemas and the developing self: Perceptions of mother and of self as joint predictors of early adolescents' self-esteem. *Developmental Psychology, 43,* no. 6, 1474–83.

Okimoto, T. G., and Heilman, M. E. (2012). The "bad parent" assumption: How gender stereotypes affect reactions to working mothers. *Journal of Social Sciences, 68,* no. 4, 704–24.

O'Reilly, A. (2010). Outlaw(ing) motherhood: A theory and politic of maternal empowerment for the twenty-first century. *HECATE, 36,* no. 1/2, 17–29.

Panfile, T. M., Laible, D. J., and Eye, J. L. (2012). Conflict frequency within mother-child dyads across contexts: Links with attachment and security. *Early Childhood Research Quarterly, 27,* 147–55.

Perren, S., von Wyl, A., Burgin, D., Simoni, H., and von Klitzing, K. (2005). Depressive symptoms and psychosocial stress across the transition to parenthood: Associations with parental psychopathology and child difficulty. *Journal of Psychosomatic Obstetrics and Gynaecology, 26,* no. 3, 173–83.

Pew Research Center. (September 2012). U.S. Bureau of Labor, Harvard Business Review.

Pipitone, R. N., and Gallup, G. G. Jr. (2008). Women's voice attractiveness varies across the menstrual cycle. *Evolution and Human Behavior, 29,* no. 4, 268–74.

Pluhar, E. I., Dilorio, C. K., and McCarty, F. (2008). Correlates of sexuality communication among mothers and 6-12-year-old children. *Child: Care, Health, and Development, 34,* no. 3, 283–90.

Porter, R. H. (2004). The biological significance of skin-to-skin contact and maternal odours. *Acta Paediatrica, 93,* no. 12, 1560–62.

Provost, M. P., Quinsey, V. L., and Troje, N. F. (2008). Differences in gait across the menstrual cycle and their attractiveness to men. *Archives of Sexual Behavior, 37,* no. 4, 598–604.

Puckering, C., McIntosh, E., Hickey, A., & Longford, J. (2010). Mellow babies: A group intervention for infants and mothers experiencing postnatal depression. *Counselling Psychology Review, 25,* 28–40.

Putnam, R. D. (2000). *Bowling alone: The collapse and revival of the American community.* New York: Simon & Schuster.

Racine, C. (2008). My darling darling: Étude on Muriel's body. *Journal of the Association for Research on Mothering, 10,* no. 2, 51–58.

Ratti, T. H. M. (2011). *I have to go on: The effect of a mother's death on her daughter's education.* ProQuest, LLC, EdD dissertation, Arizona State University.

Reynolds, A. (2001). Breastfeeding and brain development. *Pediatrics Clinics of North America, 48,* 159–71.

Rich, A. (1986). *Of woman born: Motherhood as experience and institution.* New York: Norton.

Ridolfo, H., Chepp, V., and Milkie, M. (2013). Race and girls' self-evaluations: How mothering matters. *Sex Roles, 68,* 496–509.

Romo, L. K. (2011). Money talks: Revealing and concealing financial information in families. *Journal of Family Communication, 11,* no. 4, 264–81.

Rossi, A. (1977). A biosocial perspective on parenting. *Daedalus, 106,* no. 2, 1–31.

Satyanarayana, V., Lukose, A., and Srinivasan, K. (2011). Maternal mental health in pregnancy and child behavior. *Indian Journal of Psychiatry, 53,* no. 4, 351–61.

Schoppe-Sullivan, S. J., Diener, M. I., Mangelsdorf, S. C., Brown, G. L., McHale, J. L., and Frosch, C. A. (2006). Attachment and sensitivity in family context: The roles of parent and infant gender. *Infant and Child Development, 15,* no. 4, 367–85.

Schultz, L. E. (2007). The influence of maternal loss on young women's experience of identity development in emerging adulthood. *Death Studies, 31,* 17–43.

Serido, J., Shim, S., Mishra, A., and Tang, C. (2010). Financial parenting, financial coping behaviors, and well-being of emerging adults. *Family Relations, 59,* no. 4, 453–64.

Sheehan, G., Darlington, Y., Noller, P., and Feeney, J. (2004). Children's perceptions of their sibling relationships during parental separation and divorce. *Journal of Divorce & Remarriage, 41,* 69–94.

Shlomo, S. B., Taubman-Ben-Ari, O., Findler, L., Sivan, E., and Dolizki, M. (2010). Becoming a grandmother: Maternal grandmothers' mental health, perceived costs, and personal growth. *Social Work Research, 34,* 45–57.

Song, H. (2001). The mother-daughter relationship as a resource for Korean women's career aspirations. *Sex Roles: A Journal of Research, 44,* 79–97.

Spock, B. (1945). *The common sense book of baby and child care.* New York: Simon & Schuster, Inc.

Steinberg, L. (2008). A social neuroscience perspective on adolescent risk-taking. *Developmental Review, 28,* 78–106. doi: 10.1016/j.dr.2007.08.002

Stephens, J. (2004). Beyond binaries in motherhood research. *Family Matters, 69,* 88–93.

Stern, D. N. (1995). *The motherhood constellation: A unified view of parent-infant psychotherapy.* New York: Basic Books.

Stone, E. (1988/2008). *Black sheep and kissing cousins: How our family stories shape us.* New Brunswick, NJ: Transaction Press.

Sylven, S. M., Papadopoulos, F. C., Mpazakidis, V., Ekselius, L., Sundstrom-Poromaa, I., and Skalkidou, A. (2011). Newborn gender as a predictor of postpartum mood disturbances in a sample of Swedish women. *Archives of Women's Mental Health, 14,* no. 3, 195–201.

Takemoto, S., and Nakamura, S. (2011). How infant feeding methods relate to anxiety over child-rearing and feelings toward the child. *Journal of Japan Academy of Midwifery, 25,* no. 2, 225–32.

Taubman-ben-Ari, O., Sivan, E., and Dolizki, M. (2008). The transition to motherhood—A time for growth. *Journal of Social and Clinical Psychology, 28,* 943–70.

Terry, D. J., McHugh, T. A., and Noller, P. (1991). Role dissatisfaction and the decline in marital quality across the transition to parenthood. *Australian Journal of Psychology, 43,* no. 3, 129–32.

Thomas, A. J., and King, C. T. (2007). Gendered racial socialization of African American mothers and daughters. *The Family Journal: Counseling and Therapy for Couples and Families, 15,* no. 2, 137–42.

Townsend, T. G. (2008). Protecting our daughters: Intersection of race, class and gender in African American mothers' socialization of their daughters' heterosexuality. *Sex Roles, 59*, 429–442.

Trad, P. V. (1995). Adolescent girls and their mothers realigning the relationship. *The American Journal of Family Therapy, 23*, 11–24.

Trautmann-Villalba, P., Gerhold, M., Laucht, M., and Schmidt, M. H. (2004). Early motherhood and disruptive behavior in school-age child. *Acta Paediatrica, 93*, 120–25.

Turnage, B. F., and Dotson, C. L. (2012). Parenting of female African American infants. *International Journal of Childbirth Education, 27*, 54–57.

U.S. Department of Labor, Bureau of Labor Statistics. (2011). Women in the labor force: A databook (2010 edition). Retrieved from http://www.bls.gov/cps/wlf-databook-2010.pdf.

Van Mens-Verhulst, J. (1995). Reinventing the mother-daughter relationship. *American Journal of Psychotherapy, 49*, no. 4, 526–38.

Van Mens-Verhulst, J., Schreurs, K., and Woertman, I. (1993). *Daughtering and mothering: Female subjectivity reanalyzed*. London/New York: Routledge.

Vik, T., Grote, V., Escribano, J., Socha, J., Verduci, E., Fritsch, M., Carlier, C., von Kries, R., and Koletzko, B. (2009). Infantile colic, prolonged crying and maternal depression. *Acta Paediatrica, 98*, no. 8, 1344–48.

Warner, Judith. (2012). Is too much mothering bad for you? A look at the new social science. *The Virginia Quarterly Review, 88*, no. 4, 48–53.

Weaver, J. J., and Ussher, J. M. (1997). How motherhood changes life: A discourse analytic study with mothers of young children. *Journal of Reproductive & Infant Psychology, 15*, 51–69.

White-Johnson, R. L., Ford, K. R., and Sellers, R. M. (2010). Parental racial socialization profiles: Association with demographic factors, racial discrimination, childhood socialization, and racial identity. *Cultural Diversity and Ethnic Minority Psychology, 16*, no. 2, 237–47. doi: 10.1037/a0016111

Winnicott, D. W. (1988). *Babies and their mothers*. London: Free Association Books.

Wright, T. (2013). "Making it" versus satisfaction: How women raising young children in poverty assess how well they are doing. *Journal of Social Science Research, 39*, no. 2, 269–80.

Yarcheski, A., Mahon, N. E., Yarcheski, T. J., Hanks, M. M., and Cannella, B. L. (2009). A meta-analytic study of predictors of maternal-fetal attachment. *International Journal of Nursing Studies, 46*, no. 5, 708–15.

Yoshihama, M. (1999). Domestic violence against women of Japanese descent in Los Angeles: Two methods of estimating prevalence. *Violence Against Women, 5*, no. 8, 869–97. San Francisco: Author, 2005 (Revised).

Zajicek-Farber, M. (2010). The contributions of parenting and postnatal depression on emergent language of children in low-income families. *Journal of Child & Family Studies, 19*, 257–69.

Zeskind, P. S., and Barr, R. G. (1997). Acoustic characteristics of naturally occurring cries of infants with "colic." *Child Development, 68*, no. 3, 394–403.

Index

About the Authors

Suzanne Degges-White, PhD, LPC, LMHC, NCC, is professor and chair of the Counseling, Adult and Higher Education Department at Northern Illinois University. She is a licensed counselor whose focus includes working with women and families facing transitions. Her academic research has focused on women's development over the lifespan and she has received numerous awards for her work. She is the coauthor of another book addressing the intimate, intricate female relationships, *Friends Forever: How Girls and Women Forge Lasting Relationships*. She is also coeditor of the following books: *College Student Mental Health Counseling: A Developmental Approach* (2013), *Counseling Boys and Young Men* (2012), and *Integrating the Expressive Arts into Counseling Practice* (2011). In addition to having spent much of her life trying to figure out firsthand the multilayered relationships that daughters have with their mothers, Suzanne has spent the past two-and-a-half decades, since the birth of her own daughter, trying to decipher the often complicated relationships between mothers and their daughters. She is grateful to her mother and daughter who have taught her many lessons that otherwise she might not have learned and whose treasured presence in her life provided inspiration for this project.

Christine Borzumato-Gainey, PhD, LPC, is a licensed mental health counselor and instructor at Elon University. She has extensive clinical experience working with people struggling with anxiety, body image, substance abuse, and most notably, relationship issues. Time and again she has witnessed the power of the mother-daughter bond in her clients' lives and in her own life. Christine became engaged in this current project in hopes of offering women stories that may deepen their understanding of their own mother-daughter relationship. Christine lives in North Carolina with her partner, Howard, her two active children, Brooke and Drew, and their rambunctious dog, Rugby. When she is not "in the trenches" helping people heal or otherwise better their lives, she enjoys hiking, biking, skiing, and relaxing time with good friends and her wonderful extended family.

DATE DUE
